The Making of a King

THE MAKING OF A KING

Antigonus Gonatas of Macedon and the Greeks

Robin Waterfield

THE UNIVERSITY OF CHICAGO PRESS

The University of Chicago Press, Chicago 60637

Published 2021
Printed in the United States of America

30 29 28 27 26 25 24 23 22 21   1 2 3 4 5

ISBN-13: 978-0-226-61137-2 (cloth)
ISBN-13: 978-0-226-61140-2 (e-book)
DOI: https://doi.org/10.7208/chicago/9780226611402.001.0001

Published outside North America by Oxford University Press, 2021.

Library of Congress Cataloging-in-Publication Data
Names: Waterfield, Robin, 1952– author.
Title: The making of a king : Antigonus Gonatas of Macedon and the Greeks / Robin Waterfield.
Description: Chicago : The University of Chicago Press, 2021. | Includes bibliographical references and index.
Identifiers: LCCN 2020032133 | ISBN 9780226611372 (cloth) | ISBN 9780226611402 (ebook)
Subjects: LCSH: Antigonus II, King of Macedonia, 319 B.C.–239 B.C. | Macedonia—Kings and rulers—Biography. | Macedonia—History—To 168 B.C. | Greece—History—Macedonian Hegemony, 323–281 B.C. | Greece—History—281–146 B.C.
Classification: LCC DF237.A6 W38 2021 | DDC 938/.08092—dc23
LC record available at https://lccn.loc.gov/2020032133

♾ This paper meets the requirements of ANSI/NISO Z39.48-1992 (Permanence of Paper).

For Paul Cartledge
wise adviser

Contents

Illustrations

FIGURES

MAPS

Preface and Acknowledgments

When I wrote my general history of ancient Greece, *Creators, Conquerors, and Citizens* (2018), I found that researching the third century BCE was made more difficult by the lack of any accessible book on the period. The period is riddled with scholarly controversy, and no one has tried to pull it all together in a single volume. It is true, as I explain in the introduction, that the sources for the third century are meager, so that it often receives no more than a paragraph or two in the history books, but more can be said—and deserves to be said, as this book proves. So my intention is to open up even for general readers an obscure period of ancient Greek history. I have already done this for earlier and later stretches of the Hellenistic period in *Dividing the Spoils: The War for Alexander the Great's Empire* (2011) and *Taken at the Flood: The Roman Conquest of Greece* (2014); this book completes an unintended trilogy.

There is, as is usual for Greek history, warfare to be covered. Warfare was pervasive in the Hellenistic period; it decimated families, scarred the landscape, ruined entire states, forced towns to accept occupation by foreign soldiers, and generated countless memorials in the form of monuments and texts. There are colorful characters to sketch. But there are also important political matters to elucidate. This was a critical time in the history of the Greeks of the mainland, as two events highlight. First, the Spartan reformation of the 220s. Inspired by an earlier attempt in the 240s, the reformation of a strongly conservative society was preceded by decades of soul-searching, as greed undermined their social traditions and the number of citizens plummeted to critical levels. Second, the rise of the great confederacies, which changed the political life of the Greeks forever. This was the most profound political shift in the Greek world since the original coalescence of states centuries before, and it deserves to be better known.

I chose to make Antigonus Gonatas, the king of Macedon from 276 until his death in 239, the hinge of this book. Greece had effectively been dominated by Macedon, Macedonians, and pro-Macedonian Greeks ever since Philip II defeated the Greek states at Chaeronea in 338 and formed many of them into the League of Corinth the following year, with himself as its president. By the time Antigonus succeeded to the Macedonian throne, the League of Corinth was long defunct, but he was still the representative of Macedonian dominion and hence the stimulus for at least some of the changes the Greeks were going through. He makes a good lens, therefore, through which to view this period of Greek history.

I do not mean to imply that I use Antigonus simply as a literary device; he is one of the least known and most underestimated figures in Greek history, and I want to give him the prominence he deserves. The longevity of his reign alone, in troubled times, argues for exceptional determination and strength. He inherited a Macedon that was an utter mess and turned it into a kingdom that would endure and flourish for over a hundred years, succumbing eventually only to the undeniable might of Rome. The qualities that he required do not necessarily make an amiable man, but they make a capable king.

Surely, then, it is only the paucity of sources for the period that has denied Antigonus his fame. He revived the Macedon that his predecessors had created, and put in place reforms as important and wide-ranging as theirs. He was successful in his dealings with the Macedonians, who were always his primary concern, but less so in his dealings with the Greeks, where powerful forces were ranged against him and he experienced extraordinary vicissitudes. Despite being almost constantly on a war footing, he found time to secure and reunite Macedon. He was a successful commander, more often than not, especially when it really counted. He deserves a place in the gallery of memorable Macedonian kings, and this book is intended to be a biography of Antigonus, as well as a narrative history of the period.

The writing of history is the process of sifting the sources—works of literature, official state documents, coins, works of art, archaeological data—and transforming all this disparate material into a narrative. This transformation consists of far more than just putting the pieces together. That would be enough if the facts spoke for themselves, but they rarely do. Facts gain a voice, or at least speak more clearly, only when they are put into a certain context and framework by the historian (thus, incidentally, making all history-writing to a certain extent subjective). The lack of detailed information about the third century makes the contextualizing of it both more essential and more a matter of conjecture and imagination. Readers should be aware from the start that, for some events of the third century, my version may not be the only possibility. Even the dating of events is often a matter of informed guesswork.

The structure of the book is a response to the paucity of evidence. If we had good, contemporary accounts, preserving more of Antigonus' deeds and portraying his character, there would be less necessity to infer what he and his reign were like. But, as it is, he is one of those people who only come fully into focus against a background. The book therefore falls into two parts.

In the first part, I give the background. I recount relevant aspects of history over the six decades between the Macedonian conquest of Greece and the start of Antigonus' reign (that is, what scholars call the early Hellenistic period), focusing on the main states that impinged on his work as king of Macedon: Macedon itself, Sparta, Athens, the Achaean and Aetolian confederacies, and the kingdom of Egypt. These were the powers that were lined up for or, mostly, against him. In effect, these chapters delineate the main threats or concerns that Antigonus inherited along with his throne. He was born less than twenty years after the Macedonian conquest of Greece, and so his early life is woven into these chapters, but he is rarely the protagonist. That role is often taken by his grandfather and father, however, so the first part of the book affords glimpses of Antigonus' family environment.

The same characters and events come and go in these first five chapters, with much the same span of time covered in each chapter, but from different perspectives. I would ask readers who are not conversant with the period to be patient: characters with names that at first are unfamiliar will be old friends by the time they have read on. Then, in the second part, I detail the history, insofar as it can be recovered, of Antigonus' reign itself. I cover not just the course of events, but his relations with his own people and with the Greek states, and the culture of his famous court. In a final chapter, I assess his legacy, especially in the context of the Roman conquest of Greece.

Much of the research for this book was carried out in Athens, where the staff of the Blegen Library of the American School of Classical Studies at Athens, and of the Library of the British School at Athens, were their usual helpful selves. I would like to thank (again) my agent, Bill Hamilton; my two editors at the University of Chicago Press, Susan Bielstein and James Whitman Toftness; and Charlotte Loveridge, my editor at Oxford University Press in the UK. As well as commissioning the book, Susan also went through the typescript line by line, offering many suggestions for tightening and improving the text. Because the book was being published by two university presses on different sides of the Atlantic, I received no fewer than four useful reviews of my original proposal. I profited from both their advice and their encouragement.

Various friends and colleagues sent me offprints of their work, or addressed specific questions; in the latter category, I am grateful to Tim Howe (access to research material), Richard Janko (Herculaneum papyri), Franca Landucci (a copy of her unpublished talk "Intellectuals and Culture in the Court of Antigonus Gonatas"), Andrew Lane (economics), Manuela Mari (Macedonian religion), Alexander Meeus (Greek-Macedonian relations), Shane Wallace (Greek-Macedonian relations, and unpublished Rhamnous inscriptions), Kathryn Waterfield (resources for shipbuilding, and a hundred other questions), and Liv Mariah Yarrow (Pan coinage). Shane also gets a second round of thanks for his numerous and extremely helpful comments on the finished manuscript as one of readers for the University of Chicago Press, and I profited from the second reader's comments too. It was a great pleasure to work again with András Bereznay on the maps.

The book is dedicated to Paul Cartledge, the recently retired A. G. Leventis Professor of Greek Culture at the University of Cambridge, and the still active A. G. Leventis Senior Research Fellow at Clare College, Cambridge. For twenty years or more he has unfailingly and promptly answered my questions, reviewed some of my work before publication, and been my friend. There is a familiar figure from ancient literature, the "wise adviser," whose advice is ignored at one's peril. Along with a great many others, I thank Paul for his generosity, knowledge, and wisdom.

General Maps

A. THE HELLENISTIC WORLD, c. 250 BCE
BALTIC SEA
SCYTHIA
ILLYRIS
Danube
BLACK SEA
THRACE
MACEDON
EPIRUS
SICILY
AETOLIA
Peloponnese
Byzantium
Heraclea
BITHYNIA
PAPHLAGONIA
PONTUS
GALATIA
Halys
PHRYGIA
CAPPADOCIA
CARIA
LYCIA
PAMPHYLIA
CILICIA
Crete
MEDITERRANEAN SEA
Cyprus
Antioch
PHOENICIA
SYRIA
CYRENAICA
Alexandria
Memphis
The Fayyum
EGYPT
Nile
RED SEA
ARABIA
ARMENIA
Tigris
MESOPOTAMIA
Euphrates
Babylon
BABYLONIA
SUSIANA
MEDIA
CASPIAN SEA
HYRCANIA
PARTHIA
PERSIS
Persian Gulf
CARMANIA
Aral Sea
MARGIANA
Oxus
SOGDIANA
BACTRIA
AREIA
DRANGIANA
ARACHOSIA
GEDROSIA
PAROPANISADAE
GANDARIS
Indus
INDIA
MAURYAN KINGDOM
INDIAN OCEAN
0 km 700
0 miles 400

B. NORTHERN GREECE, MACEDON, AND THRACE
PAEONIA
Pelagonia
ILLYRIS
MACEDON
THRACE
Nestus
Philippi
Strymon
Lake Prasias
Amphipolis
Thasos
Cyrrhus
Edessa
Pella
Mieza
Beroea
Thessalonica
CHALCIDICE
Pydna
Aegae
Olynthus
Dium
Cassandrea
Athos
Aeane
Olympus
PARAUAEA
ATINTANIS
TYMPHAEA
EPIRUS
Phoenice
MOLOSSIS
Dodona
Gonnoi
Corcyra
Pindus Mts.
Crannon
THESSALY
Iolcus
Demetrias
Paxoi
IONIAN SEA
Ambracia
AMPHILOCHIA
DOLOPIA
AEGEAN SEA
AENIS
Lamia
MALIS
Oreus (Histiaea)
Scyros
ACARNANIA
Medion
Heraclea Trachinia
Thermopylae
Leucas
Stratus
DORIS
PHOCIS
Elatea
Euboea
Thermum
Callion
AETOLIA
Delphi
0 km 100
0 miles 50

C. THE PELOPONNESE AND CENTRAL GREECE
ACARNANIA
AETOLIA
Thermum
Oeniadae
Calydon
Naupactus
OZOLIAN LOCRIS
Delphi
PHOCIS
Chaeronea
BOEOTIA
Thebes
Leuctra
Plataea
Euboea
Chalcis
Eretria
AEGEAN SEA
Rhamnous
ATTICA
Eleusis
Megara
Athens
Piraeus
Prasiae
Sunium
Camp of Patroclus
Salamis
Aegina
Saronic Gulf
Andros
Coressus
Ceos
Cythnos
Cimolos
Cephallania
Zacynthos
Gulf of Corinth
Patrae
Aegium
Helice
Dyme
Cerynea
Bura
Aegeira
Pellene
Pharae
ACHAEA
Leontium
Tritaea
Elis
Sicyon
The Isthmus
Corinth
Cenchreae
Phleious
ARCADIA
Caphyae
Mycenae
Olympia
Orchomenus
ARGOLIS
Mantinea
Argos
Epidaurus
Methana
Aliphcira
Troezen
Tegea
Phigalea
Megalopolis
Hermion
Hydrea
IONIAN SEA
Messene
Eurotas
Sellasia
MESSENIA
Sparta
LACONIA
Cythera
0 km 80
0 miles 100

D. GREECE AND THE AEGEAN
BLACK SEA
THRACE
BITHYNIA
MACEDON
ITALY
Byzantium
Maronea
Aenus
Lysimachea
Pella
Samothrace
THRACIAN CHERSONESE
Imbros
Hellespont
Lemnos
MYSIA
THESSALY
Lesbos
Pergamum
Scyros
AEGEAN SEA
LYDIA
Sardis
PHRYGIA
Euboea
Chios
Athens
Andros
Ephesus
Samos
IONIAN SEA
Peloponnese
Ceos
Syros
Miletus
Cythnos
Delos
CARIA
Sparta
Paros
Myndus
Amorgos
Cos
Caunus
LYCIA
Ios
Telmessus
Thera
Rhodes
Crete
Caudos
0 km 150
0 miles 100

Time Line and King Lists

338	Battle of Chaeronea; Macedon gains hegemony over the Greek states
336	Assassination of Philip II; Alexander III becomes king
334–323	Alexander the Great's eastern campaigns
323–322	Lamian War
319	Birth of Antigonus Gonatas
307–301	Demetrius Poliorcetes (Antigonus' father) ruler of Athens
301	Battle of Ipsus; collapse of Antigonid power
295	Antigonus in charge of southern Greece; Demetrius Poliorcetes takes Macedon
292	Antigonus defeats Boeotian rebellion
290s–220s	Tyrannies in the Peloponnese
286	Athenians expel Antigonid garrison from the city
285–246	Reign of Ptolemy II Philadelphus in Egypt
284	Demetrius Poliorcetes abdicates in favor of Antigonus
281–276	Repeated attempts by Antigonus to gain Macedon
280	Revival of Achaean Confederacy
279	Celtic invasion of Greece; death of Ptolemy Ceraunus; Macedonian throne becomes vacant
278	Nonaggression agreement between Antigonus and Antiochus I of Syria
277	Battle of Lysimachea (Antigonus vs. Celts)
276	Antigonus gains Macedon
276–246	Cyrenaica independent of Egypt
275	Marriage of Antigonus to Phila; birth of Demetrius II
274–272	Pyrrhus occupies Macedon

272	Death of Pyrrhus
272–239	Antigonus securely king of Macedon
c. 270	Antigonus campaigns against Ptolemy in Asia Minor
268–262	Chremonidean War
265	Death of Areus I of Sparta
263	Alexander II of Epirus invades Macedon
262–256	Athens under direct rule of Antigonus
261	Battle of Cos (Antigonus vs. Ptolemy)
258	Battle of Ephesus (Rhodes vs. Egypt)
257	Demetrius II becomes joint king with Antigonus
253	Antigonus founds festivals on Delos and builds stoa
252	Aratus' coup in Sicyon; expansion of Achaean Confederacy begins
250	Demetrius the Fair in Cyrenaica
249–245	Rebellion of Alexander of Corinth
249	Antigonus defeated at sea by Ptolemy II
246	Battle of Andros (Antigonus vs. Ptolemy)
245	Antigonus recovers Corinth
243	Aratus takes Corinth; Antigonus allies with Aetolians
239	Death of Antigonus
235–220	Alliance of Aetolians and Achaeans
229	Death of Demetrius II; Athens regains its freedom
200	Athenian *damnatio memoriae* of Antigonids

RULERS OF EGYPT (PTOLEMIES)

Ptolemy I Soter (305–285)
Ptolemy II Philadelphus (285–246)
Ptolemy III Euergetes (246–221)
Ptolemy IV Philopator (221–204)
Ptolemy V Epiphanes (204–180)

RULERS OF MACEDON

Philip II (360–336)
Alexander III the Great (336–323)

Philip III (323–317)
Alexander IV (323–308)
Olympias (for underage Alexander IV) (317–316)
Cassander (316–297)
Philip IV (297)
Antipater (297–294)
Alexander V (297–294)
Demetrius I Poliorcetes (294–287)
Pyrrhus (287–284)
Lysimachus (287–281)
Ptolemy Ceraunus (281–279)
Antigonus II Gonatas (276–239)
Demetrius II (239–229)
Antigonus III Doson (229–221)
Philip V (221–179)
Perseus (179–168)

RULERS OF SYRIA (SELEUCIDS)

Seleucus I Nicator (305–281)
Antiochus I Soter (281–261)
Antiochus II Theos (261–246)
Seleucus II Callinicus (246–225)
Seleucus III Soter (225–223)
Antiochus III Megas (223–187)

INTRODUCTION

A Time of Transition

In the winter of 252/1 BCE, a young man called Aratus took it upon himself, with the help of a few trusted friends and a band of mercenaries, to organize a coup in Sicyon, a small but prosperous state in the northeast Peloponnese, overlooking the south coast of the Gulf of Corinth. It was Aratus' native town, but he had been living in Argos ever since the assassination of his father, Cleinias, by a political rival thirteen years earlier. Besides, he was clearly at odds with the town's current ruler, Nicocles, who had only a few months earlier made himself the "tyrant," or unconstitutional sole ruler, of Sicyon by murdering the previous incumbent. Aratus' coup, vividly retold in Plutarch's *Life of Aratus*, succeeded; no blood was shed, and Nicocles fled into exile.

Despite the fact that Sicyon was in origin a Dorian town—the Dorians, one of the main ethnic groups of ancient Greece, had a strong presence in the Peloponnese—Aratus, with a mature head on his twenty-year-old shoulders, decided that its safety lay in joining the Achaean Confederacy, a federation of many towns of the north and northwest Peloponnese, which were populated by people who claimed a different ethnicity and spoke a different dialect of Greek. His youth may seem surprising, but this was an era of early death, so that men were often thrust into prominence at a young age.

Even after Aratus' coup, however, Sicyon remained troubled, and he needed funds to help quiet things down. He had invited back to Sicyon a large number of men who had been exiled by Nicocles or his predecessors, and it was going to be an expensive business to

The fountain-house of the gymnasium at Sicyon, which was built by Cleinias, the father of Aratus, when he was effectively the sole ruler of the city. Photo by author.

settle their claims for reparations, more than Sicyon could afford. He approached Antigonus Gonatas, the king of Macedon, with whom his father had been on reasonable terms, but Antigonus prevaricated. It was, in fact, a cheeky appeal by Aratus, since Nicocles, the tyrant he had ousted, had enjoyed tacit support from Antigonus, as had his predecessors. Everyone knew this, but the fact that Antigonus had left it tacit gave Aratus his opening. Aratus was planning to restore to Sicyon a large number of enemies of Macedon, turning it into an anti-Macedonian stronghold. It is no wonder that Antigonus prevaricated.

But Aratus had inherited from his father formal friendship not only with Antigonus, but also with Ptolemy II Philadelphus of Egypt, and it was to Ptolemy that he then turned. He was promptly given twenty-five talents, but it was not enough. Aratus spent it on ransoming Sicyonian prisoners of war, which left unresolved the issue of compensation for the returning exiles, so he sailed to Egypt to ask for more.

Voyages by sea were often hazardous in ancient times, and Aratus did not have an easy time of it. A storm swept him off course, and the boat barely made land on the island of Andros, where he hid while being hunted by a posse from Antigonus' garrison. But he evaded capture and did eventually make it to Egypt, traveling part of the way on a Roman ship bound for Syria.

Ptolemy gave him a generous amount of money, 150 talents (900,000 silver drachmas; millions of dollars), in cautious installments, which the young man put to good use. Antigonus felt he had to do something:

> Antigonus decided to try to win Aratus over to his side once and for all, or at least to drive a wedge between him and Ptolemy. Among his friendly gestures, none of which was at all welcome to their recipient, he once sent Aratus in Sicyon portions of the victims from a sacrifice he was performing to the gods in Corinth. And at the well-attended banquet which followed the sacrifice, he made a speech for all his guests to hear. "I used to think," he said, "that this Sicyonian boy had no more going for him than a noble and patriotic spirit, but it looks as though he's also a competent judge of the lives and affairs of kings. After all, in the past he used to ignore us. He had his gaze fixed hopefully abroad, because all the talk he was hearing of elephants and fleets and palaces gave him a high regard for Egyptian wealth. But now that he has seen behind the scenes there and realizes that everything is just play-acting and trumpery, he has come over entirely to our side. I myself welcome the young man. I have decided to involve him in all my affairs, and I require all of you to consider him a friend."

This was untrue, of course: Antigonus had not won Aratus' friendship. He was trying to start a rumor designed to undermine the relationship between Aratus and Ptolemy.

Whether or not the story is authentic—and the fact that Plutarch was drawing on Aratus' own *Memoirs* does not guarantee its veracity—it introduces us to some of the major players and themes of this book. Greece had become impoverished over the course of the fourth century, chiefly as a result of endless wars fought either between Greeks, or at least on their lands. The Greek states were weak and poor, and those with large populations were not infrequently short of food. They needed the support of kings, despite the cost in terms of subservience, and so we see Aratus appealing to both Antigonus and Ptolemy for funds. The state and status of the Greek cities, which were supposedly self-governing even in this era of absolute kingship, will form one thread of this book.

The Greek world, vastly expanded since the eastern conquests of Alexander the Great (334–323), was in the early third century essentially divided between three great monarchical superpowers. The Ptolemies had Egypt, Cyrenaica (the northeastern coastline of Libya, in today's terms), Cyprus, parts of Arabia, and a great many possessions and friends along the south and west coasts of Asia Minor and in the Aegean. The Seleucids had Syria and all the lands east to Afghanistan and the Hindu Kush, and much of Asia Minor was theirs as well, the rest being divided between a number of smaller kingdoms and Egypt. And the Antigonids had Macedon and hegemony over the states of mainland Greece. In 278, Antigonus and Antiochus I Soter, ruler of Syria from 281 to 261, came to a world-changing agreement, whereby neither would interfere in the other's territory, and so Greece became a region where Egyptians and Macedonians vied for influence, just as in the story told by Plutarch Ptolemy outdid Antigonus by funding Aratus.

This was the essential dynamic in Greece for much of the third century. The great kings of Macedon and Egypt could challenge each other, with Greeks as proxies, without (usually) coming directly to blows and creating a major international incident. It was rather as if, today, the United States and Russia were using such tactics—propaganda lies, funding, and other expressions of support—to vie for influence in some modern, developed country; for, though impoverished, Greece was not the equivalent of a third-world state, and the Greeks were always aware of their proud history.

Naturally, this situation was resented by the Greeks, and this introduces us to another major dynamic of the period: the struggle of the Greeks to gain enough power to stand up to the kings on their own. There were a number of strategies by which states forged closer relationships with one another, as when each of two neighbors granted mutual citizenship to the other, but the one that will occupy us most in this book is federation. There had been confederacies in Greece before, the most powerful being the Boeotians (led by Thebes) and the Chalcidians (led by Olynthus), but the Achaean and Aetolian confederacies were prepared to break their ethnic bounds in order to maximize their potential for expansion. That was the crucial step taken by the Achaeans when they admitted Sicyon to their confederacy. They knew that if they allowed themselves to be restricted by ethnicity, they would never become powerful enough to rival Macedon.

THE SOURCES

So Greece in the third century presents us with a fascinating swirl of currents. It was a critically important time. Antigonus stabilized Macedon after many years of appalling chaos; the Achaean and Aetolian confederacies grew and thrived, incorporating many of the formerly autonomous Greek city-states; Ptolemaic influence in the Aegean basin waxed and, thanks largely to Antigonus, waned. Athens and Sparta were the only major Greek cities to remain outside of confederacies during Antigonus' reign, but the third century saw them undergo great changes as well. Athens learned to accept that it was no longer strong enough to play a significant part in international affairs, as it had done for two hundred years, and began its long drift toward becoming a university town. Sparta refused to lie down, but underwent drastic constitutional changes as a result of internal pressures, and eventually lost its centuries-old dyarchy, its double kingship.

These are important events, but the third century also presents us with great challenges. Source material is often critically short for ancient Greek history, but it is particularly parlous for the third century. No original historical account of the period, written in antiquity, has survived. Most critical are the losses of Diodorus of Sicily's narrative of the period, and that of Hieronymus of Cardia.

Diodorus wrote a work titled *The Library* because he intended it to be a one-stop shop for the history of the known world, from its beginnings until 60 BCE. Nothing remains of his work after 302, however, except excerpts and paraphrases, and few of them are relevant to this book. But Diodorus liked to write about how kings coped with the vicissitudes that Fortune visited upon them, and he would have made much of Antigonus' reign. Hieronymus of Cardia had been a high official on the staff of Antigonus' grandfather and father, and wrote his history in the court and under the patronage of Antigonus himself. He was uniquely positioned, then, to write about the period, and so he did, covering the years from the death of Alexander the Great in 323 to the death of Pyrrhus of Epirus in 272—but none of his work remains, except insofar as we can infer its contents from its presumed influence on later writers.

Actually, there is a more-or-less consecutive narrative of the period, but it is not much use. In the late first century BCE, an upper-class Romanized Celt called Pompeius Trogus wrote, in Latin, a *Philippic History* in forty-four books. It went from the beginning of time up until the reign of Augustus, the first emperor of Rome, and like all such "universal histories" it was a compendium of earlier writers' work. But it is all lost, except that it was epitomized, perhaps late in the second century CE, by a Roman called Marcus Iunianius Iustinus, or "Justin" to us. Justin's primary intention, however, was to provide orators with moral examples, drawn from history, for them to use in their declamations. In any case, as an epitome, the historical narrative is severely curtailed, and the exploits of Antigonus Gonatas occur only in the epitomes of books 24–26. These make only fourteen pages (in the standard English translation), and Justin focused only on a few of the more sensational episodes from Antigonus' career.

Other historians are not much help. The greatest historian working in the Hellenistic period was Polybius of Megalopolis, writing in the 150s BCE. His purpose being to cover and explain the Roman takeover of the Mediterranean, he started his narrative in the year 220; and although much of his work is lost, in what remains he occasionally cast his eyes farther back in time. It is always illuminating when he does.

No other historian of the period survives in more than a few pitiful fragments. Phylarchus of Naucratis continued Hieronymus' history and took it down to the end of the 220s, but the work is lost, and the fragments that remain were mostly preserved by writers concerned to illustrate Phylarchus' sensationalist and moralizing approach to history, rather than preserving his actual historical work. Philochorus of Athens covered Greek and especially Athenian history from 320 to 260, but later writers have preserved nothing from his pen that is relevant to this book. Nymphis of Heraclea's contemporary account of the Macedonian kingdoms down to the 240s is more or less entirely lost. Aratus of Sicyon wrote his own self-admiring account of the events in which he was involved, his *Memoirs*, but it is lost, apart from its refraction through Plutarch's *Life of Aratus*.

Several of Plutarch's *Lives* are useful. Plutarch of Chaeronea in Boeotia was writing his biographies and learned essays in the late first through early second century CE, so he was working at a considerable remove from the events of the third century BCE. Moreover, he was a biographer, not a historian in the strict sense of the word, so his focus was on psychology as much as politics and events. Nevertheless, he was a good researcher, and he often preserves precious material. The most relevant of his *Lives* will be those of Demetrius Poliorcetes (Antigonus' father), Pyrrhus of Epirus (Antigonus' rival in his early years), Aratus of Sicyon (Antigonus' rival in his later years), and the reforming kings Agis IV and Cleomenes III of Sparta.

Other than these sources, we must rely on scraps. For most periods of Greek history, such anecdotes supplement our information; for the third century we have to make more of them. Isolated scraps of useful information can be found in many places, from damaged fragments of papyrus to medieval encyclopedias, but some writers preserve more than one. Polyaenus of Macedon, for instance, wrote a book called *Stratagems in War* in the second century CE, in which he described the remarkable military exploits of many past generals, including a few of Antigonus. As Pausanias of Magnesia-by-Sipylus traveled around Greece in the middle of the second century CE, collecting material for his great *Description of Greece*, he too remarks occasionally and anecdotally on Antigonus and other aspects of third-century Greek history; he is our primary source for the Celtic invasion of Macedon and Greece, and an important source for the Chremonidean War.

Antigonus was a friend of philosophers, and so there are further stories about him in Diogenes Laertius' *Lives of the Eminent Philosophers*, written perhaps in the first half of the third century CE. He also makes an occasional appearance in Plutarch's essays, known as the *Moralia*, but most of these stories are trivial. Finally, Athenaeus of Naucratis, writing in the third century CE, portrayed in his lengthy *Savants at Dinner* a banquet, in the course of which erudite men regaled one another with anecdotes from the past (usually concerning food, foodways, and luxury). Antigonus and his courtiers feature in a number of these, not least because one of Antigonus' protégés, Persaeus of Citium, wrote a *Symposium Memoirs*, which reflected life at Antigonus' court and which served as one of Athenaeus' sources.

For our purposes, we are grateful for any scrap of information, however apparently insignificant. But particular problems arise when dealing with anecdotal evidence, due to the fact that it rarely comes with any context. First, we are left in the dark about the dates of the events these sources choose to mention. Second, they often refer only to an "Antigonus," without telling us which of the several possible Antigonuses he might be—an issue that also bedevils the evidential use of coins and inscriptions.

Given the dearth of relevant literature, inscriptions become a vital source; these are official state documents that were felt to be worth preserving and so were inscribed on a durable material such as stone. At their best, they fill gaps—sometimes important ones—or corroborate testimony from elsewhere, but they are often so particular that they start hares that we can pursue nowhere because of lack of further evidence. The inscriptional record is capricious and incomplete: if, at a guess, the city of Athens (which had the epigraphic habit more than anywhere else) inscribed two hundred state laws and decrees a year throughout the third century, we never have more than half a dozen from any given year, and we have fewer than three hundred in total for the period from 300 to 228. Moreover, most surviving inscriptions were written on stone, and over the centuries the stones have been damaged, so that it frequently requires expert work to try to recover the original text, and of course interpretations differ.

Still, for the third century inscriptions are of undeniable importance, as any reader of this book will soon detect. The main additions to our knowledge of the third century over the past hundred years have come from the discovery of new inscriptions. Archaeology and numismatics shed occasional light, though the dating of Antigonus' coin issues is extraordinarily difficult and controversial; Egyptian papyri—a vital source for the Hellenistic and Roman periods that even enables bursts of microhistory—are largely irrelevant to this book.

The sources are poor and scattered, but the prospect is not entirely gloomy. A history of the third century can be written. If you have enough pieces of a jigsaw puzzle, you can gain both the broad picture and, occasionally, more detail. That will be enough to restore Antigonus to his proper place in history, and hopefully to generate interest in, and further research on, Greek history of the period.

PART ONE

The Wilderness Years (319–276)

CHAPTER 1

The Disarray of Macedon

It was the fate of Macedon in the decades immediately following the death of Alexander the Great in June 323 to be the prize that every ambitious Macedonian generalissimo wanted to win. Even if these generals succeeded in taking for themselves some slice of Alexander's eastern empire, they still longed for Macedon. It was the homeland, and they felt that the legitimate ruler of Macedon would automatically command a greater degree of respect than any other king, however great his empire. They all wanted the prestige of being able to call themselves "King of the Macedonians."

In the less than fifty years between Alexander's death and Antigonus' gaining the throne in 276, Macedon had twelve rulers—eleven kings and one queen. Five kings were assassinated, and the single queen was put to death after a show trial, precisely for having assassinated one of the kings. Two kings died in battle; two died of tuberculosis; and two were ousted from the kingdom by rivals and died abroad. Two more of Alexander's successors, Ptolemy of Egypt and Antigonus Monophthalmus ("One-Eye"), the grandfather of Antigonus Gonatas, made unsuccessful attempts on the throne in the course of these years, or threatened to do so. In the final years of complete chaos, the early 270s, when Macedon was being overrun by belligerent Celtic migrants in search of new lands, several pretenders to the throne emerged, and there was a period when there was no king at all.

This, in a nutshell, is the turmoil that beset Macedon after Alexander's death. An account of these events will afford us perspective on the achievement of Antigonus: after over four decades of turmoil, it was he who stabilized the country. He ruled for almost forty years without palace intrigues, and his Antigonid successors retained the throne for another seventy years, until the dissolution of the monarchy by the Romans in 167. To put this in perspective, the dynasty Antigonus founded lasted longer than any single dynasty of Roman emperors. Rulership was a delicate business; Antigonus had to deal with other kings, with the power-possessors of the kingdom of Macedon, with his army, and with the Greek states, and he seems to have made a good job of it. The lack of evidence (see the introduction) makes it hard to know how to judge him, but these facts alone suggest that he deserves recognition as a strong and successful king.

MACEDONIAN RESOURCES

Macedon was attractive to Alexander's successors not just because of the prestige to be gained by ruling the country, but also because of its wealth. It was far less wealthy than the other major Hellenistic kingdoms (Egypt and Syria), but that comparison hardly made it poor. Philip II, the father of Alexander the Great and king of Macedon from 360 until his assassination in 336, enormously expanded and enriched the country. It had always had the potential to be wealthy from its natural resources, but it had been held back by the fact that it was divided up into separate cantons, each with dominant baronial families, and by frequent warfare with its enemies to the west, north, and east—the Illyrians, the Central Balkan tribes, and the Thracians.

It had long been the job of the Macedonians, possessors of a frontier state, to keep these warlike tribes at bay. For centuries—as was recognized by intelligent men such as the Roman general Titus Quinctius Flamininus—Macedon had been a buffer, absorbing or repelling waves of attackers, and preventing them from reaching the southern Greeks. Hence the military nature of the Macedonian monarchy. It was Philip's foundational achievement to unite the cantons of Upper Macedon (the mountainous inland) with Lower Macedon, under central government from Pella, so that they could present a solid front and discourage such raids. Previously, Macedonian kings had had to be content with alliances with the rulers of the upper cantons.

Macedon had also been held back by the fact that it was Greeks, not Macedonians, who had made themselves the middlemen and brokers of the country's natural resources. As early as the seventh century, Greeks had started to settle in the northern Aegean, on land that lay within the geographical boundaries of Macedon, or in nearby Thrace. It was only once Macedonians began to manage these resources properly that they were able to dictate to the Greeks, whereas previously it had been the other way around. Philip was only taking this program to its logical conclusion when he ruthlessly drove the Greeks out of the area and took over their settlements. The wealth of Macedon was for Macedonians, not Greeks.

Macedon is a mountainous country, with a Mediterranean climate on the coast (supporting olive-oil production, for instance) and a continental climate inland. The mountains of Upper Macedon were covered in forests, and the broad plains of Lower Macedon were well watered all year round by rivers and streams fed by prolific snowmelt and adequate rainfall. Extensive wetlands helped to put food on tables, and the country was capable of growing a great surplus of wheat for export. Large estates specialized in cereal crops or viticulture or stock breeding, so that, as well as local markets, there was a flourishing international market economy, dependent on imports and exports. There was land to spare for luxury enterprises such as breeding horses for the cavalry elite of the country, and urban craftsmen supplied everything from everyday tableware to silverware, high-end jewelry, delicately carved furniture, tapestries, carpets, and clothing. In terms of its daily needs, the kingdom was more or less self-sufficient.

The mountains and highlands of Upper Macedon provided an apparently never-ending supply of timber, much of which was of a good enough quality to be used for ships and house-building. "The best timber that arrives in Greece for the use of carpenters is Macedonian, since it is smooth, straight-grained, and resinous," claimed Theophrastus of Eresus, Aristotle's successor as head of the Lyceum, who had visited the country. The king owned all the natural resources of his country (and as much of its land as was not otherwise in private hands), and he came to do a roaring trade in this commodity. Few regions of the Mediterranean could rival Upper Macedon's timber forests. Several of the rivers were wide and deep enough to float logs down to the coast. Good roads aided communication, transport, and the movement of armies.

As well as timber, the mountains contained minerals, especially gold and silver, in large quantities, but also copper and iron (and a small amount of tin), and another of Philip's great achievements was to hugely expand the country's potential in this respect, until he had stabilized its revenues at a very high level. According to the historian Diodorus of Sicily, the gold mines of Philippi alone (newly discovered in Philip's day) produced an annual income/weight of over 1,000 talents—though whether he meant 1,000 talents of gold, or gold worth 1,000 silver talents (the usual standard for currency) is not clear. A talent weighed perhaps thirty kilograms (sixty-six pounds). Then again, Herodotus of Halicarnassus, writing in the 420s, said that in his day the silver mines near Lake Prasias produced a talent's weight of silver every day. Whatever the details, it is clear that the Macedonian mines were a significant resource, at a time when ownership of property worth three or four talents made a private individual a member of the wealth elite. A Macedonian king's revenues dwarfed those of any other Greek state.

Macedon had a population of perhaps five hundred thousand in Antigonus' time; it was the most populous state in Greece by quite a wide margin. Proportionate to the population, there were far fewer slaves in Macedon than their southern neighbors in Greece considered normal. A good percentage of the population were pastoralists, breeding sheep, goats, and cattle, selling animal products such as leather and wool, and hiring oxen out for transport; meat constituted a higher proportion of the Macedonian diet than it did farther south. Many others were small-scale agriculturalists, but there were also large estates and a number of conurbations. As in all premodern societies, there was a great gulf between the wealthiest landowners, traders, and craftsmen, who could think about surpluses, selling to markets, and leisure pursuits, and the majority of the population, subsistence farmers who could focus on little else than putting food on the table.

This was the Macedon that Antigonus fought to make his own—a place that for him was pregnant with the sentiment surrounding a lost homeland, but a place also that, with good management, could satisfy the extravagant desires of most princes. A letter written by a Macedonian called Hippolochus in the 290s gives some idea of the wealth of the kingdom. It tells of an aristocratic wedding feast, which was a vision of richness and splendor, from the endless exotic dishes and the best wines, both in literally stupefying quantities, to the valuable tableware and the entertainments. Lighting was provided by statues holding silver candlesticks, which were revealed as darkness fell by curtains drawn aside by some hidden mechanism. Every guest, attended by slaves, received as gifts a golden wreath, a golden goblet, a large silver bowl, and a bronze plate. This was the lifestyle to which Antigonus was accustomed, and which he intended to ensure for himself and his friends.

A RECIPE FOR DISASTER

When Alexander died heirless in Babylon, in June 323, his senior officers could not decide whom to choose as the next king and ended up with a compromise, with the kingship shared between Alexander's half brother Arrhidaeus, who became Philip III, and Alexander's son, Alexander IV. This was a recipe for disaster, not least because neither king was fully competent: Philip suffered from some form of mental impairment, perhaps autism, and Alexander was an infant, born several months after his father's death. The Macedonian monarchy was a charismatic monarchy, depending essentially on the personality of the king. Neither Philip III nor Alexander IV was able to function as that kind of king. They would both be manipulated by those who claimed to speak in their names.

We do not know whether Arrhidaeus had accompanied his brother throughout the eastern campaign, but on Alexander's death he was in Babylon, and his co-king was born there a few months later. Both kings remained in the East, pawns in the early power struggles between Alexander's generals (known as the Successors), until Antipater, the man Alexander had left as his viceroy in Macedon, was able to bring them home in 319. By then, Philip III had acquired a wife, Eurydice (a half-Illyrian granddaughter of Philip II), and she had already made it clear that, as his guardian, she expected to be treated as at least the equal of whoever controlled young Alexander.

Aged Antipater died before long, bequeathing his position as guardian of the kings to another former staff officer of Alexander's, Polyperchon. But Antipater's son, Cassander, wanted it for himself, and he stirred up war. While his ally, Antigonus Monophthalmus, secured Asia Minor against Polyperchon's allies there, Cassander consolidated his hold on southern Greece, against Polyperchon's efforts to thwart him, as a preliminary to marching north.

Cassander's position was hugely improved in 317 when Philip III, no doubt at Eurydice's urging, wrote an open letter to all the Greek states, announcing that he was ordering Polyperchon to resign the regency and his command of the Macedonian armed forces in favor of Cassander. Eurydice had become the effective head of state. The court had split along the fault line that had been predictable ever since the decision to divide the kingship: Polyperchon was responsible for Alexander IV, Eurydice for Philip III, and daggers were drawn. It was clear that only one of the kings would survive the contest, or neither of them would.

Polyperchon must have known that something like this was afoot, because he had taken steps to secure the safety of Alexander IV and his mother, Rhoxane (an Uzbek princess), by sending them to Molossis, the dominant region of Epirus at the time, where the young king's grandmother, Olympias, was living. Polyperchon had been trying to persuade Olympias to return to Macedon and take over the guardianship of Alexander IV, and he now withdrew to Epirus himself, since he was no longer welcome in Eurydice's Macedon. He negotiated with the Molossian king, Aeacides, a cousin of Olympias, to borrow an army, promising in return that Alexander IV would one day marry Aeacides' daughter, Deidameia. He had no time to waste, because Cassander had not yet marched north to claim Macedon as his own. He was tied up with his forces in southern Greece, leaving Macedon as vulnerable as it ever would be.

So Polyperchon marched on Macedon, with Alexander IV in his retinue and Olympias as the symbolic head of his army. Eurydice came out to meet them at the head of her troops, but her bid for power came to an abrupt end. Her troops, "respectful of Olympias' high rank and mindful of all the good Alexander had done them," deserted her. She and Philip were walled up in a tiny cell by Olympias, leaving only a single narrow opening through which their needs were supplied. The end was inevitable:

> This abuse of the wretched prisoners went on for many days, but then the Macedonians began to feel sorry for Olympias' victims and to think badly of her. She therefore arranged for Philip to be stabbed to death by some Thracians—he had been king for six years and four months—but to her mind Eurydice deserved a worse form of punishment, since she had been making her views known and crying out that the kingdom belonged to her rather than to Olympias. She therefore sent her a sword, a noose, and some hemlock, and told her to use one of them, whichever she wanted, to kill herself. . . . Eurydice prepared her husband's body for burial, taking care of the wounds as well as she could under the circumstances, and then she hanged herself with her girdle.

This kind of savage purge was far from uncommon in Macedon when one ruler took over from another. Olympias was now the queen of Macedon, and she turned to eliminating the friends and supporters of Cassander. Immediately after the death of Alexander the Great, Olympias had been responsible for spreading a rumor that Antipater and his family had poisoned her son, and she now desecrated the tomb of Cassander's brother Iollas, whose hand was supposed to have personally delivered the poisoned chalice at a party. Cassander's loathing of Olympias was deeply personal, and he abandoned his war in the south and marched north. He knew he could expect support in Macedon from the survivors of the same factions that had supported Eurydice and allowed her to declare for him, but his enemies raised three armies against him and must have been confident of victory.

Cassander launched a blitzkrieg and displayed tactical genius. First, he transported his men by boat around the Aetolians, who were holding the pass at Thermopylae against him. He then split his army into three. One division checked Aeacides in Epirus, another did the same to Polyperchon on the southern border of Macedon, and while these two enemies were occupied, Cassander defeated Olympias' forces in Macedon itself. Polyperchon's army was bribed away from him, and he fled. One of Cassander's first moves as the new ruler of Macedon, once he had captured Olympias and put her to death, was to foment rebellion in Epirus against Aeacides and install a puppet on the Epirote throne in his place. His victory was swift and overwhelming, and he held the remaining Macedonian king, Alexander IV, along with his mother, Rhoxane, under house arrest in Amphipolis. Cassander was perhaps thirty-five years old and he would rule Macedon for twenty years, until his death in 297.

KING CASSANDER

Cassander was a strong and effective ruler, and his reign was good for Macedon. Once he had secured its borders against the northern tribes and the Illyrians to the northwest—no easy job, but Cassander handled it well, both militarily and diplomatically—his main foreign-policy concern was the growing strength of his former ally, Antigonus Monophthalmus, who by 315 had made himself the master of all Asia, and made no secret of the fact that he was eyeing the Macedonian throne. He was close to making himself a second Alexander. Cassander accordingly arranged an alliance with the other Macedonian rulers, Lysimachus of Thrace and Ptolemy of Egypt, and four years of warfare began. The so-called Peace of the Dynasts brought the war to an end in 311, with the status quo not much altered from what it had been at the outset.

One effect of this war, however, was extremely important. In Diodorus' words, "The treaty specified that Cassander was to be the

General of Europe until Alexander, Rhoxane's son, should come of age; that Lysimachus should be master of Thrace and Ptolemy of Egypt and the neighboring cities in North Africa and Arabia; that Antigonus Monophthalmus should have supremacy in all Asia; and that the Greeks should be autonomous." In other words, the treaty recognized for the first time the basic divisions of the empire Alexander had created. Each of these dynasts had a core territory; he would of course try to expand his territory at the expense of the others, because that was the ethos of these kings, but nevertheless the treaty moved them all closer to being rulers and possessors of distinct territories.

By acknowledging that the empire had been divided up, the Peace of the Dynasts made Alexander IV expendable. Technically, each of the Successors was merely the governor of one or more of the provinces of his empire, but none of them was now going to return to being a subordinate when Alexander came of age and claimed the entire empire as his inheritance. And the first throne he would claim would undoubtedly be that of Macedon—so, perhaps in 308, Cassander quietly had the teenager and his mother poisoned. When the secret leaked out, there was a telling lack of protest from any of the others.

Cassander had now killed the mother, wife, and son of Alexander the Great. Alexander's illegitimate son Heracles was eliminated as well; his mother, Barsine, had been Alexander's mistress for a few years from 333. It was Polyperchon who killed Heracles and Barsine, but he did so at Cassander's insistence, as part of the deal that secured peace between the two of them. It was the end of the main branch of the Argead line, which had been the ruling dynasty of Macedon for centuries. Only one of Alexander's half sisters remained alive (Thessalonice, who was married to Cassander and had three sons), and his full sister, Cleopatra, was soon to be killed by Antigonus Monophthalmus because she was poised to marry Ptolemy and thereby legitimate his claim to the Macedonian throne.

Alexander IV's death removed the last obstacle to kingship. Antigonus Monophthalmus had been recognized as the king of Asia for some time, and by 307 the Athenians were hailing both him and his son as kings, but now they all assumed the title—Antigonus first in 306, making his son Demetrius joint king at the same time (so that thirteen-year-old Antigonus Gonatas, Demetrius' son, immediately became the heir to the most powerful realm in the world at the time), with the others soon following suit. Lysimachus became king of Thrace, Ptolemy became simultaneously king and pharaoh of Egypt, and Cassander became king of Macedon.

So Cassander was relatively secure in Macedon; he must have been accepted by the surviving Macedonian power-possessors, and his marriage to Alexander's sister helped to legitimate his claim to the throne. On seizing the throne ten years earlier, he had also made a big show of burying the bodies of Philip III and Eurydice with royal honors, since it was the duty of the new king to see to the funeral of his predecessor. And he undertook kingly duties such as accelerating the urbanization of the country by founding cities: Cassandrea and Thessalonica (named after his wife). He was showing the world that he was the right king for Macedon.

THE BATTLE OF IPSUS

The ambitions of the Successors ensured that the Peace of the Dynasts would not last. War broke out again in 307, and once more all the other dynasts lined up against Antigonus and Demetrius. The anti-Antigonid alliance now included Seleucus, the former governor of Babylonia, who had taken the eastern provinces of the empire from Monophthalmus and declared himself king. Most of the fighting took place in Asia and the eastern Mediterranean, and by 304, Cassander, left to his own devices, had won back, by force or diplomacy, many of the Greek cities that had previously been attached to the Antigonids, and the whole Antigonid enterprise in Greece was at risk. Demetrius broke off a year-long siege of Rhodes, where his ingenuity at inventing siege engines earned him his sobriquet Poliorcetes ("Besieger"), and returned to Greece.

After two years of tough campaigning, Demetrius had recovered much of southern Greece, and was poised to invade Macedon itself. Cassander sent an army to Asia Minor, where Lysimachus was keeping Antigonus Monophthalmus at bay while waiting for Seleucus to arrive from the east with reinforcements, including a force of several hundred war elephants, the most terrifying military unit in the world. Cassander then marched south to confront Demetrius in Thessaly. But nothing happened.

For weeks the two armies remained close to each other, doing nothing—perhaps maneuvering for a favorable position, but failing to find it. But Antigonus Monophthalmus felt that the critical action was going to take place in Asia Minor, between him and Lysimachus, and was even prepared to abandon Greece, at least temporarily. On his father's orders, Demetrius left Greece and joined the others in Asia Minor. Once Seleucus arrived in 301, battle was joined at Ipsus in Phrygia. Each side was commanded by two kings and fielded about eighty thousand men; all the peoples of Alexander's empire were represented. It was the greatest battle of the Successors, and the most significant. If the Antigonids won, they would soon have the entirety of Alexander's empire.

But it was an outright victory for the anti-Antigonid alliance. Antigonus died, Demetrius fled, and Macedon remained safely in Cassander's hands. He also regained control of much of Greece, except that Demetrius and Antigonus Gonatas held Demetrias (a heavily fortified port town in Thessaly, and an important center of northern Aegean trade), Chalcis in Euboea (another valuable naval base), Piraeus (the port of Athens), and Corinth. These were precisely the four harbor towns the importance of which for controlling Greece was acknowledged by a later Macedonian king, Philip V, when he described them as "the Fetters of Greece." Actually, Philip omitted Piraeus, but only because in his time it was free. The Greek delegates to the Roman Senate in 197 who quoted this remark of Philip's recognized the importance of the Fetters. "As long as Chalcis, Corinth, and Demetrias remained in Macedonian hands," they said, "it was impossible for the Greeks to have any thought of liberty." But the importance of these places was economic as well, and the Antigonids depended heavily on harbor dues and other commercial taxes. Their taxes were steep, which did not endear them to their subjects.

The Antigonids thought they had Athens too, but the Athenians refused Demetrius entry and expelled those members of his family who were there. The Antigonids were massively wealthy, they still had the most powerful fleet and an army of nine thousand mercenaries remaining after Ipsus (many of them veterans of Alexander's conquests), and they had some overseas possessions, most importantly some of the Cyclades islands, Cyprus, and the Phoenician cities of Tyre and Sidon. They expected to survive by moving between havens and making raids as opportunities arose, like pirate kings. In Greece, they made Corinth their main residence. They built a royal mansion there on the northern slopes of the Acrocorinth, commanding wide views north, east, and west. The Antigonid garrison, installed on the Acrocorinth in 303 (replacing a sequence of other Macedonian garrisons that had been there since

The rugged Acrocorinth, 600 meters (2,000 feet) high, rises out of the plain just south of the ancient city of Corinth. It dominates the surrounding countryside, and anyone who garrisoned it could prevent the passage of enemy armies through the narrow isthmus that joins the Peloponnese to mainland Greece. Photo by author.

337), would remain there for sixty years, until the position was lost under Antigonus Gonatas when he was king of Macedon.

ANTIGONUS AND HIS FAMILY

Demetrius had seven, possibly eight, wives, and a number of mistresses. Several of Alexander's successors were polygamous. This "bedroom diplomacy" was a sign of the insecurity of the times: they contracted multiple marriages as a way of making alliances with other power-possessors who threatened or could be useful to their plans. It meant that many of the crowned heads of Antigonus' time were his cousins. But, because of his father's promiscuity, Antigonus had a number of half brothers, and one younger half sister, but he also had one full sister, Stratonice, who became the wife of both Seleucus of Syria and his son Antiochus, one after the other.

Antigonus' and Stratonice's mother was Phila, Demetrius' first wife. Phila was the sister of Cassander, and the eldest daughter of Antipater, the former viceroy of Macedon and regent of the kings; she was given to Demetrius in 320, to seal the alliance between their two fathers, despite the fact that she was considerably older than him (very unusual in the Greek world) and had been married twice before. She was born c. 350 and Demetrius c. 336, so he was still a teenager. Despite rumors of Demetrius' dissatisfaction with the arrangement, Antigonus was born within a year or two, and the usual date given for his birth is 319. It is possible that he was born in the month of July, since, as we will see later, there is evidence of a celebration in his honor in that month, in the Attic town of Rhamnous, and the normal occasion for such celebrations was a birthday.

Phila was a formidable woman and a real catch for Demetrius. She was an early prototype of the semi-independent queens of the later Hellenistic period. She was the first royal woman to be assigned the title *basilissa*, "queen," invented by the Antigonids as a way of identifying the most important woman in the court. Even when she was young, her father, Antipater, used to consult her on matters of policy, and she deployed her personal wealth in ways designed to sustain her husband's power, such as presenting troops with back pay and giving impoverished families dowries for their daughters.

An inscription from the island of Samos honors a man who was "in Queen Phila's retinue and the captain of her bodyguard"; such a guard was a dignity that seems to have been awarded only to those royal wives who were most active in the public sphere. At Athens, she was worshipped as a goddess, Phila-Aphrodite (that is, the perfect woman and wife). She seems to have been a loyal wife to Demetrius, and he trusted her enough to use her as an ambassador to her brother Cassander at a critical juncture (when he was taking Cilicia over from her and Cassander's brother). But her ultimate act of loyalty was that, after Demetrius' expulsion from Macedon, when all seemed lost, she committed suicide, aged in her early sixties.

Most of Antigonus' half siblings are no more than names to us—Corrhagus, Alexander, Demetrius the Meager, Demetrius the Fair, and another Phila, the daughter of one of Demetrius' mistresses. Phila, Corrhagus, and Demetrius the Meager we know nothing about. All we know about Alexander is that he was given as a hostage to Ptolemy when he was a child; he seems to have died in Egypt. Only Demetrius the Fair has any kind of history; on one occasion that we know of, he acted as his brother's agent, and I shall cover the episode in its proper place. Antigonus' maternal half brother Craterus, the product of one of Phila's earlier marriages, also worked for him, as his viceroy in the Peloponnese. He may have been a scholar as well. There is a Craterus that we know of from this period, though his work has not survived, who made the first collection of Athenian decrees (up to the end of the fifth century) as a resource for historians and other scholars, and it is probable that this far-sighted antiquarian was the brother of Antigonus.

Craterus' son, however, as we shall see, turned against his uncle. This incident is something of an anomaly in the Antigonid court. Antigonus Monophthalmus had troublesome nephews as well, but essentially the Antigonids were a close family, far less prone than the Ptolemies or Seleucids to internal rivalries and assassinations, and far more likely to make use of family members in positions of responsibility. Antigonus Monophthalmus used to boast that he allowed Demetrius into his presence armed, and throughout the whole history of Antigonid rule of Macedon there was only one assassination in the immediate family, that of the younger son of Philip V, another Demetrius, who was suspected of being a Roman puppet and was killed by his father in the winter of 181/0. When Demetrius Poliorcetes was imprisoned by Seleucus, Antigonus Gonatas offered to surrender all his possessions, and himself as a hostage, for his father's return.

We do not know where Antigonus was born. His grandfather, Antigonus Monophthalmus, was in Asia Minor at the time, and Celaenae in Phrygia was usually his base, so that may be where his family stayed. Demetrius was still a little too young for independent command. The ancient idea that Antigonus' name Gonatas derives from his birth in Gonnoi in Thessaly is nonsense: "man of Gonnoi" is *Gonneus* in Greek. "Gonatas" is undoubtedly a Macedonian word whose meaning we do not know, Macedonian being an obscure dialect of Greek, interlaced with non-Greek elements.

But that has not stopped people, ancient and modern, from speculating. "Gonatas" is very similar to the genitive of the Greek word for "knee," *gonatos*, and this derivation has found favor. One late Latin version of his eponym was *geniculosus*—Antigonus Geniculosus; the word is corrupt, but related to *geniculum*, meaning "knee." So for many people he is "Antigonus the Knock-Kneed," or something. But there are so many Antigonuses around in the early and middle Hellenistic periods that ancient writers would certainly have identified him by a knee-related affliction, if he had one. Could "Gonatas" have meant "firstborn" in the Macedonian dialect? It is possible.

It is impossible for us to know what Antigonus looked like. If a passage by the Roman writer Seneca the Younger (first century CE) refers to him, as seems likely, he was apparently short and ugly; but his father and grandfather were so famously tall, handsome, and charismatic that Antigonus probably suffered in the contrast. He was once taunted from the walls of a town he was assaulting for his unsightliness. "Oh, but I thought I was good-looking," he self-mockingly replied—and, once he had captured the town, he sold as slaves those who had jeered at him. On some of the coins he minted, showing the head of the god Pan, the god has a fleshy, jowly appearance (see the front cover of this book). This is probably a portrait of the elderly Antigonus, assimilated to the god. To judge by these coin portraits, Antigonus went clean-shaven, following the trend set by Alexander the Great and adopted by the majority of the Successors.

Scholars are so desperate to pinpoint a likeness of Antigonus that almost any possible and unattributed portrait is liable to be roped in. A bust from the Villa of the Papyri in Herculaneum in Italy has been suggested, but it is probably Ptolemy II. Others have argued for one of the paintings from the villa at Boscoreale, on the Bay of Naples in Italy, built by Publius Fannius Synistor in the first century CE and buried by the eruption of Vesuvius in 79. It is certain

It has been suggested that the central figure in this painting from the villa at Boscoreale could be Antigonus. But it is not very likely, and so coin portraits (as on the cover of this book) afford us our best impressions of what Antigonus may have looked like.

enough that these paintings are copies of Antigonid originals, but it is sheer guesswork which, if any, of the portraits is our Antigonus. The best bet is the one reproduced here, where Antigonus might be the central figure, with a staff and a Macedonian shield, and the seated woman may be his mother, Phila; they both appear to be listening to the philosopher on the left. But the "Antigonus" figure is rather effeminate for a Macedonian king and is more likely to be just a personification of Macedon, identified by the typically Macedonian hat and the emblematic shield.

ANTIGONUS AND THE PHILOSOPHERS

We know virtually nothing of Antigonus' early life. His main teacher in his teenage years was perhaps the polymath Euphantus of Olynthus, who later addressed a treatise on kingship to an Antigonus. We know that, even as an adult, Antigonus liked to relax by playing ball games, which presumably stemmed from his teenage years. He does not seem to have been present at his father's great siege of Rhodes in 305–304. He was probably dividing his time between Corinth and Athens.

Antigonus also visited Athens on and off in the 290s and early 280s, accompanying his father. His sojourns in Athens may have been relatively settled periods in his young-adult life, which was so frequently disturbed by warfare—although we should remember that a good portion of the Athenian population was hostile to Macedonian rule. Nevertheless, it was while living in Athens that the prince gained a lifelong reputation as a bon vivant—good training for a future Macedonian king, who was expected to be able to drink his courtiers under the table. More importantly, the city was a center of culture, and Antigonus seems to have made the most of it, rounding out his earlier schooling.

In later life, Antigonus was on good terms with a number of philosophers, including Zeno of Citium (in Cyprus), the founder of the Stoic school, and Zeno's protégé and adopted son, Persaeus. He reputedly used to visit Zeno whenever he was in Athens. His court poet was the Stoically inclined Aratus of Soli (in Cilicia). It is clear that Antigonus appreciated the brilliance of this philosophy, and the fact that its ideology permitted and even encouraged political activity. So he had Persaeus tutor his son Halcyoneus—but also made him the military commander of the vital Acrocorinth, the citadel of Corinth.

The ideology of Stoicism also saw the patronage of kings as a legitimate source of income. As we shall see, Antigonus used his position as king of Macedon to attract a number of intellectuals to his court, including philosophers, as temporary or long-term visitors, and where he could not help them by such direct patronage, he helped them financially: he gave the princely sum of 3,000 drachmas, for example, to the Stoic Cleanthes of Assos, the second head of the school.

But none of this adds up to Antigonus' being a philosopher himself, as is sometimes claimed, let alone that Platonic ideal, a philosopher-king. There is no indication of this in the anecdotes about him, and certainly no evidence to suggest that, as king, he tried to put Zeno's or anyone else's political thought into practice. It would only be plausible to entertain the idea that he was a Stoic, but an anecdote in which Antigonus teases Persaeus for being less indifferent to money than a Stoic should shows little understanding of Stoicism, which was a matter of constant striving and self-improvement.

When Zeno died, Antigonus is reported to have said that he had lost the opportunity to see his work objectively: "I have lost the theater of my actions." He took Zeno's advice, then, but that does not make him a philosopher either. He also used to travel from Athens to the island of Euboea, perhaps to attend to business in the Antigonid fortress of Chalcis, but also to attend the circle of intellectuals centered on Menedemus of Eretria, an important Stoic philosopher who had also been admired by his father; but these were probably only occasional visits, falling short of a full course of philosophy.

It was traditional for a well-off young man, even a prince, to complete his higher education (with its focus on grammar and rhetoric) by attending the classes of a philosopher or two, and Athens was the best place to find them. Zeno started his school there in 300, a few years after Epicurus had established his commune, the Garden, as a base from which to promulgate his ideas; perhaps, in less high-minded moments, he also communicated to his followers his loathing for Macedonian rule and his aversion to all involvement in public life. The Platonic Academy (pro-Athenian in its politics) was flourishing, and so was the pro-Macedonian Aristotelian Lyceum. There were also unattached teachers willing to impart their views on a vast range of topics. We will not be far off the mark if we imagine Antigonus dipping into this lecture course and that, rather than committing himself to one school. He might have been a scholarly king, but he was no philosopher-king.

ANTIGONUS COMES OF AGE

The final years of Cassander's reign were peaceful for Macedon, but soon after his death in 297 the country descended into civil war. Cassander had always been somewhat frail; he had not marched east with Alexander the Great, for instance, as he might have been expected to. He probably suffered from tuberculosis. His eldest son inherited the Macedonian throne as Philip IV, but he followed his father into the grave within a few months, probably succumbing to the same disease. Cassander's two other sons then divided the country between them, with Alexander V west of the river Axius and Antipater I to the east.

There was bad blood between the two teenage kings—and Demetrius felt that the unsettled situation boded well for him. He returned in force to Greece from the eastern Mediterranean. In the years since the battle of Ipsus, he had not been idle. Most importantly, he had taken Cilicia, thus securing an eastern Mediterranean kingdom consisting of Cilicia, Cyprus, Tyre, and Sidon (as well as retaining his possessions in Greece and the Aegean). But rulership of Macedon remained his goal.

When Antipater murdered his mother, Thessalonice, who was favoring his younger brother, and drove Alexander from his half of the kingdom, Alexander retreated to Thessaly and appealed to

Demetrius for help. This was the opportunity Demetrius had been waiting for. When the appeal arrived, he had already starved Athens into submission, and was poised to take Sparta, for the first time in its history, but he gave up even that claim to fame.

Antigonus, by now in his early twenties, gained military experience with his father in the eastern Mediterranean, and then in his campaigns in southern Greece. When Demetrius marched north in response to Alexander's appeal, he left his son in charge of southern Greece, the first official position we know that Antigonus held. Alexander, however, had also turned to Pyrrhus of Epirus, the son of Aeacides and a cousin of Alexander the Great.

Born in the same year as Antigonus, at the age of eighteen Pyrrhus had fought for the Antigonids at Ipsus (while Antigonus had not), and it was in Pyrrhus' hands that Demetrius had left his Greek possessions when he and Antigonus fled after the battle. Demetrius had recently married Pyrrhus' sister, Deidameia. But Pyrrhus subsequently transferred his allegiance to Ptolemy of Egypt, and it was with Ptolemy's support and Ptolemy's stepdaughter Antigone as his wife that in 297 he regained the throne of Epirus that he had lost in 302. Ptolemy was doubtless keen to have a strong ally in Greece. From then on, Pyrrhus became a constant thorn in the Antigonid flesh.

Pyrrhus' assistance to Alexander was costly. Having unified the peoples of Epirus, he was anxious to expand, and he demanded the two cantons of Macedon that bordered Epirus to the east (Parauaea and Tymphaea), and the right to annex without Macedonian interference the Greek peoples to his south in Amphilochia and Ambracia. Alexander agreed. Pyrrhus quickly chastised Antipater and then, with the help of Lysimachus, the neighboring power, reconciled the two brothers. Ambracia (modern Arta) became Pyrrhus' capital, and at the same time he added Atintanis to his vastly extended kingdom. At a stroke, Epirus became a major power in the Greek world.

But when Demetrius arrived, he killed Alexander and terrified Antipater into flight. Lysimachus was disinclined to take action, preferring to trade his recognition of Demetrius' right to Macedon for Demetrius' abandonment of the remaining Greek cities of Asia Minor that still owed him allegiance, but were now, since Ipsus, within Lysimachus' territory. Over the next few years, Demetrius also lost almost all his other territories to his rivals: Ptolemy gained Cyprus, Seleucus took Cilicia.

But Demetrius secured his control of Greece by taking Thessaly (which had been a satellite of Macedon since Philip II's time) and installing garrisons in the most important Greek cities, reversing his father's policy of allowing the Greeks their freedom. Antigonus remained in the south as his father's viceroy there, and his eldest son, Halcyoneus, was born in Athens in 290 or thereabouts. Halcyoneus' mother was Antigonus' mistress Demo, so he was technically illegitimate, but Antigonus kept him by his side and gave him full honor; indeed, it was not until Antigonus was in his early forties, by which time Halcyoneus was an adult, that he became the father of a legitimate son, and up until then Halcyoneus had been treated as the crown prince.

In 292 Antigonus served Demetrius well by containing a Boeotian rebellion. He had to raise a scratch force to do so, because his father was adventuring abroad with the army, but Demetrius hastily returned, joined his son, and besieged the city of Thebes into submission, despite Pyrrhus' attempts to distract his attention by raiding Thessaly. There was considerable loss of life among the Macedonian besiegers, and an anecdote survives that is designed to tell us that Antigonus was made of less stern stuff than his father. When he queried whether so many deaths were really necessary, Demetrius snapped back at him: "What's that to you? Do you owe the dead wages?" But ancient writers with a moralistic bent liked to contrast Antigonus with Demetrius, as the good son of an immoral father. On another occasion, Antigonus is reliably reported to have said that, in military matters, he preferred timing to force. He was a cool-headed rather than an impetuous commander—but that is also to say that he lacked the military brilliance of an Alexander or a Pyrrhus.

THE DOWNFALL OF DEMETRIUS

For much of the late 290s and early 280s, Demetrius defended Thessaly and Macedon against Pyrrhus' threatening, but ultimately futile attempts to further expand his territories. By 288, Macedon was reasonably secure. This was good for Macedon, but bad for Demetrius, because he immediately began to dream of recovering all the former Antigonid territories in Asia. He was planning to amass an army of one hundred thousand (mainly mercenaries), and a fleet of five hundred warships was being prepared in his shipyards.

Once again, Antigonid schemes forced all the other kings, now including Pyrrhus, into a coalition. In 287, while Ptolemy's admiral sailed for southern Greece to stir the Greek states into rebellion, Lysimachus and Pyrrhus invaded Macedon from the east and west, respectively. Demetrius took steps to meet the threats, but resentment had been building up in Macedon over his autocratic style of kingship and his assumption that Macedon was no more than a springboard for eastern conquest. He had anchored his kingship by conquest and by marriage to Antipater's daughter, but it was not enough. Whether or not it was true, the story circulated that he had been seen tossing a bundle of petitions he had received from his subjects into a river, and there were other signs that he did not care for them as a king should.

His Macedonian troops abandoned him, just as they had abandoned Eurydice thirty years earlier; no doubt they or their officers had been suborned in advance. It was an inauspicious start to the attempt to establish an Antigonid dynasty in Macedon. Lysimachus and Pyrrhus gained the eastern and western halves of Macedon almost without a blow. This was different from the earlier division of the country between the teenage kings, Cassander's sons, because now Macedon was ruled from outside, from Thrace and Epirus. Antipater, in exile in Thrace, pointed out that he was the rightful king of Macedon, so Lysimachus, his father-in-law, had him killed; so expired the Argead house, which had ruled Macedon for over three hundred years.

Demetrius fled to what remained of his Greek possessions, and he and Antigonus used their wealth to rebuild their strength, even if not to the extent Demetrius had dreamed of. And then, driven by his insane dreams of conquest, in 286 Demetrius invaded Asia Minor, leaving his son in Greece. Antigonus had work to do: Lysimachus' response to Demetrius' invasion of his territory was to persuade Pyrrhus to go on the offensive in Greece. The Epirote king tried to stir up rebellion in Thessaly and attacked some of Demetrius' garrisons in the Greek cities.

It was Antigonus who kept things safe for the Antigonid cause, proving himself to be a competent general and diplomat. He lost the Phocian town of Elatea, where, with Lysimachus' help, the Antigonid garrison was bribed to leave, and the town was never recovered; but he installed garrisons in some of the Peloponnesian towns, joining the great garrison at Corinth in the task of keeping the Greeks there quiescent.

A year later, Demetrius was trapped in the Taurus Mountains between Asia Minor and Syria. Lysimachus' son Agathocles was blocking his way north into Asia Minor, and Seleucus blocked his other routes. Seeing the hopelessness of the situation, his men were deserting in droves, and Demetrius soon fell into Seleucus' hands. He died in captivity two years later, having drunk himself to death, according to rumor. Seleucus sent his ashes back to Antigonus in Greece:

> When Antigonus heard that his father's remains were on their way home, he put to sea with his entire fleet [from Corinth] and sailed for the islands to meet them. The urn, which was of beaten gold, was handed over, and he placed it in his largest flagship. . . . As the fleet sailed into Corinth, the urn, decorated with royal purple cloth and a diadem, was clearly visible in a prominent position on the prow, with an honor guard of young men standing by it. . . . But it was Antigonus himself who stirred the most pity and sorrow in the spectators crowding the shoreline, when they saw how he grieved and wept.

Antigonus toured the Greek cities by sea to receive their recognition of his kingship, and buried the urn in Demetrias in Thessaly, where Demetrius was revered as the city's founder. From his prison, Demetrius had bequeathed his kingship to Antigonus, and Antigonus took the Macedonian year 284/3 to be the first year of his reign, to establish dynastic continuity. He was at the time a king without a country, and later king-lists style him at this time the "king of Greece," not of Macedon, even though he held only enclaves in Greece. But the important point is that Antigonus felt himself to be the rightful king of Macedon, by direct inheritance from his father. That belief dictated his actions over the following years.

DESCENT INTO CHAOS

On the expulsion of Demetrius in 287, Lysimachus and Pyrrhus of Epirus divided Macedon between them, but in 284 Lysimachus drove Pyrrhus out and claimed all Macedon as part of his now enormous kingdom (Thrace, much of Asia Minor, and Macedon, with a newly built capital at Lysimachea on the Thracian Chersonese). Lysimachus' court was in trouble, however, with his two main wives each fighting for her son to become Lysimachus' heir. Arsinoe, a daughter of Ptolemy, came out on top, and Agathocles, Lysimachus' son by Nicaea, the daughter of Antipater, the former viceroy of Macedon (and therefore a cousin of Antigonus), was assassinated. The kingdom fell apart, but not quite into civil war, because Agathocles' wife and supporters persuaded Seleucus to get involved. Seleucus, following the imperialist impulse of all Alexander's successors, saw his chance. If he took Lysimachus' kingdom, he would have all of Alexander the Great's former empire except for Egypt—which would probably fall next to him or his heirs.

Seleucus invaded Asia Minor, and at the battle of Corupedium in February 281, west of Sardis, he defeated and killed Lysimachus. It was the last of the great battles of Alexander's successors. Arsinoe fled with a mercenary force to the fortress town of Cassandrea in Macedon, which had been favored and probably refounded by Lysimachus; she hoped that she would be able to install her eldest son, Ptolemy (who was about eighteen years old), on the now vacant Macedonian throne. She might even have arranged for him to be declared king, because Justin tells us that the Macedonian throne rightly belonged to Arsinoe's children.

Seleucus now held all Asia from the Aegean to the Tigris, and in 293 he had made his son Antiochus joint king, responsible for the provinces east of the Tigris up to the borders of Pakistan. Ptolemy II (who had inherited the Egyptian throne in 285) must have felt threatened, especially since Seleucus had accepted his elder half brother, Ptolemy Ceraunus ("Thunderbolt"), into his court when he fled from Egypt.

Ptolemy Ceraunus had an excellent claim to the Egyptian throne, and Seleucus was promising to help him get it; Ceraunus was the son of an earlier marriage than the one that had produced Ptolemy II and Arsinoe, and the eldest son by about ten years. His mother was Eurydice, another daughter of Antipater, the former viceroy of Macedon, who, blessed with a large family, had made prolific use of them for diplomatic purposes; Ceraunus was therefore another cousin of Antigonus. Seleucus spent a few weeks organizing his new territories in Asia Minor, before setting out for Europe to take Lysimachus' former possessions there as well. He had not seen Macedon, the country of his birth, for fifty years. We can only imagine what had been happening in Macedon during those few months; perhaps the leading families took responsibility for their own territories, so that Macedon effectively reverted to cantonization. But Ceraunus wanted Macedon for himself, and he treacherously stabbed Seleucus to death with his own hand.

The murder of the most powerful king in the world was bound to lead to chaos. Seleucus' son Antiochus urgently needed to prevent Asia Minor from falling apart, but he had to deal first with uprisings in the Middle East that were supported by Ptolemaic troops, and it was not until 279 that he was able to arrive in person with an effective army. In the meantime, Asia Minor had been in the care of one of his generals, but he had been unable to prevent some disintegration.

By the time Antiochus got there, several countries in Asia Minor had become independent kingdoms, some of the autonomous Greek cities (most importantly Heraclea and Byzantium) had formed a confederacy that was hostile to his rule, and much of the southern and western coastlines had fallen into Ptolemaic hands. Taking into account the fact that he also had the friendship of the rich mercantile islands Rhodes and Cos, Ptolemy II effectively held the entire eastern Mediterranean and southern Aegean coastline. After the downfall of Demetrius, he had the strongest fleet in the eastern Mediterranean.

PTOLEMY CERAUNUS AND THE CELTS

In Europe, Ptolemy Ceraunus, who must have laid his plans carefully and made suitable friends in advance, was acclaimed king of Macedon by the army, "because they had no alternative," as one historian suggests. He had already been welcomed by the inhabitants of Lysimachea, Lysimachus' capital city, who were loyal to their founder's memory and therefore opened their gates to the killer of his killer. The Macedonians might have considered Antigonus a possibility, but many of them still hated the memory of his father.

Late in 281 or early in 280, however, Antigonus launched an invasion of Macedon by land and sea, to claim the country as his by inheritance. But he was repulsed in a sea battle by Lysimachus' former fleet and ships supplied by the people of Heraclea, all under the generalship of Ceraunus, and he retreated to Greece.

As for Arsinoe, to avoid warfare and to gain Cassandrea, Ceraunus agreed to marry his half sister (which was considered unusual, but not quite incestuous) and adopt her children as his heirs. But he immediately butchered her two younger sons, the eldest, Ptolemy, having sensibly fled. Arsinoe too fled, and ended up in Egypt, where she became a queen for the third time. Ptolemy soon returned to Macedon at the head of an army of Illyrians, and although he failed to defeat Ceraunus and establish himself on the throne, he seems to have remained nearby, perhaps based in one of the cantons of Macedon that was loyal to him, and ready to take advantage of any further opportunities that presented themselves.

Ceraunus established himself in a fractured Macedon and recovered all Thessaly, except for Demetrias, which remained in Antigonus' hands. He negotiated nonaggression pacts with Antiochus and Pyrrhus, but failed in an attempt to reconcile with his half brother, Ptolemy II of Egypt. It was lucky for him that Pyrrhus, a charismatic and talented war leader, was now seeking adventures in Italy and Sicily, rather than casting covetous eyes on Macedon. Ceraunus even loaned him some troops to help him on his way westward, and Antigonus may have loaned him some transport ships. But in 279 a huge war party of Celts approached from the northern Balkans, where they had settled after being displaced from north-central Europe a hundred or so years earlier, when one large band had even sacked Rome. They had been gradually moving east along the Danube ever since, and in all probability earlier incursions had been checked only by the formidable reputation of Lysimachus. But now Lysimachus was dead.

The Celts sacked Seuthopolis, the capital of the Odrysian kingdom of Thrace, overran the country, and continued onward, taking advantage of Macedon's troubles to launch a massive invasion. They were in search of new lands to settle, and were accompanied by their families and wagons laden with belongings, so there may have been as many as three hundred thousand people on the move. Archaeologists have uncovered evidence of the destruction of rural estates with their fortified farmsteads; smoke from burning fields and houses bruised the sky.

When it came to battle, the Macedonian army was cut to pieces. Ceraunus had refused to pay off the Celts, which was the usual method of dealing with them; he had refused an offer of help from the Thraco-Illyrian Dardanians of what is now Kosovo, because he did not want to let these traditional enemies of Macedon be responsible for its deliverance; and he had lent thousands of troops to Pyrrhus. Ceraunus' head was paraded on a spear as a deterrent to further resistance. Justin, ever the moralist, presents this as divine retribution for Ceraunus' slaughter of Arsinoe's children.

Ceraunus left no heir, and a man called Meleager, almost certainly Ceraunus' brother, was deposed by common consent after only a few weeks on the throne, which was apparently long enough for him to demonstrate his incompetence. Meleager was succeeded by a man called Antipater, a nephew of Cassander, who reigned for only forty-five days; since this was held to be the length of time the seasonal Etesian winds blew (called the *meltemi* today), he became known as Antipater Etesias. It is not clear why he was deposed, but we have not quite seen the last of him: like Ptolemy, the son of Lysimachus and Arsinoe, he lived on and was in a position to make a nuisance of himself when Antigonus launched his final, ultimately successful bid to gain Macedon.

Antipater Etesias was replaced by Sosthenes, a competent general, because the Celts were still on the rampage and a strong hand was needed at the helm. Luckily, the Celts lacked siegecraft, so that people were able to huddle in towns and fortresses. But although Sosthenes kept the country relatively safe for a couple of years, he refused the kingship when it was offered to him. He probably had to put down the attempts of further pretenders to the throne—and possibly a second attempt by Antigonus Gonatas as well. At any rate, in 277 Antigonus was not far away, on the Thracian Chersonese, as we shall see. In the meantime, Macedon had no ruler, and the country had effectively split up. Cassandrea, for instance, fell under the rule of a tyrant of legendary cruelty called Apollodorus, and we may imagine that other towns and cantons likewise made their own arrangements. Philip II's Macedon had fallen apart, and it would take a strong hand to reunite it.

CHAPTER 2

The Pride of Sparta

Sparta had always been a champion of Greek freedom. The famous Peloponnesian War of 431–403, in which the Spartan alliance fought and defeated Athens and its many allies, was explicitly undertaken to free the Greeks from the tyranny of Athenian imperial leadership. The Athenians had gradually subordinated their allies until the "alliance" scarcely differed from an empire. The Spartans undertook to set matters right.

Even before that, because they had never been ruled by a "tyrant," a sole ruler who seized power by unconstitutional means, the Spartans had the reputation of being opposed to tyranny and of aiding states that wished to throw off their tyrannies. The reputation was unfounded, since the Spartan-led Peloponnesian League was originally formed at the end of the sixth century in part to try to impose a tyrant on Athens, and when the Spartans succeeded in destroying the Athenian alliance at the end of the Peloponnesian War, they immediately set about changing it into an alliance of their own, with themselves in the dominant position previously occupied by Athens.

As long as they were in power, the Spartans, along with everyone else, deployed the slogan of "freedom" cynically, with an eye to their own advantage. Greek politicians were always quick to make use of the emotive terminology of "tyranny" and "slavery." Nevertheless, the Spartans' reputation persisted, and when the Greek states became part of the Macedonian empire, it was natural for them to resist.

SPARTA AND THE LEAGUE OF CORINTH

After Philip II, the father of Alexander the Great, had defeated the Athenians and the Thebans at the battle of Chaeronea in 338, he bound the mainland Greek states together in a common peace, to prevent the internecine warfare that had always troubled them and kept Greece disunited. The Greeks were not only to avoid internal strife within their states and take steps to keep the restive poor in their place, but were to respect one another's autonomy and territorial integrity, and act in concert against any offenders, or risk the armed might of Macedon. They were to provide delegates for a common parliament, the Council of the Greeks, which would debate and vote on issues that concerned them, and its decisions were to be binding on all the cities of the league. The Greeks were careful to select their delegates from among men who would be pleasing to Philip.

The council is nowadays called the League of Corinth, because Corinth was the primary meeting place. It went a long way toward unifying the Greeks as a nation for the first time. Philip, and then his heirs, were to be presidents for life—virtually the presidents of the United States of Greece. The Spartans, however, refused to recognize Philip's supremacy and stayed aloof from the league. They had not fought against Philip at Chaeronea, but that decision was based mainly on their long-standing loathing for the Thebans, who had been responsible for the severe diminishment of Spartan power in the 370s and 360s. Since then, the Spartans had withdrawn somewhat from international affairs. But, although they had not fought against Philip, they had not fought for him either, as he had requested, and that, along with Sparta's residual strength, made it one of the Greek cities that Philip singled out for special treatment.

In the autumn of 338, Philip invaded the Peloponnese to deal with the Spartans. A nice story arose later—typical of the laconic style the Spartans adopted—that when Philip wrote to them asking whether they would prefer to receive him as a friend or a foe, they replied, "Neither." Philip's intention was not to destroy Sparta, but to neutralize it and to show the other Peloponnesian states that, thanks to him, it would be possible for them in the future to exist without the constant fear of Spartan dominance. He used his military supremacy to rearrange the borders of Laconia, the territory of Sparta, in favor of its neighbors. Argos and Megalopolis were the main beneficiaries (joining Elis and Sparta as the major centers of power in the Peloponnese), but Tegea and Messenia also came off well. Spartan territory was limited to the Eurotas valley and the two eastern peninsulas of the Peloponnese. Philip had not only weakened Sparta by reducing its territory, but had surrounded it with a cordon of cities that had reason to be grateful to Macedon for their renewed prosperity. Some of these cities—in particular, Mantinea, Messene, and Megalopolis—were also heavily fortified.

So, when the League of Corinth was formed in 337, why did Philip not incorporate Sparta into the league? He could have forced the issue. Its omission usefully drew attention to the fact that membership of the league was voluntary, but that hardly seems a sufficient reason. The probable answer is that Philip felt that Sparta would be a disruptive force within the league, since it would push constantly for a restoration of its position as leader of the Peloponnese rather than focusing, as the league was supposed to, on matters of common concern to all Greeks.

At several points in the 350s and 340s the Spartans had attempted to regain territory that had been removed from them by the Thebans. A story arose that a senior Spartan politician, on hearing that Philip had given the Messenians back some of their land, asked if he had also given them the ability to prevail in battle when the Spartans tried to reclaim the land. It was clear that the Spartans were still obsessed with their irredentist claims to possession of Messenia and hegemony in the Peloponnese. If they had been brought into the league, they would have had to swear oaths recognizing the legitimate existence of Messenia as an independent entity, and that they would never do. Whether inside or outside the league, they were going to cause trouble, and Philip preferred them to remain outside, relatively bereft of friends.

FALLING NUMBERS

Writing at the end of the first century CE, Plutarch of Chaeronea lavished praise on the Spartans for their resistance to Macedon. As long as they adhered to the "laws of Lycurgus" (as the Spartan constitution was known), he claimed, they retained some strength even when their society began to be corrupted:

> Although impaired by greed, yet after the victory of Philip of Macedon at Chaeronea, when all the Greeks first proclaimed him their leader on land and sea, and then after the subjugation of Thebes did the same for his son Alexander, the Spartans alone, despite the fact that their city had no defensive walls and their numbers had been reduced by constant warfare, and despite the fact that they had become much weaker and would be easy to defeat, still, as long as they kept alive some faint sparks of the laws of Lycurgus, they refused to take part in the campaigns of these kings or of those who succeeded to the Macedonian throne, nor did they join the common council [the League of Corinth], nor did they pay tribute.

Two of the causes of Spartan weakness in this account of Plutarch's deserve more emphasis: greed and the reduction in the number of Spartans capable of serving in the armed forces. These two causes are more closely connected than they might at first sight seem.

As is well known, all true-blue Spartan citizens—Spartiates, as they were called—were brought up in a rigorous educational and physical training program known as the *agōgē* ("the raising"), which was designed to weed out the weak and to indoctrinate teenagers into the moral imperative of serving the state in any capacity they could, especially as soldiers. Spartan society was rigidly hierarchical, and only Spartiates were full citizens of Sparta, with the rights of assembly and voting, and of serving on administrative and judicial committees. Their land was worked by serfs called "helots" ("captives"), and trade and industry were in the hands of free Laconians. For much of their lives, Spartiates were focused on the barracks and the messes to which they were assigned: they ate there, bonded with their messmates through dancing, simulated battle, and athletic competition, and put a proportion of the wealth they gained from their possession of land toward the maintenance of the mess.

One important consequence of this is that they were away from home a great deal, and responsibility for the maintenance of their households naturally fell to their womenfolk. This was unusual in ancient Greece. Generally speaking, ancient Greek women led fairly restricted lives, largely confined to the household, and limited to religious duties, domestic chores, and bringing up the children. On the whole, men dictated how women behaved and what they did with their lives. Spartan women, however, left such chores to their serfs or slaves, and entered more fully into male-dominated society.

The critical difference was that Spartan women could own property, which came to them as a dowry or by inheritance. On the death of her father, if a Spartiate woman had a brother or brothers, she received half the amount of land that he or they did; otherwise, she inherited it all, or shared it with a sister or sisters. Over the course of the fifth and fourth centuries, male Spartiate numbers went into a steep decline, so that there came to be many husbandless Spartan women, who had to take care of their estates by themselves.

By the middle of the third century, the richest people in Sparta were women, and despite their inability to hold political office or vote they wielded considerable influence through their many male clients and dependents. Many Greeks, especially Aristotle, were shocked at the license allowed Spartan women and saw it as a real flaw in their system. If women have wealth, they gain influence over the male leaders of the community, and so Aristotle asked scornfully: "What is the difference between women ruling and rulers being ruled by women?"

However, the freedoms allowed Spartan women opened a calamitous flaw in the system. Because women could inherit, in some cases—in increasingly many cases—the sizes of farms that men inherited shrank until they could no longer contribute to their messes, which meant that they lost their citizenship, were relocated out of the city of Sparta itself, and could, among other things, no longer form part of the Spartiate phalanx in battle. Messes became sites for the display of luxury by those who could still afford to contribute to them, rather than centers of military austerity, as they had been before. The process was accelerated by the tendency of wealth to marry wealth. This meant that fewer and fewer families accumulated wealth, as already rich men and women combined their estates, and then had few children so that they would not have to divide the estate too much. Spartan society was ruined in part by greed.

In 479, there were eight thousand Spartiates, full Spartan citizens; by the 240s, there were only about seven hundred, and only about a hundred families still owned land. The problems created by the inheritance rules and greed were accelerated by an earthquake that flattened Sparta in 465, and then the Spartans were almost continuously at war for sixty years from 431. In military contexts, they could make up the shortfall by recruiting their serfs, free Laconians, partially disenfranchised former Spartiates (called "Inferiors"), allied troops, and mercenaries, leaving senior posts and homeland defense to Spartiates, and by making sure that Spartiates did not bear the brunt of the fighting. When the Spartan king Agesilaus II invaded Asia Minor in 396, for instance, to free the Greek cities there from Persian rule, his army included only thirty Spartiates, his staff officers. But in political terms, from the middle of the fourth century Sparta was dominated by an increasingly small elite of super-rich men and women.

Why did they not correct the situation? Why did they not extend citizenship to a larger number of men, or even ban women from owning property? Clearly, the self-interest of the wealth elite was an inhibiting factor, along with the tradition that citizenship came only by birth and could not simply be assigned or granted to a non-Spartiate. Some remedial steps were taken. Around 500 it became the custom to treat unmarried Spartiate men with insulting disdain; only men who had already fathered sons were allowed to join the Three Hundred and die resisting the Persians at Thermopylae in 480; a regulation was introduced after the earthquake of 465 exempting a man from military service if he fathered three sons, and from all taxes if he fathered four. At much the same time, a form of eugenics was introduced: a Spartiate husband could get a younger man to sleep with his wife if he felt that a good soldier would be the result, and brothers might share wives. But these were Band-Aids, not solutions.

In addition to elite greed, it was probably pride that stopped them from taking the necessary steps—the same pride that kept them from fortifying their city with a defensive wall until the cusp of the third and second centuries, and sustained their long resistance to Macedon. They were proud of their ability to maintain their position high in the pecking order of Greek states even with fewer citizen soldiers than their rivals. There was also considerable inertia in Spartan society, due to indoctrinated reverence for the constitution; they were, quite simply, slow to change. It would take the work of two revolutionary kings later in the third century to remedy the situation—to try to restore Sparta to a position where it could challenge Macedon.

SPARTAN RESISTANCE

Excluded from the League of Corinth, the Spartans were free to pursue their own agenda, which consisted largely in the determination to recover Messenia and neutralize Megalopolis, the two most important of the hostile states that ringed their city. After Philip II's assassination in 336 and the ascension to the throne of Alexander III, later Alexander the Great, the Spartans remained outside the League of Corinth. Alexander invited them to join, but they rebuffed him, replying proudly that it was not their custom to follow others, but to take the lead themselves.

Alexander later pointedly chastised them for their aloofness: in 334, after his massive defeat of a first Persian army at the Granicus River in Asia Minor, he sent three hundred Persian shields back to Athens, for dedication on the Acropolis. The gesture resonated with the fact that the ostensible reason for his eastern expedition was to punish the Persians for their crimes against the Greeks, and especially Athens, in 480 and 479, during the Persian invasion of Greece. But the number of the shields was a pointed reference to the Three Hundred Spartans who had defended Thermopylae in 480, and the message that accompanied the captured weaponry was "Alexander, the son of Philip, and all the Greeks except the Spartans dedicated these spoils, taken from the barbarians occupying Asia." Alexander's expedition was supposed to be a panhellenic crusade, representing the Greeks collectively, and Spartan defiance irritated him and spoiled the propaganda, especially since they had been the leaders of Greek resistance to the Persians.

In 335, the year before Alexander set off on his eastern expedition, the Thebans had rebelled and suffered terribly after he defeated them: the city was razed to the ground, and all of its inhabitants were either killed or sold into slavery. Alexander undoubtedly meant the fate of Thebes to deter future Greek uprisings, but the Spartans ignored the lesson. They waited until Alexander was hundreds of miles away, deep in the Persian empire, and then in 331 they rose up against Macedonian leadership.

Sparta had two kings, one from the Agiad and one from the Eurypontid house. Agis III had come to the Eurypontid throne in 338. He shared a common Greek hope that Alexander would be crushed in the East by the Persians, and that the Greeks could regain their freedom from Macedon in the aftermath of such a momentous defeat. Already in 333 he had been in touch with the Persian forces in the Aegean, seeking military and financial support for a rebellion. But Alexander's unexpected success in the autumn of that year at the battle of Issus in Cilicia, his second great victory in the East, put paid to any expectations Agis might have entertained of substantial Persian support.

Instead, Agis recruited Greek mercenaries who had fought on the losing side at Issus, and united the perpetually warring Cretan states enough to gain another force from them as well. Meanwhile, Antipater was faced with a simultaneous rebellion by the Macedonian governor of Thrace, and while he was dealing with that, Agis brought his troops over from Crete to the Peloponnese, defeated a Macedonian army, and sent envoys around all the Greek states, asking for help in the cause of liberty.

Agis received positive responses from many Peloponnesian states, especially the Achaeans, Mantinea, Tegea, and Elis. The most notable Peloponnesian absentees were Corinth, Megalopolis, Messene, and Argos—Corinth because the Macedonian garrison there stifled rebellion, and the others because of their long-standing hatred of Sparta. The Athenians, whose help was vital, remained uncommitted after furious debate in the Assembly. Along with many other Greek states, they knew that they had contingents serving with Alexander who were effectively hostages for their good behavior. Still, Agis was able to muster a formidable army of perhaps thirty thousand.

Over the winter of 331/0, however, Antipater came to terms with the rebel Thracians, and in the spring he marched south to confront Agis, gathering more forces on the way, until his army numbered some forty thousand. Agis had Megalopolis under siege, the city that had been founded in 370 in Arcadia, close to the border with Laconia, precisely in order to curb Sparta. He waited on the plain near the city for Antipater's arrival. The Greeks, and especially the Spartans, fought brilliantly, but there was little they could do against such overwhelming odds. By the end of the day, over five thousand Greeks lay dead, and among them was Agis, who died a heroic death, ordering his men to leave while he held off the enemy, because he knew that his city could afford to lose no more Spartiates.

The League of Corinth dictated the punishment of those of Agis' allies who were league members, and pro-Macedonian governments were installed in rebel towns, but the decision about Sparta's fate was passed on to Alexander himself. But by the time the envoys reached Alexander in the East, he had made himself master of all Asia, and the affairs of Greece seemed insignificant to him. Sneering at Antipater's great victory as "a battle of mice," Alexander left the Spartans unpunished, probably judging it sufficient that they had been defeated with considerable loss of life, and that Antipater had taken fifty high-ranking Spartiates as hostages, further depleting their stock of citizens.

SPARTA QUIESCENT

Defeat at Megalopolis was a severe blow for the Spartans on top of all they had suffered in recent decades. In fact, they had to take steps to avoid the total collapse of their society. By Spartan custom, Spartiates who surrendered on the battlefield (rather than winning or dying) were called "Tremblers"; they were treated with disdain and lost some important citizenship rights. But since Sparta was critically short of citizens, the convention was not applied to the Spartiates who had surrendered at the battle of Megalopolis. The Spartans had waived this regulation once before, after the battle of Leuctra in 371. Realizing the dire consequences of further reducing citizen numbers, Agesilaus II, by far the dominant king at the time, had "allowed tradition to sleep for that day." The Spartans allowed it to sleep again after Megalopolis. This irritated the traditionalist hard-liners, but they really had no choice.

So the Spartans once more withdrew from international affairs for some decades. No king had the vigor of Agis. Subsequent events would show that the Spartans were searching their souls, trying to decide whether the dominance of a small, wealthy elite warranted a thorough shake-up of their society, and whether a restoration of the "laws of Lycurgus" would enable Sparta to regain its position as leader of the Peloponnese and rival to Macedon. Plutarch says that, in those decades, the Spartans were "constantly on the lookout for opportunities for revolutionary change." The pressure eventually built up to the reformation initiated in the 240s, while Antigonus was king of Macedon.

In 324, however, the Spartans at least debated and probably instituted the worship of Alexander the Great as divine, as many other Greek states did, probably at Alexander's request. A leading Spartiate, Damis, said, with devastating irony: "Since Alexander wants to be a god, let him be one." The following year, they signally refused to take part in the most significant of the Greek rebellions against Macedonian rule, the conflict known as the Lamian War. Led by the Athenians and Aetolians, the Greeks came close to defeating the Macedonians, commanded by Antipater, and came off worst only when he was reinforced by two of Alexander's former generals from Asia Minor. This was a major effort by the Greeks, but the Spartans, still smarting from their humiliation, had nothing to do with it. Twenty years later, when Demetrius Poliorcetes had gained enough control in Greece to revive the League of Corinth, he too did not bother to incorporate Sparta, but tolerated its refusal to join.

For forty years after the death of Alexander the Great in 323, his successors tried to carve out for themselves a piece, or even the totality, of the empire he had created by conquering the Persians. Almost constant war raged in Greece, the Near East, and Asia, but there were only a couple of occasions when the Spartans involved themselves in the fighting. First, in 294, Demetrius Poliorcetes invaded the Peloponnese as part of his campaign to secure as much as possible of southern and central Greece before attempting to make himself master of Macedon.

Demetrius had already secured much of the Peloponnese in recent years, but Sparta refused to capitulate and remained a potential troublemaker. After all, even a weakened Sparta was stronger than most Greek states. The Eurypontid king, Archidamus IV, came out to meet him at Mantinea, in Arcadia north of Sparta, but was easily defeated. Demetrius then invaded Laconia and won a second battle near Sparta itself, which was defended by no more than a moat and a palisade (and they were relatively new, built in 317). He was poised to take the city, for the first time in history, but, as we have seen, his attention was distracted by more important game.

This affair was an anomaly, a matter of necessity; the Spartans had no choice but to defend their city from a direct attack, and their basic position was still quiescence. But, still, almost forty years had passed since Agis' defeat at Megalopolis, and there were clearly those who were inclined to take a more aggressive stance toward Macedon. There is a telling anecdote about Eudamidas I,

Agis' successor on the Eurypontid throne, who reigned from 331 until 305 before being succeeded by Archidamus IV. In the face of near-universal approval in Sparta for making war on Macedon, he spoke in favor of keeping the peace. If we date the anecdote to the final years of Eudamidas' reign, the chief hawk in Sparta at the time was the other king, Areus I, who had ascended to the Agiad throne in 309, and who was consistently hostile toward Macedon. The war party in Macedon was clearly in the ascendant again, and in the year following Demetrius' near capture of Sparta, the Spartans sent a force to help their allies, the Boeotians, defend against an attack by Demetrius.

The force was led by Cleonymus, the uncle of Areus, but the Spartan intervention soon fell apart:

> Since Demetrius already had most of the Peloponnese, and, outside the Peloponnese, Megara and Athens were his, he next marched against the Boeotians. At first, they made reasonable attempts to arrange a pact of friendship with him, but then Cleonymus the Spartan arrived in Thebes with an army. The Boeotians' confidence rose and . . . they came out in rebellion. But when Demetrius brought up his engines and put Thebes under siege, Cleonymus took fright and stole away, and the terrified Boeotians surrendered.

Plutarch makes it seem as though Cleonymus' expedition was a total failure, no more than a sharp reminder that, even in alliance with the Boeotians, Sparta was no match for Macedon. But there may be more to the expedition than Plutarch has told us or realized. In order to reach Boeotia by land from Sparta, Cleonymus must have led an army past the Macedonian garrison at Corinth. This was a strong garrison, and it was usually able to prevent such excursions by creating a line of defense across the narrow Isthmus. Unmentioned by Plutarch, then, a battle probably took place between Cleonymus' forces and the Macedonian garrison, in which Cleonymus prevailed. As for the Boeotians, they rebelled again in the following year, 292, but were quelled in part by Antigonus, as we have seen.

SPARTA RESURGENT

If it is right to assume that Cleonymus defeated the Antigonid garrison at Corinth, his expedition was far more of a success than Plutarch makes it seem, and would have restored Spartan confidence in their prowess. This expedition to Thebes is one of the few times we find Cleonymus actually working directly for his native city, rather than for himself. He was largely an adventurer and a mercenary commander, but arguably even his self-interested exploits had the effect of reviving Spartan confidence and military ambitions.

When the Agiad king Cleomenes II died in 309, his successor, Areus, was still underage, and Cleonymus, Areus' uncle, acted as regent for him for a few years until he attained his majority. Cleonymus wanted the throne for himself; he was Cleomenes' second son, but his elder brother, Areus' father, was already dead. Nevertheless, the Spartan authorities had preferred Areus' claim, and Cleonymus had to be content with the regency.

In 303 the Greek city of Taras (modern Taranto) on the heel of Italy, the second greatest city in Italy after Rome, appealed to the Spartans for help in its ongoing war against the native Italian people, the Lucanians, who were its neighbors. Taras, the major power in southern Italy, had originally been founded by Spartans about four hundred years earlier, and so they had the right of appeal to the mother city for such aid, but it is unlikely that any such sentiment was involved. All they wanted was a strong commander, and they felt that the Spartans could supply one.

This was not the first such appeal from the Tarentines: in 342 the Eurypontid king, Archidamus III, had led a mercenary force there, but died in battle a few years later. In 333, the Tarentines had summoned Alexander I of Epirus, who had achieved significant successes against the Lucanians and others before being killed in battle. Now it was Cleonymus' turn; his skills as a general were recognized in Sparta, and he was sent off at the head of a force of five thousand mercenaries.

In Italy, Cleonymus successfully cowed the Lucanians into submission, but before long his high-handed and corrupt ways had alienated his employers, the Tarentines, and he ended up as a kind of warlord on the island of Corcyra (modern Corfu), which he seized and occupied, before returning to Sparta a few years later when he was driven off the island by the Syracusans of Sicily. It was undoubtedly Cleonymus' success as a warlord that led to his being chosen to lead the Spartan forces to Thebes in 293, to confront Demetrius.

The next sign of the Spartan resurgence that we know of was an expedition undertaken by Areus in 281. There was no mistaking the anti-Macedonian thrust of the expedition. But the Spartans were aware that they were still too weak to take on the Macedonians directly, so they chose to attack the Aetolians, who were then, unusually, in alliance with Macedon. The Aetolians were consolidating their hold on Delphi, the most important religious center in Greece and the home of the main oracle of Apollo, and Areus launched a "sacred war," as the Greeks called wars that were intended to right some wrong at Delphi.

In fact, Areus' war was secular as much as sacred. Delphi had for centuries been administered by a board known as the Amphictyonic Council (the "council of neighboring states"). Since members of the board came from a plurality of states and it was unusual for so many Greeks to reach consensus on any political issue, their decisions carried considerable international weight, and Areus and his allies must have been concerned to ensure that the Aetolians' policies did not always prevail in the council. Areus gained wide support; the Boeotians, Megara, Epidaurus, and several of the Achaean and Arcadian towns all responded favorably to his call, but in the event, when his men turned to plundering, they were badly mauled by the Aetolian guerrillas and withdrew in ignominy.

Nevertheless, the Spartans had clearly set out their anti-Macedonian stall, and it was only because Macedon was about to descend into chaos that they remained unpunished. Moreover, even if only temporarily, they had once again commanded a coalition of Peloponnesian states. However, when Areus tried to regain these allies after his defeat, they turned him down, fearing that he was intending to resuscitate something like the old Peloponnesian League, which was always dominated by Sparta. An anecdote about a Spartan king called Archidamus, plausibly Areus' colleague Archidamus IV, claims that the Greeks rejected his advice to break with Antigonus because they felt that the Spartans would be harsher masters than the Macedonians.

CLEONYMUS' BID FOR THE THRONE

After Areus' setback, Cleonymus continued to be used by the Spartans for military ventures. In the early 270s, he spearheaded Spartan attempts to regain lost territory in Messenia; in Argolis, he drove the Macedonian garrison out of Troezen and replaced it with a Spartan garrison; and, in Arcadia, he did the same at Alipheira. He also achieved some successes in Crete, reconciling warring towns.

But he still hankered after the Agiad throne, and in 272 he set in motion an attempt to take it. The trigger for his break with Areus and departure from Sparta was the humiliating affair that his much younger wife, Chilonis, was publicly conducting with Areus' son, the future Agiad king Acrotatus II. As we have seen, it was possible for a Spartiate man's wife to have other lovers, but only with her husband's permission. No such permission was granted in this case.

Cleonymus turned for help to Pyrrhus, by then the king of much of northern Greece. Seeing this as an opportunity to take the Peloponnese for himself, the ambitious Epirote launched a massive invasion at the head of twenty-five thousand foot, two thousand horse, and twenty-four war elephants. He tricked the Spartans into believing that the purpose of his expedition was to expel the Macedonian garrisons from the Peloponnesian towns; that was undoubtedly part of his aim, because his primary and constant concern in these years was to weaken Antigonus and seize the Macedonian throne, but he concealed the fact that he was also trying to install Cleonymus as king. Both Pyrrhus and the Spartans were on good terms with Egypt, and linked by their mutual hostility to Macedon; perhaps that was why the Spartans did not suspect treachery.

With Areus away fighting in Crete, Cleonymus' success seemed so certain that his friends in Sparta decorated his house in prep-

Pyrrhus, the ambitious and gifted king of Epirus, who was a constant enemy of Antigonus as he tried to gain the Macedonian throne and get himself established on it. Photo © Marie-Lan Nguyen / Wikimedia Commons. CC BY 2.5 (Unported).

aration for his triumphant return. Somewhere south of Sparta there was a place that became known as "the Camp of Pyrrhus," presumably after one of his bases during this campaign. But Pyrrhus' forces met strong resistance from the Spartans, and when the Spartans were reinforced by troops from the Macedonian garrison at Corinth, commanded by Antigonus' general Ameinias of Phocis, and Areus brought two thousand troops over from Crete, Pyrrhus withdrew.

We will meet Pyrrhus again, for his final showdown with Antigonus, but we hear no more of Cleonymus after this, and he presumably died or disappeared into exile. Nevertheless, his importance is clear. Despite his maverick nature, it was he who revived Spartan pride. In the short term, the Spartans resuscitated their claims to lost territory in Messenia and elsewhere, and in the longer term they began to dream again of driving the Macedonians out of the Peloponnese and making it their own. Pyrrhus' invasion had united the Spartans and Macedonians to defeat the common enemy, but this rapprochement was very temporary, and their basic position was still one of mutual suspicion and hostility. However, it may have been at this time that Antigonus gave the Spartans a large amount of wheat to relieve a severe shortage, which had perhaps been induced by Pyrrhus.

So by the time Antigonus secured Macedon in the late 270s, the continued hostility of the Spartans was a given, and he could not be certain of a number of other Peloponnesian states either. Argos, Elis, Messenia, and Megalopolis were his most important allies, but few of the others could be relied on. Antigonus' aim was never to secure blanket control of the Greek states—he did not need to garrison every single town—but he still had reason to worry about the Peloponnese. The historically minded geographer Strabo described the Peloponnese as the acropolis of Greece, meaning, among other things, that it was easy to defend: its narrow land entrance was guarded by the Acrocorinth, which was large enough to house a sizable garrison; many stretches of coastline were short of harbors of any size; and the inland was often very rugged. In Plutarch's opinion, whoever controlled the Acrocorinth controlled Greece as a whole.

The Peloponnese may have been remote from Macedon, but it could serve and had served as a base for men or states whose ambitions extended to attacking Macedon, and Antigonus would have to take steps to make sure that did not happen. In a fictional speech written by the great historian Polybius and assigned to the year 211, the speaker looks back on Antigonid policy regarding the Peloponnese and says that no Macedonian king could be sure of his rule if the Spartans acquired supremacy in the Peloponnese. The historian was, in part, explaining why Antigonus felt it necessary to adopt a repressive approach to controlling the Greeks, and especially the Greeks of the Peloponnese.

CHAPTER 3

The Democratic Spirit of Athens

After the Greeks, defeated at Chaeronea, fell under Macedonian sway in the winter of 338/7, Philip treated the Athenians with surprising generosity. They had instigated the Greek coalition that had resisted him and had been prominent in the battle itself, and so, after their defeat, they fully and fearfully expected the city to be put under siege. Demosthenes and the city's other leaders proposed emergency measures, but Philip was lenient, probably out of respect for Athens' glorious past and his need for a counterweight to Thebes, with which Athens was normally on bad terms. He did not attack the city, and even sent his son there, a dashing seventeen-year-old prince, the future Alexander the Great, bearing with honor the ashes of the Athenians who had died in the battle.

The terms of the settlement were that the city would retain its democratic institutions and its navy; it would remain ungarrisoned, and was not required to surrender its anti-Macedonian politicians—Demosthenes and his faction—for punishment. But the league of allies it had in place around the Aegean was dissolved, except for the few islands it traditionally owned or exploited: Lemnos, Imbros, Scyros, Salamis, Delos, and Samos. However, even these became less secure possessions over the following decades; Delos was out of Athenians hands from 314 until 167.

By contrast, the Thebans, who had been just as prominent as the Athenians in the resistance, but had broken a treaty with Philip in order to take up arms against him, were harshly treated: Theban prisoners of war were sold into slavery; the Thebans had to pay an indemnity; they lost their leadership of the Boeotian Confederacy;

a Macedonian garrison was installed on their acropolis; and Boeotian towns that had been destroyed by them in the 370s, when they were establishing their dominance in the confederacy, were rebuilt and populated with returnees who had long memories and good reasons to hate the Thebans. Elsewhere, Ambracia, Corinth, and Chalcis had garrisons installed, not in punishment, but because they were three of the best and best-equipped harbors in Greece.

The Athenians capitalized on their good fortune and, under the leadership of a statesman called Lycurgus, entered a period of renewed prosperity. There was a downside to the Lycurgan reforms, however. Stable finances and a massive navy stoked Athenian pride and aggrandized their dreams. No sooner had Philip died than they were in touch with a rival of Alexander's, proposing to back his bid for the throne in opposition to Alexander's succession. That came to nothing, because Alexander had the rival murdered, along with his family. By 330, the Athenians were provocatively honoring enemies of Macedon, and Demosthenes was delivering his most famous speech, *On the Crown*, which is replete with anti-Macedonian sentiment. By the time Lycurgus died in 324, the Athenians imagined themselves great enough to lead resistance to Macedonian rule, and they were already extending feelers to other Greek states, to see what enthusiasm there might be for rebellion.

THE EXILES DECREE

Alexander inherited his father's position as president of the League of Corinth. According to the league constitution, the Greeks sitting in council were to make decisions (albeit often when prompted to do so by the president), and the president was to carry them out. But as Alexander conquered Asia, his style of monarchy became more high-handed and much less consultative. In August 324, from his base in Media he sent a representative called Nicanor (probably the nephew of the philosopher Aristotle) to the festival of Zeus at Olympia in the Peloponnese, knowing that he would find the largest audience of Greeks there, for the quadrennial Olympic Games.

Rumor had already alerted everyone to the content of the announcement, and the usual large crowd had been swelled by thousands of men who had, for one reason or another, been exiled from their states. Their hopes were fully realized:

> King Alexander to the exiles from the Greek cities: Although we were not and are not responsible for your banishment, we will be responsible for restoring you to your homelands. Only those of you who are under a curse are excluded. We have written to Antipater about this, instructing him to use force in the case of cities that refuse to comply.

There were sound reasons for the edict, because there were thousands of rootless Greeks, political exiles or demobilized professional soldiers, in both Asia and Europe, and they threatened disorder if the former put their wealth toward hiring the latter and tried to get back to their native cities by means of violence, or if they turned to brigandage or piracy. As the Athenian political writer Isocrates put it, “Larger and stronger armies may now be formed from footloose men than from those who live in cities.” Besides, Alexander wanted to seed the Greek cities with men who would be grateful to him. But he had unilaterally issued this order without involving the League of Corinth, as he should have for matters relating to the Greek states. It might have been a charade to have got them involved, but protocol and the maintenance of good relations still demanded it.

The disruption caused by the Exiles Decree would be both political, stemming from the return of opponents of current regimes, and economic, due to the need to accommodate thousands of men and to settle claims for long-lost property. To make matters worse, these were years of drought and grain shortages. Alexander’s arrogant gesture made the Greeks afraid; they had been terrified by his destruction of Thebes in 335, and they could only see more of the same autocratic and extreme behavior from him in the future. The result was an increased determination to resist.

The worst affected by the Exiles Decree were the Aetolians and the Athenians. This was probably Alexander's intention, since they were the two most powerful states in Greece, now that Thebes and Sparta had been reduced. The Aetolians, in need of a good western harbor, had recently taken over Oeniadae, which belonged to their Acarnanian neighbors; they had expelled its inhabitants and repopulated it with their own people. The Athenians had done the same with the entire island of Samos earlier in the century. Hence no less a person than Demosthenes also visited the 324 Olympic festival, seeking an audience with Nicanor, in the hope of negotiating a better solution for the Athenians on Samos.

If the Samian exiles returned home, they would evict Athenian families who in some cases had been there for forty years. Many thousands of Athenian citizens were involved, and the Athenians were unwilling either to give up the island or to receive so many refugees. At the time of Alexander's death the following year, in June 323, many of the Greek states were up in diplomatic arms over the decree. Exiles were massing on borders, anticipating their imminent return, and local conflicts were already breaking out as some tried to sneak home before the decree came into force.

THE LAMIAN WAR

Greece was a powder keg, and the Athenians lit the fuse. The Spartans, still reduced by their defeat in 331, stayed away, and the Boeotians, profiting from Alexander's destruction of Thebes, fought for Macedon, but many of the other central and southern Greek states flocked to the banner raised by the Athenians in the name of freedom from Macedonian dominion. The Athenian general Leosthenes marched north at the head of twenty-five thousand men. The army included for the first time several thousand professionally trained Athenian citizen soldiers, since the institution known as the Cadet Corps (the *ephēbeia*) had been instituted in 335. The war is known nowadays as the Lamian War, after the town that was the focus of the early action, but to the Greeks it was the Hellenic War, emphasizing their professed unity against the enemy and the alleged foreignness of their opponents. As a matter of fact, the Macedonians were both ethnically and culturally Greek, but it suited Greek rhetoric to present them as "barbarians."

The size of the Greek forces would have been greater had the Macedonian garrison at Corinth not prevented most of the Peloponnesian contingents from linking up with the central Greek forces. There is no way to tell, but it would not clash with what we know of Peloponnesian history to conclude that they saw their primary objective as a more parochial one, ridding the Peloponnese of this garrison, and that they deliberately spent their time over this rather than join up with Leosthenes. After all, they could have found some other way to get to central Greece—across the Gulf of Corinth, for instance.

Nevertheless, when Antipater marched south to meet the Greeks, Leosthenes defeated him in battle and put him under siege in Lamia, the main town of the district of Malis (which had sided with the Macedonians), before forcing him to withdraw to Macedon. Even after Leosthenes fell, Greek hopes were high, but Antipater had arranged to be reinforced by armies from Asia Minor, and in August 322, after decisive defeats at sea, the outnumbered Greek land forces were defeated at Crannon in Thessaly.

Many in Athens expected their city to be destroyed. Intense negotiations secured less harsh terms, but they were still devastating. The philosopher Xenocrates, head of the Platonic Academy in Athens at the time, described the terms as "fair if Antipater regarded the Athenians as slaves, but harsh for free men." After 180 years, the city that was synonymous with democracy was turned into an oligarchy.

Democracy was replaced by a limited franchise, with the threshold of citizenship set at a property level of 2,000 drachmas, so that thousands of poorer citizens were disenfranchised at a stroke, and power was transferred from the people to men of property. The Assembly continued to operate, but only to rubber-stamp the measures proposed by Antipater's friends; it was monitored by officials called the "guardians of the law," who made sure that those attending the Assembly knew their place. It was the end of the great Athe-

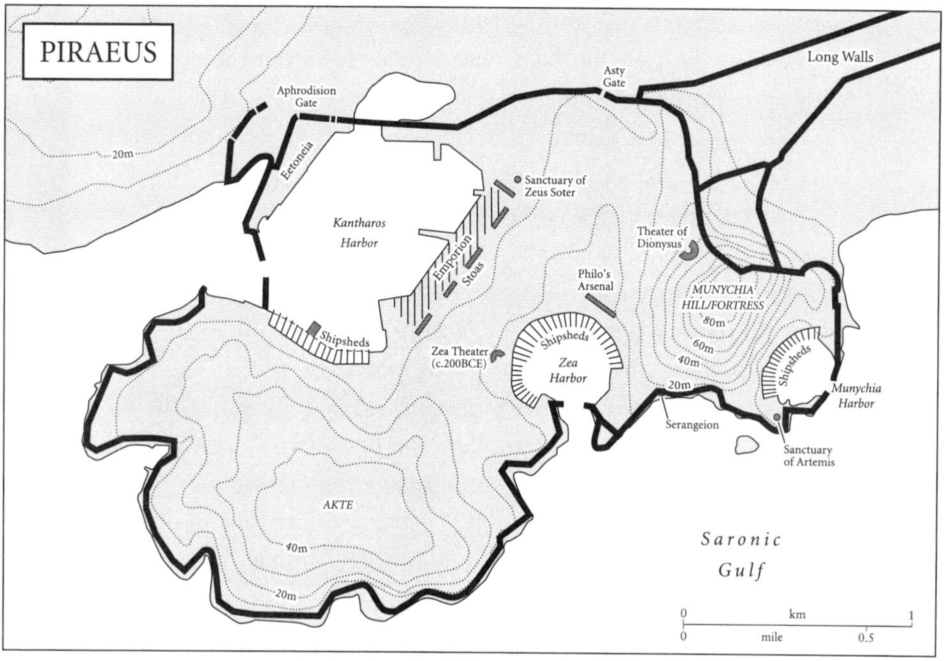

nian democratic experiment. Democracy was reinstated several times over the decades, always with great fanfare, but it was never quite the same.

A garrison was installed on the Munychia hill in Piraeus—the first time Athens had been occupied by a foreign power since 403, at the end of the Peloponnesian War—and a massive indemnity was imposed. The size of the war fleet was greatly reduced, and Athens was never again the sea power that it had been in the past. Since sea power had always been the foundation of its prosperity and military might, this was a major blow. The *ephēbeia* was abolished.

The island of Samos was finally returned to the Samian exiles, and the Athenian settlers were evicted. Among them was a teenager called Epicurus, who sixteen years later would establish his school of philosophy in Athens. His lifelong hostility toward Macedon presumably dated from his family's banishment from the island. Over ten thousand of the newly disenfranchised Athenians were relocated to Macedonian-controlled Thrace, perhaps to make room for returnees from Samos. Naturally, the most prominent anti-Macedonians were killed. Demosthenes took poison rather than fall into Antipater's ungentle hands.

Nor was it just Athens that was reduced. The Aetolians lost Oeniadae, of course, and they survived a massive invasion by Antipater in 321 partly by guerrilla warfare in the mountains, but mainly because Antipater was called away to Asia Minor for more urgent business. Many future Macedonian kings and generals would regret Antipater's decision not to annihilate the Aetolians, or at least break up their confederacy.

So the Athenians and Aetolians were adjusting, each in their own way, to defeat in the Lamian War. The League of Corinth had broken up of its own accord, and Antipater replaced it with more direct, less benign means of control. He made sure that all the major states in Greece were governed by pro-Macedonian oligarchies or sole rulers, supported where necessary by garrisons of mercenaries under Macedonian commanders. These sole rulers were known as "tyrants," and they deserved the title because they were immune to constitutional methods: they were removable only by rebellion or their own resignation. Their regimes were not usually oppressive, but they were living symbols of Macedonian dominance. Mainland Greece was effectively occupied territory, and resentment of Macedonian rule seethed below the surface.

REGIME CHANGES

Unlike Sparta, Athens was often caught up in the wars of Alexander's successors, or at any rate those that were fought on Greek soil. Athens was one of the most attractive prizes, not just because of its formidable prestige, but because Piraeus, its port, was both one of the major centers of commerce in the Aegean and a naval base capable of housing and servicing a large fleet. After about seventy years of peace, then, Attica, the territory of Athens, became a war zone.

In this phase of its history, the city was tormented by regime changes between democrats, fervently desiring to retain or regain the democratic institutions of the fifth and fourth centuries, and oligarchs or autocrats, who were equally fervent in their ideology and were often backed by one or another of the Macedonian potentates. In 322, Antipater's oligarchy replaced the long-standing democracy, but democracy briefly returned in 319, only to be replaced by tyranny between 317 and 307. This tyranny was supplanted by democracy, but another tyrant arose at a time of trouble and ruled Athens between 300 and 295, until being succeeded by an oligarchy. Democracy returned in 286, and had a good run before being replaced in 262 by a pseudo-democracy overseen by Antigonus Gonatas. Democracy finally returned in 229, along with the expulsion of the Macedonian garrisons. The Athenian commitment to democracy is remarkable; they resurrected it every time it was suppressed, and it is no wonder that Antigonus attempted to curb such enthusiasm.

In 319, when Cassander decided to use force to make himself, instead of Polyperchon, the regent of the two Macedonian kings, his first moves were to ally himself with Antigonus Monophthalmus in Asia Minor, who had the resources to support his effort, and to write to the commanders of all his father's garrisons in Greece, ordering them to place their forces at his disposal. Piraeus was so important that he secured it with one of his own men.

Polyperchon responded by issuing a proclamation in the name of Philip III, designed to stop the garrison commanders inclining toward Cassander. In the proclamation, blame for the oppressive regimes under which the Greek states were suffering was placed squarely at Antipater's door, and Polyperchon explicitly encouraged the Greeks to rise up and restore more democratic systems in their cities, with less interference in the future from Macedon. He included his own version of Alexander's Exiles Decree, by ordering the Greek cities to take back the democrats exiled by the Antipatrid regimes. All this would have been enough to excite the Athenians with the prospect of the restoration of their democracy, but Polyperchon added a sweetener: "Samos we give to the Athenians."

So in the winter of 319/8 the Athenians put to death the men who had led them under Antipater's regime, and returned to democracy. Polyperchon marched south and encamped near the city (draining its resources), in an attempt to force Cassander's garrison in Piraeus to leave. But the attempt was a failure, and in 317, after Polyperchon had also been badly defeated by his enemies in Asia Minor and had failed, in the Peloponnese, to take Megalopolis (where the governor put in place by Antipater was refusing to submit), the Athenians realized that they had looked to the wrong man for protection. Cassander, meanwhile, had arrived in Piraeus in person, and had taken the islands of Salamis and Aegina from Athens. The Athenians entered into negotiations with him, gave up all hope of recovering Samos, and surrendered the city.

Athens and Piraeus were reunited, therefore, but democracy was dissolved again in favor of a limited franchise (though less limited than the one imposed by Antipater a few years earlier), and the essential democratic instrument of sortition (a lottery) for choosing certain officers from lists of volunteers was abandoned. These and other measures were seen through by an oligarch called Demetrius of Phalerum, who was put in place by Cassander as the governor or tyrant of the city. He was a noted author in the Aristotelian tradition, and he ruled Athens for ten years. The year before, he had taken refuge from Athenian democratic wrath with the Macedonian garrison in Piraeus, and had been condemned to death in absentia.

ANTIGONID ATHENS

This was a period of peace and prosperity for the Athenians; they were able to exploit the expanded markets opened up by Alexander's eastern conquests for their products. But the fact that thousands of Athenians chose, in 310, to join one of Ptolemy's former generals, Ophellas, the governor of Ptolemaic Cyrenaica, in a doomed expedition against Carthage argues for considerable discontent with Demetrius' tyranny, and some elements in Athens were secretly in touch with Antigonus Monophthalmus, asking him to free the city. So in 307 the Antigonids, who now held all of Alexander's former empire apart from Macedon, Greece, and Egypt, decided to make Greece their own as well. Their alliance with Cassander was already a dead letter. If they controlled Greece, they could hope eventually to take Macedon as well.

Antigonus Gonatas was only twelve, and presumably remained in Asia Minor, but in 307 his father, Demetrius Poliorcetes, brought enormous forces into the Aegean. It did not take him long to recapture Piraeus and drive Demetrius of Phalerum out of Athens. The Athenians undid the most antidemocratic of the measures that had been put in place, and for several years enjoyed a return to democracy, which was marred only by the fact that Demetrius' yes-men were prominent. But this is only to say that the democratic leaders found it expedient to acknowledge and honor the genuine good Demetrius was doing the city, in order to keep him happy. He gave the city abundant wheat, and enough timber to rebuild a fleet, their fortifications, and their pride.

The Athenians greeted Demetrius and his father as kings, made offerings to them as Savior gods, and awarded them other extraordinary honors. But in fact the Antigonid victory ushered in several difficult years for Athens, as the citizens tried to reconcile democracy with Demetrius' tendency toward autocracy (for instance, when he insisted on the quashing of a fine legally imposed on one of his friends), and endured repeated attacks and raids by Cassander's forces. In order to ensure that Athens was well defended against Cassander, Demetrius took the unusual step (though it would be followed by his son) of personally appointing a loyal man, Adeimantus of Lampsacus, as general for two consecutive years. Democracy suffered further when Stratocles, Demetrius' chief lackey among the Athenian politicians, got the motion passed that "whatever King Demetrius should ordain is righteous in the eyes of the gods and just in the eyes of men."

But Demetrius' father, Antigonus Monophthalmus, was determined to make an all-out assault on Ptolemy of Egypt, and he recalled Demetrius from Greece for a successful takeover of Cyprus, an unsuccessful invasion of Egypt, and then a long and ultimately unsuccessful siege of Rhodes, an Egyptian ally. In the meantime, Cassander was not idle in Greece, and in 304 he had Athens under siege. The fleet the Athenians had intended to build had never fully materialized (though in 306 they had sent thirty ships to support the Antigonid takeover of Cyprus), since they were too busy defending the countryside against Cassander.

The Antigonids were close to losing Greece altogether, so Demetrius returned, again in terrifying force; the Antigonids at the time had by far the greatest resources of any of Alexander's successors. Demetrius drove Cassander from Athens and chased him all the way to Thessaly before returning to expel his garrisons from the Attic border forts of Phyle and Panactum, control of which returned to Athenian hands. The situation of the Athenians' other northern defenses, the fortified villages of Aphidna and Oenoe, is unclear, and they may have been little used at this time.

A splendid monument celebrating the victory of the Athenians over Cassander's cavalry was still visible in the second century CE. Athenian pleasure at the victory, however, was tempered by Demetrius' occasional use of his authority to make sure that his own men were elected, while his opponents (such as Demochares, the nephew of Demosthenes) disappeared into exile. A year later, Demetrius had recovered much of the Peloponnese as well, and he revived Philip's and Alexander's League of Corinth to organize the Greek states and keep them at peace. Adeimantus of Lampsacus was chosen to preside over the league.

All such arrangements were voided, however, by the Antigonids' defeat at the battle of Ipsus in 301. The Athenians refused to allow Demetrius into the city and expelled the members of his family who were living there. Gonatas is not mentioned in this context, so he was presumably in Corinth. For a while (starting in 300), they were led by a man called Lachares, who appears to have been the sole ruler of the city. With the implicit backing of Cassander, Lachares seized power on the pretext of restoring peace to a troubled city, and had all his opponents executed after a mass trial. But Demetrius returned in 295, two years after Cassander's death, and put the city under siege. His forces occupied the countryside (especially the strongly fortified towns Rhamnous and Eleusis), and he deterred traders from sneaking grain into the city by summarily executing one of them, along with the captain of the ship he had hired.

The earlier 290s had already been a time of crop failure and inflation, and now, during the siege, anecdotes tell of a father fighting his son for the right to eat the corpse of a mouse, and of the philosopher Epicurus counting out the daily ration of beans for the members of his commune. The price of wheat rocketed to about 120 times its normal level. When the horror became too much, Lachares fled (ending up in Lysimachus' court), and the Athenians surrendered. They had insulted Demetrius in 301 by closing their gates to him, and they did not know what to expect. On the previous two occasions, he had come to Athens in the guise of a liberator and a restorer of democracy; now he came as a conqueror.

REBELLION

This time, the period of Demetrius' third residence in Athens, the restoration of democracy was a farce, despite being greeted with joy—though the joy may have been due to the vast quantity of wheat that Demetrius gave the citizens to relieve their starvation. In reality, once Demetrius had made himself king of Macedon and had moved his court there, an oligarchy of Antigonid supporters formed the ruling clique in Athens, and he made sure that his supporters were there by ordering the return of all the oligarchs who had been exiled during recent bouts of democracy. Opposition was repressed, and garrisons were installed not only in Athens and Piraeus, but also in outlying fortresses, once Cassander's men had been expelled.

The Piraeus garrison, on the Munychia hill, would remain in place for over sixty years, throughout Antigonus' reign, and much of the history of third-century Athens can be read as the attempt to recover control of their port and its facilities, by diplomacy or force. Piraeus continued to function as a commercial port, but the Athenians lost their privileges and their rights to favorable deals, which had been in place for many decades. Athens was treated as just another customer for goods that were now under Macedonian control. The Athenians became relatively impoverished, unable to sustain themselves, and often had to rely on the generosity of others.

In 286, exploiting the opportunity presented by Demetrius' ejection from Macedon, the Athenians threw his garrison off the Museum Hill (the modern Philopappos Hill) and recovered their freedom. It was a famous assault, long remembered, and aided by the fact that one of the Macedonian officers, a man called Strombichus, was persuaded to change sides, along with a number of his men. After repulsing an attack by the Macedonian garrison, the aged Athenian general Olympiodorus stormed the hill at the head of a scratch force of the oldest and youngest men of military age, because the rest of the citizen army, commanded by Phaedrus of Sphettus, was out of the city, protecting the grain harvest.

The details of the rebellion are significant. Some years later, the Athenians erected an impressive marble stele, thanking an Athenian called Callias of Sphettus, the brother of Phaedrus, for his help in freeing Athens at the time of the rebellion and enabling the collection of the grain harvest despite the Macedonian garrisons, and awarding him the highest honors they could grant. Callias had long been an officer in Ptolemy's army, and he sailed to Athens from the island of Andros. This island had been in Egyptian hands since 308, and just the year before, in 287, the rest of the Cyclades (so called because the islands form a circle around Delos) had been taken over by Egypt and formed into a federal state, the Confederacy of Islanders.

Callias was a Ptolemaic general, and the thousand men he came with, to support his brother in the countryside, were Ptolemaic troops, mercenaries hired with Egyptian money. The decree, published in the Athenian year 270/69, when Antigonus was on the Macedonian throne, states that Callias came to help Athens, "acting in accordance with the goodwill of King Ptolemy toward the Athenian People," and Ptolemy is effusively thanked alongside Callias. Ptolemy was always prepared to support Greek resistance to the Antigonids, and even instigate it if he could. Far from being a superpower itself, Athens had become a field of conflict between superpowers. Demetrius briefly put Athens under siege in the summer of 286, but he was in a hurry to launch his invasion of Asia Minor, and he was persuaded to allow the city its freedom by delegates

This marble stele was inscribed and erected in Athens in 270/69 as a snub to Antigonus, since it celebrated the liberation of the city from his father's dominion. It thanks Callias of Sphettus, an Athenian general employed by the Ptolemies of Egypt, for his part in the liberation. Courtesy of American School of Classical Studies at Athens: Agora Excavations.

from Ptolemy and Lysimachus, and by Pyrrhus, Ptolemy's main ally in Greece. The affair was brought to an end by a peace treaty not between Demetrius and the Athenians, but between Demetrius and Ptolemy, given the state of war between them.

Of course, what the Athenians recovered was no more than a fitful freedom: Antigonus, Demetrius' viceroy in his absence, had Piraeus garrisoned (despite Pausanias' mistaken claim that Olympiodorus evicted that garrison too) and the other fortresses in the Attic countryside. And the Athenians, having evicted the Museum garrison, were now Antigonus' enemies, not just subjects, so that over subsequent years he continued to use his garrisons in Attica to make it difficult for them to harvest their crops, receive incoming cargoes by sea, or use their war fleet. In a story preserved by Plutarch, Antigonus gave the commander of the Munychia garrison in Piraeus metaphorical instructions, telling him that controlling a dog requires more than a strong collar; the beast itself must also be made lean.

This was an intolerable situation, and took the edge off Athenian delight in having simultaneously rid themselves of an oligarchic government and the occupation of a foreign power. In a letter written in 283 BCE, Epicurus spoke (if the gaps in the papyrus fragment have been properly filled) of "destroying the hated Macedonians." Over the following years, the Athenians had to solicit help in the form of grain from a number of foreign dignitaries, as well as wealthy locals, and were forced to use other harbors, so that we find, for instance, that the bay at modern Vouliagmeni, near the ancient town of Aexonides Halae, was fortified and that more use was made of it than usual. Other protected harbors were at modern Porto Rafti (near the ancient village of Prasiae), Rhamnous, and Eleusis, all of which had been recovered, while Antigonus was at his weakest, by the end of the 280s. It must have been at one of these that the Ptolemaic naval commander Zeno landed in 286, escorting grain ships from Egypt; his blockade-busting achievement is equated in the decree thanking him with "supporting the struggle for the salvation of the city." Both Lysimachus and Ptolemy were expressing their hostility toward Demetrius and Antigonus by helping the rebel city.

"THE DEMOCRACY OF ALL ATHENIANS"

The Antigonids and the Ptolemies had consistently been enemies since the mid-310s, but the critical part the Egyptians played in removing the garrison from the Museum Hill must have driven home to Antigonus, more than any earlier event in his experience, just how deep and relentless that hostility was. Ptolemy was represented for the peace negotiations by a friend called Sostratus, better known as the man who designed and funded the building of the Pharos, the lighthouse of Alexandria, which was soon regarded as one of the Seven Wonders of the World. This was an era that admired bold and large-scale structures.

In Athens, democracy was restored with such fervor that it was described as "the democracy of all Athenians" to distinguish it from the less-than-full democracies that had preceded it, and the Athenians promptly undid many of the undemocratic changes that had been made to the constitution and the administration. Demochares returned from exile, and one of his measures was a decree awarding posthumous honors to his uncle Demosthenes, forging a symbolic link between this democracy and the fully fledged democracy of the mid-fourth century, before the Macedonian victory at Chaeronea.

However, the fact remained that if the Athenians were for the moment not answerable to the king in Macedon, they still depended for their survival on the generosity of others. Hence, one of the first major religious festivals they held after the revolution was a Ptolemaia, newly instituted by Ptolemy II in commemoration of his father. With the support of Ptolemy above all, but also others, the Athenians remained relatively independent for twenty-five years, under democratic leadership, until they rose up in war against Antigonus and were defeated. By the start of that war, the Chremonidean War, they had recovered most of their outlying for-

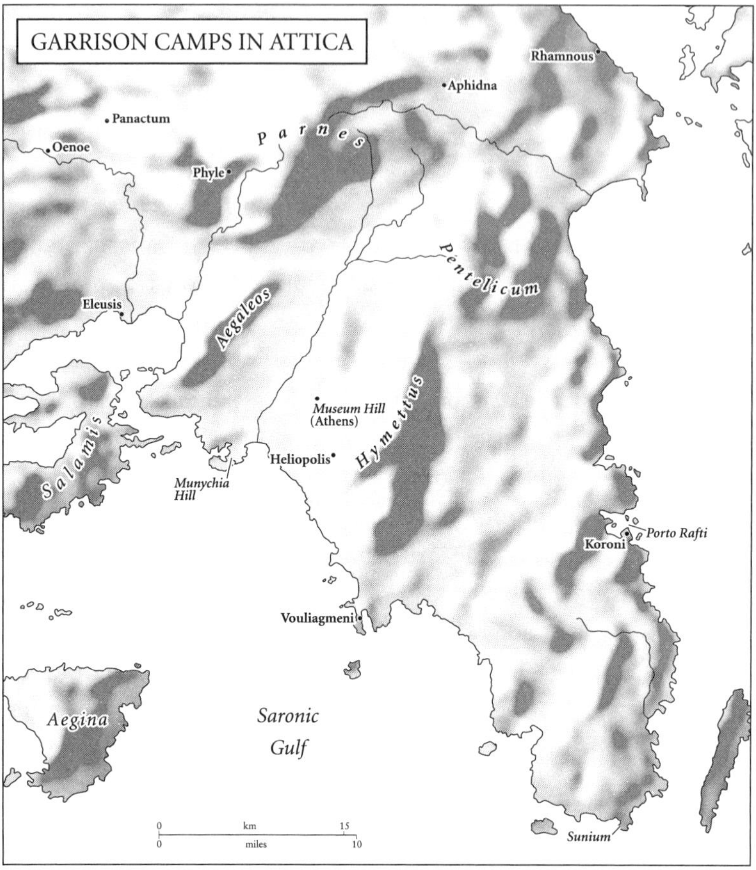

tresses, and evicted the Macedonians from them, but they never expelled the garrisons from either Piraeus or Sunium. They made repeated attempts on the Munychia hill of Piraeus, and many lives were lost in the mid-280s, but to no avail.

GARRISONS

The garrisoning of Greek states—in effect, the militarization of much of Greece—was the preferred policy of successive Macedonian rulers, starting with Antipater. They had the money to hire mercenaries for the job and maintain them for years, if necessary. Polybius has one of his characters assert in a speech: "And is there anyone who does not know what Cassander, Demetrius, and Antigonus Gonatas did? Either by installing garrisons in cities or by planting tyrannies in them, they forced every city to accept slavery."

The size of garrisons varied considerably, depending on the size and importance of the location. The garrison at Corinth must have been large enough to be hard to dislodge and impossible to leave intact in one's rear. The other Fetters of Greece—Chalcis, Piraeus, and Demetrias—must have had sizable garrisons too, as perhaps did Ambracia on the west coast. Anywhere in Greece that the Macedonian kings considered important, in the short or long term, was liable to be garrisoned. To garrison a place was to occupy it militarily, and by extension to exercise control over nearby towns and villages as well. It would not take many garrisons to control Greece, or at least its likely trouble spots.

But it is important to distinguish between two kinds of garrison—a distinction made, for instance, by Philip V of Macedon (reigned 221–179), who was careful to differentiate between "protecting" a town and "garrisoning" it. At a time of war, if a town was on the front line or otherwise in danger, a garrison was not primarily a means of political control (though it could double up as such), but a way to protect the place. As such, it may even have been requested by the townspeople themselves. In such cases the garrison was tolerable, and the troops, even if they were foreign mercenaries, were among friends; in all likelihood, the garrison would be removed once the danger was over. Moreover, in places smaller than Piraeus and Athens, garrisons could stimulate the local economy, as the soldiers used their pay (typically in Macedonian coinage) to buy goods and services.

Garrisons of a more permanent kind, however, were a hated burden and a humiliating symbol of subjection to a foreign power, forcing citizens to behave obsequiously and to endure checkpoints and patrols. A garrisoned city was denied the dignity of managing its own militia. The garrison troops were answerable to their Macedonian paymasters, not to any local authority, and were often scarcely subject to the local law code; their commander reported directly to the Macedonian king or his representative. If the city was required to pay tribute or war indemnities to the king, or to subsidize the garrison, it was the garrison troops who saw to the collection of the money. The keys to the city gates were held by the garrison commander.

The mercenaries who were employed on garrison duty (albeit with a more trustworthy man in command) might be little better than "murderers, mutilators, thieves, and burglars." Garrisons commonly consisted of an assortment of mercenaries from all over the Mediterranean. Discipline is always more difficult under such circumstances, and so is integration into the community; not all of the soldiers stationed in a town would have been able to take part in local religious rituals, for instance. Even if they were good, disciplined troops, they changed the face of the town they occupied. If the town had an acropolis—and most did—it became the mercenaries' fortress and living quarters. At least they were not billeted on the townspeople, which was always liable to cause trouble, but their presence still changed the acropolis from a place of refuge and worship to a place of fear or at least caution.

A lead curse tablet has been found in Athens, dating from the end of the fourth or beginning of the third century, and the targets of the inscribed curse were the garrison in Piraeus and four named senior Macedonians. Time and again, in the sources, we find that garrisons were a major bone of contention; time and again, when treaties were drawn up, central topics for negotiation were whether or not a garrison was needed, and, if so, for how long. To remain ungarrisoned became almost synonymous with freedom.

In many towns the anniversary of the removal of a garrison became a public holiday and day of thanksgiving; if a garrison commander had behaved well—that is, contrary to worst fears—he might be awarded honors by the citizens of the town of which he had the command. In 229, Diogenes, the commander of the Macedonian garrisons in Piraeus and Rhamnous, and on the island of Salamis, was persuaded to accept a large sum of money to pay off his troops, disband the garrisons, and return these places to Athenian control. He was granted the title of "Benefactor," a gymnasium was named after him, he received regular sacrifices, and an annual festival was instituted in his name.

The expulsion of the garrisons in 229 was the culmination of long striving. The tale of Athens in the early decades of the Hellenistic period is one of the gradual surrender of its government to men who were prepared to compromise its democratic institutions in order to remain on good terms with their masters. Nevertheless, the enthusiasm with which the Athenians restored democracy or some version of it every time, as soon as they could, contained a warning to Antigonus: there was still no lack of spirit among the leaers of Athens.

CHAPTER 4

The Vigor of Confederacies

The formation and growth of federal states was a major phenomenon of the fourth and third centuries, not just in mainland Greece, but elsewhere in the Greek world as well. Previously, the majority of Greeks had lived in separate communities. There had been federal states before, most notably the Boeotian and Chalcidian confederacies, and there had been a number of military alliances that were large enough to be termed "leagues." I have already mentioned the Peloponnesian League, headed by Sparta, and Philip II's League of Corinth, but there were others: most importantly, the two leagues that had Athens at their head, the Delian League of the fifth century and the Second Athenian League of the fourth. And another example of the centralization of authority was the Amphictyonic Council. The new confederacies could look back to a number of precedents.

Federation in the third century was generally a form of military and economic protection: in the new world of superpowers such as Macedon, strength lay in numbers and the reduction of local competition in favor of cooperation. The actions of Elis early in the second century show this clearly. Having supported a war against the Romans that the Greek allies lost, the Eleans' position was extremely precarious, and they expected retaliation from Rome. They made this more difficult by voluntarily joining the Achaean Confederacy, so that the enemy would be faced with a mighty power, not just a single town.

The prospect of safety and prosperity was enough to persuade towns that chose to join a confederacy to accept the necessary sacrifice of a degree of autonomy. The Achaean and Aetolian confederacies, the focus of this chapter, evolved in mountainous regions that had been considered backward, and without federation would have remained so. One of the first advantages of federation for these regions was that coastal towns were incorporated, creating an integrated economy of upland and coastline, so that the region could begin to prosper and hold its own against other states. The constant expansiveness of the two great third-century confederacies is understandable as an attempt to achieve greater economies of scale, a greater variety of resources, a greater pooling of economic risks, the reduction of transaction costs, and greater physical security. The more members they had, the more tribute was generated, and the larger the army that could take to the field; economic and military concerns were the spurs to federalization.

In the great majority of cases, towns and villages joined confederacies voluntarily. This was a major shift of attitude, away from the separatism and particularism of the Greek city-states—a shift toward a larger sense of belonging, so that a man was a citizen of a geographically larger political entity as well as his native community. A citizen of a federal state was, for instance, "an Acarnanian, from Stratus," to indicate the two tiers with which he identified, the confederacy and the member community.

Confederation was the most significant political movement in the Greek world for centuries. Earlier Greek history is largely the history of city-states such as Athens, Sparta, Corinth, Argos, and so on; in the third century, confederacies became greater drivers of history. We have already seen how difficult Athens and Sparta were finding it to stand up to Macedon. The speed and ease with which the confederacies grew suggests that, on the whole, there was widespread enthusiasm for joining. It must have been thrilling for a Greek to be alive in the third century and to participate in the movement that was sweeping Greece and promised to offer effective resistance to Macedon.

POLIS AND *KOINON*

A city-state, or *polis*—since the word refers to a unique kind of polity, it is impossible to translate accurately—was a small, self-governing community of citizens and their dependents, living in a town and its hinterland, where its farms and harbors were (if it had coastline), and sharing common political, social, and religious institutions. *Poleis* varied greatly in extent; in modern definitions of a city, size is a relevant factor, but that was not the case for a *polis*. The largest might indeed have a population in the hundreds of thousands, and a dependent territory containing towns and villages as well as hamlets and farmsteads; but the smallest occupied no more than a single valley or coastal plain or small island, with a population more readily counted in hundreds than thousands.

For all the fame of the *polis*, however, it was not and never had been the only form of political community in Greece. The people who occupied the various regions of Greece thought of themselves as kin, met together at fairs and religious festivals according to their own calendar, and gave themselves a shared history. At some point, not unnaturally, they began to add a layer of political and economic institutions. If at this point a single community did not emerge as dominant over the rest, which was the *polis* system, the result was a *koinon* (literally, a "shared venture"), a federal state, in which the member communities were all theoretically equal, and government was shared between the common institutions and the member states. Federation was a genuine alternative to *polis*-formation, suitable for the governance of large territories.

Koina grew out of a sense of kinship, whereas kinship was the outcome of the *polis* system, not the start of it: everyone in Attica perforce became "Athenians," because Athens was the political center. But *koina* could and did overstep their ethnic boundaries, by granting citizenship to foreign communities. Once a constitution and an administrative structure had been developed, the system could be transferred to others, whatever their ethnicity. Ethnic outsiders had exactly the same rights and obligations as insiders; at a stroke, they became "kin." Official meetings of the larger confederacies either rotated among member states or convened at a shared sanctuary, in order to avoid privileging one member over the rest, or the original homeland over the newly acquired territories.

The right of citizens of member communities to live, work, and intermarry elsewhere in the federal state was always an important aspect of *koina*; it was a concrete recognition of kinship (real or fictive) and created a strong social fabric. In *poleis*, citizenship was often a closely guarded privilege. When the Romans conquered Macedon in 167 and divided the kingdom into four small republics, one of their first measures was to ban intermarriage between the four statelets, to make it less likely that the country could re-form.

Koina came together by agreement, and that is enshrined in the term "federalism," the Latin root of which is *foedus*, "a compact." Federal states find themselves in a difficult, almost paradoxical position. They have to allow their member states a fair degree of autonomy, while at the same time retaining enough power themselves to maintain the state as a whole. The institutions of a federal state are necessarily a compromise: neither the center nor the peripheral members can gain too much strength. The nature of the compromise is often exposed in North American politics today, in the continuing debate over states' rights. The balance of power can be delicate, and at times of stress the compact between center and periphery might be up for renegotiation.

In the Greek confederacies, each of the member communities usually remained responsible for its own internal affairs—its finances, farmland, citizenship rolls, sanctuaries and local forms of worship, offices and officers, choice of delegates for the federal council, laws and courts (provided they did not contravene federal laws), and nonmilitary forms of interaction with others—but any decisions that affected the confederacy as a whole were referred to central government. In the ancient Greek world such decisions very often concerned war and peace, and the two great confederacies, the Aetolian and the Achaean, were far from alone in each having a General, the man responsible for the armed forces, as their annually elected leader.

This division of responsibilities between the federal center and the member states was modeled on earlier leagues. The Athenian leagues of the fifth and fourth centuries, for instance, also permitted a high degree of local self-government (though as the fifth century progressed, the Athenians' attitude toward league members became increasingly domineering), and had a central council made up of representatives of the member states. They had efficient systems for the collection of taxes, and although we have little evidence for how the Achaeans and Aetolians handled this aspect, it may well have been based on the Athenian system; the Athenians divided the members of the Delian League into five districts and put tax collection in the hands of elected Athenian specialists. And the Athenians promoted the worship of their chief deity, Athena, throughout the league.

Like the Athenians, every federal state elected officials to take care of diplomatic, financial, and military matters, had a common meeting place for political assembly, shared military duties, had common judicial, deliberative, legislative, and executive systems, exacted financial contributions from its members, employed standard weights and measures to aid commerce within the state, took care of infrastructure such as roads and harbors, and acknowledged its presiding deity with a common sanctuary, which was often also where federal meetings took place. In short, the federal state facilitated cooperation among its members and provided goods that they could not provide on their own. In the third century, this deal proved hugely attractive to individual communities.

FEDERAL STATE STRUCTURES

Both the Achaean and Aetolian confederacies were flexible enough to adapt their institutions to changing circumstances, especially the ever-increasing numbers of their members. Both confederacies had similar institutions, and in fact probably imitated each other, as well as drawing on the experiences of earlier leagues. Basically—and in imitation of the typical Greek city-state—each confederacy had a tripartite structure, consisting of a general assembly, a council, and annually elected officers.

The general assembly was, in theory, the legislative branch of government. It could be attended by all male citizens over the age of twenty (that is, of military age), but given the huge geographical extent of the confederacies, it is not clear how well attended assemblies were. The practice of rotating meetings helped to ensure that everyone at least had a chance to attend once in a while. But the general assembly met rarely. It could be summoned for emergency meetings, but the basic structure was two meetings a year in Aetolia, and four in Achaea.

In both cases, the assembly was advised by a council, which met between assembly meetings and discussed issues to present to the assembly for debate and decision. Members of the council were chosen by their hometowns and could be chosen year after year. Other boards, with specialized missions (such as finance or law-drafting) were created as subcommittees of the council. But this council became unwieldy: it consisted of representatives of all the member states, with the number of representatives each state provided based proportionately on its population, and when the confederacies had reached their largest extent, the councils numbered in the high hundreds. In 167, when the Aetolians were severely divided over the question of whether to side with Rome, no fewer than 550 councilors were murdered in the council-house, with others sent into exile, and they were only the pro-Roman faction.

Both confederacies adopted the same solution to this unwieldiness, and created small permanent boards, which met frequently and took care of daily business. The assemblies officially delegated their powers to these boards, so that they could make decisions and act on them without further consultation. This board therefore was the effective ruler of the confederacy. It still presented matters for voting at the general assembly, but some of these matters were necessarily faits accomplis, which the assembly was required merely to rubber-stamp. The big issues, however, such as war and peace, were still reserved for general assemblies.

These boards consisted largely of the senior officers of the confederacy, who also attended and chaired the main council meetings and the assemblies. It was the senior officers, then, who wielded power. The historian Polybius, who came from Megalopolis, an Arcadian city that had joined the Achaean Confederacy, loyally claimed that the Achaean system was a model democracy, but in reality both the Achaean and Aetolian confederacies were oligarchies of landowners, just like pretty much everywhere else in the third and second centuries. Only the leisured rich had the time to devote to administration. Analysis of the names of senior officeholders in both the Achaean and Aetolian confederacies shows that they came from relatively few politically engaged families.

Throughout the third century, the meeting place for the Achaean assembly was the town of Aegium, and specifically the nearby sanctuary of Zeus Homarios, "Zeus the Unifier." It was only later, early in the second century, that meetings began to move from place to place, because Aegium was no longer central to the expanded state. Elections were held at first at the spring meeting, but later (after 217) they came to be held in the autumn, so that the General had time to prepare for the next year's campaigning season. The Aetolians held one of their meetings in the autumn at Thermum, sacred to Apollo and long the acknowledged center of the region—this was the meeting at which elections took place—and another in the spring, which rotated from town to town. The only towns that hosted the spring meeting were ethnically non-Aetolian, so this rotating meeting must have been introduced only once the confederacy had expanded beyond Old Aetolia. It gave even far-flung members the chance to pack a local meeting.

Each year, in both confederacies, a General was appointed as the head of state, and he was supported by a small group of other elected officers, responsible for, say, military levies or state finances. The second-in-command was a Cavalry Commander, and in Achaea, but not in Aetolia, there was a third senior officer, a Fleet Commander. The General had to leave an interval of one year in the Achaean Confederacy, and perhaps three years in the Aetolian Confederacy, before being reelected, but within this constraint reelection was common.

In theory, the regulation that no one could be General in consecutive years was supposed to impede the acquisition of personal power, but it was a failure. The Achaeans, especially, had the habit of elevating one person at a time to a position of authority, making him virtually a sole ruler. Aratus is the prime example; he was

General every other year—that is, whenever he was legally allowed to be—from his first election in 245 at the age of twenty-six until his death in 213, with only one self-imposed interval. Even when out of office, he dictated Achaean policy. In the second century, Philopoemen was another, and his career demonstrated what a supreme General could get away with, such as ignoring orders and acting as *he* thought best for the confederacy. The Aetolians seem to have been less liable to heroize their leaders—or perhaps they just never had leaders of the caliber of Aratus and Philopoemen.

THE ACHAEAN CONFEDERACY

The Achaeans of the northern Peloponnese had long had a sense of ethnic identity, certainly since the sixth century. They spoke the same dialect, lived close to one another, traded at the same fairs and harbors, and worshipped at the same temples. They felt themselves to be tied by blood and a shared history. They had also occasionally acted in common, but we can be certain of the existence of federal structures only in the first half of the fourth century. Subsequently, the imposition of tyrants on the Peloponnesian cities by Antipater and others broke up the confederacy, since the cities acted as independent entities, but then it began to reform in the late 280s. The first General of the renewed confederacy was elected for the year May 280 to May 279, just as the migrant Celts were streaming into Macedon.

The reformation of the confederacy was undoubtedly in part a response to the defeat of Areus of Sparta and the weakness of Macedon, both factors that revived political self-confidence in Achaea. They were, at least temporarily, free from their two major threats. Four Achaean towns—Dyme, Patrae, Tritaea, and Pharae—expelled their tyrants and their Macedonian garrisons and formed themselves into a federal body; not coincidentally, these four were farthest from the Macedonian headquarters at Corinth. If they performed some formal act of inauguration of the renewed federation, we have no knowledge of it; no observers at the time seem

These powerful fortifications on the acropolis of Dyme must have been a factor in the town's decision to secede from Macedonian dominion and cofound the Achaean Confederacy. Photo by author.

to have appreciated the importance of the move. If Antigonus was concerned, there was nothing he could do about it: he was too busy trying to secure Macedon.

In 275, three other Achaean towns—Aegium, Bura, and Cerynea—followed suit, and the following year Leontium, Aegeira, and Pellene joined as well. These ten towns were the original members of the reformed confederacy, but a significant moment came late in 252 or early in 251, when Aratus, a political exile from his native Sicyon, on the south coast of the Gulf of Corinth, returned and gained control of the city. Sicyon was still racked by factional fighting, but it seems that the one thing the majority could agree on was that they should join the Achaean Confederacy, despite the fact that they were not Achaeans. Economic and defensive considerations outweighed those of ethnicity, and Aratus was allowed to see this idea of his through to completion. There was a precedent for this extension of Achaean citizenship to non-Achaeans: in the first manifestation of the confederacy, in the fourth century, the Achaeans had occupied the Aetolian town of Calydon and made the Calydonians Achaean citizens, perhaps against their will.

From the time of Aratus' first Generalship in 245, the aim of the Achaean Confederacy was to incorporate all the towns and city-states of the Peloponnese, even their most powerful neighbor, Sparta. The Peloponnese had been more or less unified once before, in the fifth century with the Peloponnesian League, and Aratus intended to resuscitate that sense of being Peloponnesian, rather than Achaean or Argive or Sicyonian or Spartan. Polybius, writing in the second century, approved of both Aratus' vision and his plan for the Peloponnese:

> There had been many attempts in the past to unify the Peloponnesians, but none of them succeeded because each state was interested only in its own supremacy, not in freedom for all alike. In my time, however, this cause has made considerable progress. It has been so successful, in fact, that not only have the Achaeans formed the states into a community of allies and friends, but they have also adopted the same laws, weights and measures, and coinage, and they share statesmen, council and law courts. In short, the only way in which almost the entire Peloponnese fails to be a single state is that its inhabitants are not enclosed within a single wall; in all other respects, the public aspects of their lives are more or less identical from town to town.

And when Polybius goes on to ponder why all these towns wanted to join the confederacy (although he admits that "the timely application of force" was sometimes required), he argues that it was the attraction of the fact that they would all count equally within the confederacy. There is a degree of exaggeration in Polybius' enthusiastic account—he underplays the extent to which member states retained their own identity—but he was right to highlight the relative success of Aratus' policy. But it was a policy that would inevitably lead them to clash with Antigonus, above all because they wanted to deprive him of Corinth, the guardian of the Peloponnese.

THE AETOLIAN CONFEDERACY

The Aetolian Confederacy had a parallel history. There had long been people identified as "the Aetolians," as though they were ethnically distinct, and Thermum had evolved into an important regional meeting place by the middle of the seventh century. It was a sacred center, and the place where people discussed Aetolian affairs and settled disputes among themselves, so that it was natural for it to evolve into the main meeting place of the confederacy. The coastal and inland communities, however, seem to have been separate blocks for much of the early history of the region, each of them divided among various village-dwelling tribes. For some of the fifth and fourth centuries, in fact, the "Aetolian" coastline was not in Aetolian hands—as just mentioned for Calydon.

By early in the fourth century, however, federal structures were in place. The goal of the Aetolians at this time appears to have been the recovery, and incorporation into the confederacy, of the coastal towns within its territory. This aim was successfully realized over the following decades, culminating in the recovery of Naupactus by the end of the 330s and the seizure of Oeniadae in the 320s. By the end of the century the Aetolians had taken over western Phocis as well, by peaceful assimilation of these non-Aetolians into the confederacy.

The Aetolians continued to expand. In 280, they took advantage of Macedonian chaos to seize Heraclea Trachinia—a very useful outpost—and then successfully defended it against the Celts. Aetolian possession of Heraclea, where they installed a substantial garrison, had the potential to be a major irritant to Macedon, since it gave them control of the two best passes that a Macedonian army might want to take as it marched south, Thermopylae and Dyo Vouna. The Aetolians also expanded, settlement by settlement, into Ozolian Locris. Members of the wealth elite themselves, the statesmen of the confederacy were good at winning over the elites of the towns they wanted to incorporate, especially by holding out the possibility of their holding office in the confederacy.

The turning point for the confederacy was its leadership in repelling the Celtic invasion of 279. After ravaging Macedon and Thessaly, the Celts marched south. At Thermopylae, they were blocked by a combined Greek army; only the Peloponnesians stayed away (apart from the Achaeans of Patrae), because they did not feel threatened. Unable to break through the pass, the Celts divided their forces; some went to the Aetolian town of Callion and massacred the civilian population, in order to draw the Greeks from Thermopylae; the atrocity was long remembered. The rest marched on Delphi, intending to plunder its wealth. To the Greeks, this was a shock of equivalent magnitude to Pearl Harbor or 9/11, and ever afterward the Celts had the reputation of striking terror into their opponents. They had not come to stay, but only to ravage, rape, and pillage.

Exactly what happened at Delphi will remain forever unclear, because later tradition ascribed the repulse of the Celts as much to divine intervention (earthquakes, rock falls, tempests) as to Greek prowess, but the upshot was that the Celts were forced back north in tatters, and their leader, Brennus, was killed in the action. It may be true that the Celts were terrified by these natural forces, because we are told that when a delegation of Celts was asked by Alexander the Great what they most feared, they replied that they were afraid only of the sky falling on them.

The defense of Delphi had been undertaken by a combined Greek force, but the Aetolians claimed leadership and gained much-deserved kudos. Over the subsequent decades, they translated their new standing in the Greek world into dominance over Delphi (with which they had long enjoyed good relations) and the incorporation of its non-Aetolian Amphictyonic neighbors; by 259, they had nine votes on the council, out of a total of sixteen. They were in the process of taking over the entirety of central Greece.

Up until their defeat of the Celts, the Aetolians had been regarded as backward bandits, who preyed on their neighbors and everyone else in ways that had not been seen in civilized Greece for centuries. In a hymn to Demetrius Poliorcetes, for instance, composed in Athens in 291/0, the Aetolians are called brigands and are likened to the monstrous Sphinx of legend, which occupied a rocky perch (here, the Aetolian mountains) and snatched people and their possessions; Demetrius is urged to hurl the Sphinx off its cliff and reduce it to ashes. Even in the second century, an Achaean ambassador to Rome said that "the Aetolians have only the tongues of Greeks, just as they have only the appearance of men." Their poor reputation was due to the fact that the state had long tended to turn a blind eye toward, and even to sponsor, individual acts of piracy and brigandage.

But Aetolian success against the Celts gave them moral authority, and they entered the economic and military mainstream of Greek history. Thermum became one of the most magnificent locations in Greece. Its agora, with its abundant freshwater spring, was graced by huge stoas, a monumental temple to Apollo, and around two thousand statues in bronze and marble. Over the subsequent decades, a great many Greek states, on the mainland, in the Aegean, and even in Asia Minor, were happy to enter into diplomatic relations with the Aetolians. By promoting the Celts as the new barbarian threat, now that the Persians had been defeated, they made themselves out to be the saviors of Greece, even though in fact their priority had probably been the preservation of Aetolia.

The Aetolians instituted a new festival at Delphi, the Soteria, or Festival of Deliverance, which became one of the most important and popular festivals in the Greek world and a reminder, for as long as it was held, of what the Aetolians had done for Greece. For decades, they issued coinage showing Aetolia personified and seated on a pile of Celtic spoils, and they erected similar statues at both Delphi and Thermum. The Aetolians were at the forefront of the attempt to keep Greek pride alive—to keep it from being crushed by Macedonian dominion.

At the time of Antigonus' accession to the throne, before the full flourishing of the Achaeans later in the century, the Aetolians were, and were recognized as, the only Greek state capable of offering serious resistance to Macedon. They had already proved their credentials in this respect by their opposition to Cassander and then Demetrius Poliorcetes. They had been one of the few Greek states that Demetrius had failed to incorporate into his revived League of Corinth. His son knew what to expect from them.

A CAUSE FOR CONCERN

A great many countries today are federal states: the United States, Russia, Canada, Mexico, Switzerland, Germany, Austria, Brazil, India, Pakistan, Nigeria . . . the list is long. But the Greeks invented the first federal states in the world. The Aetolians and Achaeans were not the earliest Greek confederacies, but they were the most successful. And one of the reasons for their success was their willingness to experiment, to find the best way to satisfy the member states and create a stable system. The Achaeans and Aetolians laid the foundation and created a model for future federal states to follow. It is very likely that the Founding Fathers of the United States, who were steeped in Greek history, looked in part to the two great third-century confederacies as their models.

By the time that Antigonus had secured his throne in the late 270s, the Aetolians were already a powerful force in central Greece, and the Achaeans were a rising force in the Peloponnese. To his undoubted dismay, both federations were relatively stable. They drew on the political knowledge and wisdom of their member states to create systems that were good compromises, and hence proved less liable to the factional fighting that had marred individual city-states—at any rate until the Romans came and stirred things up in the second century. They were also large enough to field sizable citizen armies, and wealthy enough to hire mercenaries; and, even though, during Antigonus' lifetime, these two confederacies were more usually enemies than friends, they were both founded on the same determination to resist the Macedonians and any other form of imperialism.

The growing power of Macedon forced the Greeks to make the necessary adjustments. The nature and structure of the confederacies endowed them with strength and resilience, and made them a real threat to any Macedonian king, if he could not get on good terms with them. Antigonus proved good at playing one of the confederacies off against the other, but the enthusiasm the confederacies met as they expanded would have concerned him, since it was clear that the Greeks collectively had not yet given up hope of extricating themselves from Macedonian dominion. Federation was a new, vigorous manifestation of the Greek love of independence, and Antigonus had every reason to be concerned.

CHAPTER 5

The Empire of the Ptolemies

Toward the end of 309, Ptolemy of Egypt was waiting on the island of Cos for the birth of his son, the future Ptolemy II Philadelphus. He was also finalizing his plans to invade Greece. He had prepared the ground well. He had spent the previous two years seizing bases to support the invasion by increasing his grip on the cities of Cyprus and attacking Antigonid possessions in the southwestern corner of Asia Minor. Then he softened up all the Greek cities, on the mainland and elsewhere, with a propaganda initiative, designed to make them sympathetic to him rather than his rivals. Next he detached Polemaeus, a renegade Antigonid general (a nephew of Antigonus Monophthalmus) who controlled central Greece, from his alliance with Cassander in Macedon. Finally, he proposed marriage to Cleopatra, the full sister of Alexander the Great, and she accepted. She was past childbearing, but marrying her would help legitimate his claim to the entirety of Alexander's former empire. They saw themselves as the king and queen of Macedon.

There should never have been any doubt about Ptolemy's ambitions. All Alexander's immediate successors wanted to emulate the conqueror and take the entire empire for themselves, and Ptolemy was no exception. After Alexander's death, when the provinces of the empire were shared out, to be held in trust until the kings demonstrated the competence to rule in their own names (in effect, until Alexander IV came of age), Ptolemy received the prize of Egypt. The country was a relatively self-contained unit, geographically speaking; it consisted of the Nile delta on the Mediterranean, and a strip of fertile floodplains a thousand kilometers (620 miles) south up the river valley to the First Cataract (the first stretch of shallows), bounded by desert to east and west. The kingdom comprised about 23,000 square kilometers (about 8,880 square miles) and had a population of four or five million.

Settlements along the river were perched on high ground to avoid the annual mud-depositing floods, the source of the country's great wealth; at the time of the floods, they were turned into islands. Until the Aswan High Dam was completed in 1970, every summer, from June until October, the water level rose, in good years as much as twelve or even fifteen meters (forty to fifty feet), flooding the plains to either side, and then gradually subsided until the following spring. Every time the river flooded, it deposited large amounts of fertile silt on farmers' fields, making them fabulously productive by the standards of the ancient world, year after year. The location is otherwise harsh, with minimal rainfall; without the Nile, Egyptian civilization would never have happened.

There were three main areas of settlement. Lower Egypt, the delta region in the north, was densely settled; it was in the far west of the delta that Alexander the Great chose to site Alexandria, which became the greatest city in the Mediterranean before the rise of Rome. To the southwest of the delta lay a large, fertile depression called the Fayyum, where the amount of arable land was hugely increased by a massive drainage and canalization project undertaken by the first two Ptolemies. Then Middle and Upper Egypt sprawled up the Nile, and included two great cities, Memphis in the north, the religious heart of Egypt for native Egyptians, and Thebes in the south, famous for the temples of Karnak and Luxor. Ptolemais, founded by Ptolemy I, became another major center in the south—and a defense against the frequent rebelliousness of the southerners. The north became highly hellenized, the south (apart from Ptolemais) considerably less so; people there tended to the view that Egypt should be governed by Egyptians.

But Ptolemy immediately showed that he had ambitions beyond those of a mere governor of a province. He did away with the old guard, those who had been placed in positions of authority in Egypt by Alexander himself; he responded to an appeal by the exiled oligarchs of Greek Cyrenaica to establish a puppet regime in the cities of this fertile region of North Africa, with his general Ophellas as governor; he entered into alliances with kings of the Cypriot statelets; he demonstrated interest in Arabia; and he hijacked the corpse of Alexander the Great in order to bury it in Egypt instead of Macedon. The point of this astonishing last move was that it was the job of a new Macedonian king to see to the funeral of his predecessor. By burying Alexander in Egypt, Ptolemy was claiming himself as the legitimate successor and Egypt as the headquarters of the new empire. Right from the start, he had his eye on the empire as a whole.

A LESSON LEARNED

So, early in 308, Ptolemy set out for Greece. Our only informant is Diodorus, and all he says is the following:

> Ptolemy put to sea from Myndus with a strong fleet. As he sailed through the Aegean islands, he liberated Andros and installed a garrison. When he reached the Isthmus, he was ceded Sicyon and Corinth by Cratesipolis. . . . Ptolemy's plan was to liberate the rest of the Greek cities as well, the idea being that the goodwill of the Greeks would greatly increase his power.

Cratesipolis, the aptly named "Holder of Cities," was the formidable (and apparently very beautiful) wife of Alexander, the son of Polyperchon, who in 315 had declared himself an independent ruler of the enclave of Corinth and Sicyon in the northeastern Peloponnese. When Alexander died, the victim of a murder plot, his wife took over and ruled for several years, until Ptolemy's arrival. Ptolemy must have prepared the ground well, because Cratesipolis immediately ceded her realm to him, despite the fact that her mercenaries were encouraging her to put up a defense. We hear no more of her after this episode.

When Diodorus says that Ptolemy intended to liberate the rest of the Greek cities as well, he probably means that he intended to form them into a self-governing (and so "free") league, like Philip and Alexander's League of Corinth. But all of his plans came to nothing. Diodorus' account goes on:

> But when the Peloponnesians, who had undertaken to supply him with grain and money, did nothing of the kind, the aggrieved dynast made peace with Cassander, by the terms of which each of them would retain the cities he currently possessed. Then, after securing Sicyon and Corinth with garrisons, he sailed back to Egypt.

The response he had hoped for from the Greek cities never materialized. Diodorus focuses on the Peloponnesian cities, but central Greece failed to take up his cause either. Ptolemy had killed Polemaeus before setting out, probably because the renegade wanted Greece for himself, but he had clearly failed to secure the allegiance of Polemaeus' former friends, on which he must have been depending. We can perhaps detect the hand of Antigonus Monophthalmus here; it would have been natural for him, after Polemaeus' death, to get back on good terms with the central Greeks. Antigonus had recently finished an unsuccessful war against Seleucus in Babylonia, and was now free to concentrate on his other enemies, giving Ptolemy another good reason to return to Egypt.

Ptolemy's failure to find support in Greece was matched by his failure to secure Cleopatra as a wife. She set out from Sardis, where she was resident, to join him, but Sardis was within Antigonus Monophthalmus' domain, and he had no desire to see her used as a springboard to promote another man to the Macedonian throne. So he had her murdered; these were brutal times. It seems possible that Ptolemy had not heard about her death before setting out from Myndus, and that it was the arrival of the news while he was in Greece that finally brought his campaign to an end, with the realization that, without her by his side, he was never going to gain the Macedonian kingdom. When Demetrius Poliorcetes took Corinth and Sicyon in 303, Ptolemy did not attempt to recover them.

This failure generated a fundamental shift in Ptolemaic policy. The kings of Egypt learned their lesson. They still saw themselves as the future leaders of the entire Greek world, but they went about it more cautiously, by gradual expansion rather than sudden invasion, and also, as we shall see, by a powerful propaganda offensive.

In geographical terms, they spent many decades slowly expanding from their core territory. In an illuminating passage, Polybius stressed the importance of these foreign possessions. After criticizing Ptolemy IV Philopator for his attitude toward kingship—"he ruled for all the world as though he were on holiday"—he goes on:

> His predecessors, however, had paid more attention to their foreign possessions than they had to ruling Egypt itself. It was their possession of Coele Syria and Cyprus that had enabled them to threaten the kings of Syria on land and sea; their mastery of the most notable cities, regions, and ports along the entire coastline from Pamphylia to the Hellespont and the district of Lysimachea had allowed them to influence the Asiatic princelings and the islands as well; and their possession of Aenus, Maronea, and even more remote cities had enabled them also to watch over Thrace and Macedon. In this way, they had maintained a long reach, and with the principalities as distant buffer zones, they never had to worry about their rule in Egypt.

The buffers were not just physical, in the sense that any enemy would have to get past many Ptolemaic garrisons before reaching Egypt itself, but also economic, in that they supplied Egyptian deficiencies (especially in minerals and timber), raised useful revenues, and gave the Ptolemies access to expertise and manpower. Important elements of this empire were located in the Aegean, building on the foundation created by Ptolemy I's seizure of Andros in 308; but here the Ptolemaic policy of gradual expansion was impeded by the growing naval strength of Antigonus. For a while, the Egyptians were on the back foot, compelled to react rather than act. They nurtured greater ambitions, but had to be content with trying to preserve what they had and with undermining Antigonus, not least by trying to win the allegiance of anti-Macedonian politicians in the Greek states.

SIBLING MARRIAGE

In 305, Ptolemy became king and pharaoh of Egypt, after the murder of Alexander IV had finally done away with the pretense that Alexander the Great's empire might remain intact. The Ptolemies formed the thirty-first and final dynasty of Egypt, and the longest lasting: Egypt fell to Rome after the deaths of Mark Antony and Cleopatra VII in 30 BCE. In 285, Ptolemy abdicated in favor of his son, and he died two years later. Ptolemy II became known as Ptolemy Philadelphus, where his father had been Ptolemy Soter ("Savior"). The Hellenistic kings of Syria and Egypt regularly took on bynames that indicated how they wanted to be thought of by the wider world. Philadelphus means "Sibling-Lover."

When Arsinoe fled from Ptolemy Ceraunus and Cassandrea in 280, she found refuge first on the island of Samothrace (a sacred island, and so a place of asylum), and then she was invited to join her younger brother, now Ptolemy II, in Alexandria. One of Ptolemy's chief concerns early in his reign was to secure his rule against the possibility of any interdynastic disputation of the throne. He was aware of the potential Ptolemy Ceraunus held for causing trouble, and of the troubles within Lysimachus' court, in which his sister had been involved, and he wanted to make sure that his court was free of such strife. When Arsinoe arrived, he made her marry him and adopt his children, so that there were no loose ends.

Marrying his full sister was an extraordinary step for Ptolemy to take, even if he took it more for symbolic reasons than for procreation; even marrying a half sister was barely acceptable by Greek tradition. The fact that, in myth, some of the gods had done it only proved that the practice was restricted to the gods. It was something that pharaohs had occasionally done, however, and fourth-century dynasts of Caria, such as Mausolus, for whom the world-famous Mausoleum was built, had married siblings, but none of these rulers had been Greek. For all its riskiness, Ptolemy gloried in it. Gigantic statues of him and Arsinoe greeted visitors at the main entrance to the harbor of Alexandria; but, above all, he made the royal couple objects of worship.

Around 272, he inaugurated a joint cult of Alexander and the Sibling Deities—himself and Arsinoe, though both were still alive. They were the Philadelphoi, the Sibling-Lovers, or the Theoi Adelphoi, the Sibling Deities. The incestuous relationship was recognizable by both of the two main categories of their subjects: Greeks could recognize them as avatars of the sibling deities Zeus and Hera, and Egyptians as Osiris and Isis. Nor were these minor cults: the priests and priestesses of dynastic cults were always important people, and royal appointees.

It may seem surprising that a living human being could be worshipped as a god, but apotheosis was possible within Greek religion. Of course, there were uncrossable gulfs between humanity and divinity, not least the fact that the gods, by definition, do not die. But it was always possible for a person to be taken over temporarily by a god. A sexy woman was temporarily possessed by Aphrodite, for instance, and in the biblical Acts of the Apostles, the Lycaonians took Saint Paul to be Hermes and his companion Barnabas to be Zeus. Some intellectuals believed that all gods had originally been human benefactors of humankind.

So, as long as a king was performing apparently miraculous deeds, he could be regarded as an incarnate god. Alexander's incredible conquest of the East propelled him to divinity, and all of the immediate Successors were worshipped, in some places, at some point during their lives. The worship of Arsinoe was a phenomenon of the second generation of the Successors: she was not so much the doer of great deeds herself as a representative of the greatness of the dynasty to which she belonged.

Brother-sister marriage was supposed to guarantee the purity of the bloodline, advertise the solidity of the royal family, and secure stability by eliminating the possibility of rival claimants to the throne; the king's offspring would effectively be clones of himself, and so every generation of Egyptian kings took the same name. Moreover, starting with Ptolemy II and Arsinoe (though they also retrojected it back on to their parents), every generation of rulers was presented as a loving couple.

Perhaps surprisingly, there is no real evidence of genetic dete-

Brother and sister, husband and wife, the original power couple: Ptolemy II and Arsinoe II. They seem almost to be two heads of a single body. The bulging eyes are a sign of potency and magnanimity. Photo: The Metropolitan Museum of Art, New York.

rioration over the more than two hundred years that the Ptolemies practiced sibling marriage. Strife within the royal family became increasingly savage, but savagery has characterized many courts throughout the ages. Sibling marriage was a symbol of power, a way for the Ptolemies to claim that conventional morality applied as little to them as it did to the gods. If the reaction of the poet Sotades of Maronea is typical, the Greeks were appalled: "Unholy the hole into which you push your prick." Sotades dared to pen this line even though he was resident in Alexandria, but he paid for it with long imprisonment, and then, after he escaped, in the early 260s he was caught and killed on the island of Caudos, off the south coast of

Crete. Ptolemy's general Patroclus had him placed inside a lead coffin and thrown into the sea.

GREATER EGYPT

A major concern of Ptolemy II's was, of course, the preservation and expansion of the empire his father had bequeathed him. In a poem written ten or twelve years after his accession, one of his court poets, Theocritus of Syracuse, claimed:

> He takes portions of Phoenicia and Arabia,
> Of Syria, Libya, and the land of the black Ethiopians.
> All Pamphylians and the spearmen of Cilicia he commands,
> The Lycians, the war-loving Carians, and the islands of the Cyclades,
> For there are no finer ships than his that sail the sea.

If Theocritus had been penning historical truth, rather than currying favor with his king, he would not have implied that all this was Ptolemy's doing; some of these possessions had been bequeathed to him. And "Libya" (that is, Cyrenaica) was in fact at the time in rebellion, and remained out of Ptolemaic control between 276 and 246. Nevertheless, it is true that by the time of Ptolemy's death in 246, he had both consolidated and extended his father's empire.

Ptolemy wanted control of all the trade routes and harbors of the eastern Mediterranean, the Aegean, and the Black Sea approaches, in order to give the abundant wheat his kingdom produced the best chance of dominating the market. Wheat was a staple all over the Mediterranean, and was by far the most widely traded commodity. Confederacies were easier to manage than a great number of separate towns, and an essential plank in Ptolemy's policy was to form his dependencies into federal states. The Cyclades, Lycia, and at least some of the Carian communities all became confederacies. In addition, Ptolemy gained control over, or got on good terms with, a number of important harbor towns and islands on the west coast of Asia Minor. If he ever had wanted to invade Greece like his father, he controlled most of the approaches.

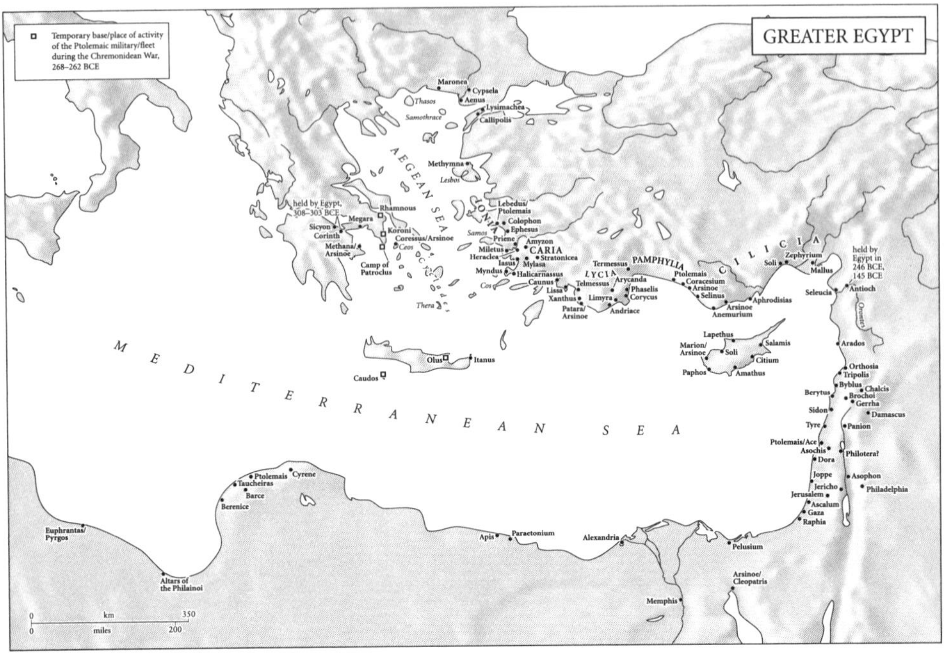

But the Ptolemies never penetrated much farther. In the 260s, one of Ptolemy's generals—Patroclus, again—achieved the great coup of seizing, fortifying, and garrisoning an excellent harbor actually on the mainland of Greece, by occupying the volcanic peninsula of Methana in Argolis. But it was not until the reign of Ptolemy III Euergetes that outposts were established farther north, in Thrace (at Aenus and Maronea), and on the Hellespont (especially Lysimachea), from where sea traffic through the narrows could be monitored, and intercepted if necessary. Essentially, and thanks to Antigonus, by the middle of the century security had become the Ptolemaic priority in the Aegean, not growth.

PTOLEMAIC OUTREACH

The Ptolemies had two main foreign-policy goals. The first, as we have just seen, was domination of the sea lanes of the Aegean and eastern Mediterranean. The second was trying to gain or retain Coele Syria, the region made up of Palestine, Lebanon, and southern Syria. The wars for Coele Syria took place far from Greece, and so will play little part in this book, but it is worth bearing them in mind, because these were times when the Ptolemies were inevitably distracted, and less able to focus on the Aegean.

For much of the third century, the Ptolemaic empire was very healthy, not just in material terms, but also in the boldness of how it was presented to the wider world. The Ptolemies presented their empire as *the* world empire for Greeks, a universal empire; the Seleucids were doing much the same. There was a common belief in the ancient Mediterranean world in a succession of empires. It is found, for instance, in the biblical Book of Daniel (written in the second century), where we read of four empires: Babylonian, Median, Persian (Achaemenid), and Macedonian.

Some, including Daniel, held that the sequence was theoretically endless, as each new empire replaced the previous one; others, however, held that the final empire was the end point of history, and this seems to underlie the Ptolemaic presentation (as it does later versions of the theory, where the Roman empire is seen as the end point). Both Ptolemy II's main court poets, Callimachus of Cyrene and Theocritus, chimed in by prophesying rule over the entire world for him.

Any empire is a complex construct, and one of its elements is always spiritual. More than any other ancient empire, the Ptolemaic empire was an ideological as well as a geographical construct. All empires use ideology and the perpetuation of certain spiritual values to win the hearts and minds of their subjects, and to appeal to further potential subjects. The ideology of the British empire was civilization and Christendom; of the Romans, romanization and peace; of the Third Reich, Aryanism. The Ptolemies claimed to bring concord—to unite potential enemies throughout the eastern Mediterranean as friends under their aegis—and security, whether that came as money, wheat, or spiritual salvation.

ARSINOE, UNIVERSAL GODDESS

It is not easy to pinpoint the year of Arsinoe's death, but it was probably 270. Having promoted his sister and himself as the living Sibling Deities, her early death was awkward for Ptolemy, but he grasped the nettle firmly: he never remarried, and undertook a campaign of further deification of his sister-wife, with cults on her own or combined with those of himself and others, and promoted her worship throughout the empire, as a force for the unification of all its disparate parts. Her death did not put an end to her career; she continued to support her brother's enterprises.

In Egypt, where she was worshipped by the Greek population as Arsinoe-Aphrodite, she had her own temples, but she also joined every single one of the deities of the Egyptian pantheon in their temples; in the great temple of Ptah, for instance, in Memphis, she was recognized as Ptah's consort, and the priest of Ptah managed her cult too. A new nome (county) was created in the Fayyum, the Arsinoite nome, so she was the nome goddess for all the inhabitants there and the recipient of appropriate forms of worship.

Within the wider Greek world, Arsinoe Philadelphus received cult, at least for a while, in Phoenicia, Cyprus, Lesbos, Delos, Paros, Ios, Amorgos, Samos, Thera, Caunus, Miletus, Rhamnous, and Eretria; she was even worshipped as far away as the Crimean peninsula. The evidence for this consists of chance survivals, so the full tally of places would in reality have been much larger. Her apotheosis was celebrated in a hymn by Callimachus, one of Ptolemy II's finest court poets. Many towns in Greater Egypt were named after her. They cluster especially in Cyprus and the Aegean islands, but there was an Arsinoe on the Suez Gulf, in Crete, and at Methana in mainland Greece. And it was naturally in these towns that her cult was particularly important. She was sometimes worshipped in these places, which were harbor towns, as the protector and deliverer of sailors.

In short, under Ptolemy's guidance, the divinized Arsinoe gained a rather bewildering array of identifications, but the most important of them was Isis, because this raised her to the level of universal mother goddess. One of the most remarkable phenomena of the Hellenistic period was the very rapid spread of the worship of the Egyptian deities Serapis/Osiris and Isis. They were worshipped even in Antigonus' Macedon—though, not surprisingly, Arsinoe was not. Their popularity was due to the fact that they were imagined as being more responsive to human needs than the older Greek gods, the gods of Olympus. There was an increased demand in the Hellenistic period for salvationist and other kinds of cult designed to appeal to the individual; the Ptolemies responded to this need.

Serapis already existed as an Egyptian deity; he was thought of as an amalgam of Osiris and the living Apis bull after it died, and as such had already received cult, as Osorapis, from Greek residents of Memphis. But Ptolemy I tweaked the name to be more acceptable to Greeks, and developed his cult and iconography in a European direction, which downplayed the Apis connection. Serapis was worshipped on his own, but his cult was also joined, during the reign of Ptolemy II, with that of his sister-wife Isis, and this very soon merged with the cult of the Sibling Deities.

Devotees came to regard Serapis/Osiris and Isis as the primordial masculine and feminine principles of the universe. Isis became "the Goddess of Countless Names," and absorbed the functions of almost every other female deity in the Egyptian and Greek pantheons. Those devotees who assimilated the Sibling Deities to Serapis and Isis were therefore elevating Arsinoe to a great height. As well as unifying the Ptolemaic empire, she was offering the rest of the Greek world, the part that still lay outside the empire, the chance to partake in what was being presented as a universal salvationist cult, and to join an empire that was being presented as the end point of history. This was heady, powerful propaganda.

THE GREATEST FESTIVAL IN THE WORLD

Sometime late in the 270s, Ptolemy II put on the most astounding and expensive festival recorded from the ancient Greek world. It is not entirely clear whether it was an existing festival, upgraded for a special occasion, or a one-off. If the former, it was probably the festival called the Ptolemaieia (or the Ptolemaia, in the scaled-down versions put on by Ptolemaic sympathizers outside of Egypt). Ptolemy had inaugurated this festival in 280/79, to commemorate his dead father, and had written to all the Greek states asking them to give official recognition to the new festival by sending delegates to represent them at it, and to accept it as equal in status to the festival held every four years at Olympia in the western Peloponnese, the Olympic Games. The competitive aspects of the festival closely followed the Olympic model, and the Ptolemaieia too was held every four years. The extravaganza that concerns us now may have formed part of the first, second, or third occurrence of the festival.

Grandiosity was well entrenched within the Macedonian tradition of kingship, and Hellenistic kings had the money to do it in style: their palaces and temples were huge and magnificent, their extravagances legendary, their costumes and banquets cost fortunes, their ceremonials were meant to be remembered for generations. This was not just a form of megalomania, but served a practical purpose too: these were new countries, and grand gestures attracted potential immigrants. By the same token, the Ptolemies always played a magnificent part in the Olympic Games and the other most important games in mainland Greece, since they afforded the best opportunities to put on a display for the Greeks.

This particularly extravagant performance of the festival cost Ptolemy the equivalent of hundreds of millions of dollars, although some of the expenses were offset by the gifts that visitors from other states were obliged or expected to bring. It consisted largely of an enormous procession, games, and stupendous sacrifices. The procession began on Day One with a float celebrating Dawn and the Morning Star, and ended several days later with one dedicated to the Evening Star.

Tens of thousands of soldiers paraded in gleaming armor, on foot or horseback. Music and singing filled the air from orchestras and choirs. Exotic animals from all over the world—a particular interest of Ptolemy's—announced the Ptolemies' claim to world domination, and competed for the crowd's attention with colossal gold and silver artifacts and state-of-the-art contraptions such as a robot that could stand up, pour a libation of milk from a jug, and sit down again—the creation of the genius inventor Ctesibius, the son of a barber. On Ptolemy I's golden throne rested a crown made of ten thousand gold coins; 120 boys carried trays of saffron. Images of the Ptolemies mingled with Dionysus, Zeus, and the divinized Alexander the Great, stressing the legitimacy of their rule under divine protection. The pageant just went on and on, with every event surpassing the one before in splendor and costliness.

Overall, the festival, especially the procession, left the audience with an indisputable impression of Ptolemaic power. It was, in effect, the announcement of a new era. The whole world was being presented as under Ptolemaic sway, now or in the future. All the riches of the world flowed into Egypt. It was a symbolic representation of the empire as a whole, designed to legitimate the Ptolemies' universalist ambitions.

Honored guests, invited from all over the Mediterranean, were feasted and entertained in their hundreds in an enormous pavilion; their "party favors" were the items of golden and jewel-studded tableware with which they had just eaten the choicest food and drunk the most celebrated wines of the Mediterranean. Since the guests were representatives of the Greek states, the symbolism united them all in that particular place; Alexandria was the center, and they represented the peripheries. Ptolemy circulated freely among them all, on a floor strewn deep with flowers.

The propaganda was both general and particular. At a general level, in presenting their empire as *the* Greek empire, the Ptolemies were saying that it was that toward which all Greek affairs tended. But the festival was also designed more directly to cast doubt on Antigonus' legitimacy as ruler of Greece. One sequence of floats portrayed the Greek cities of the mainland, Asia Minor, and the islands as free thanks to Alexander the Great and the Ptolemies. The woman portraying the city of Corinth was particularly prominent, standing next to an image of Ptolemy I. The message was plain: Corinth (and the rest of the Greek cities) were properly part of the Ptolemaic realm, which was a continuation of the empire of Alexander the Great, and it was all under the protection of the gods. Delivering the Greeks from Macedon was the manifest destiny of the Ptolemies.

THE MUSEUM OF ALEXANDRIA

The city of Alexandria was the Ptolemies' flagship. It was built on a grid plan, and its broad and breezy avenues, as well as its spacious parks, were famous the world over. But the seafront and the harbors—that is, the areas that would give a visitor his first impression—were where the most awe-inspiring buildings were concentrated: the palaces, the Sema (a mausoleum for Alexander and the Ptolemies), the barracks, the harbor facilities and warehouses, and the most important temples. The fabulous discoveries of archaeologists since the 1990s, often working underwater, give some idea of the splendor of the waterfront, which was swamped in the fourth century CE by a tsunami.

Then there was the Pharos, built in 287—the multistoried, white marble tower named after the island at the mouth of the harbor on which it was located, and one of the Wonders of the World for its design and huge size. It was the world's first lighthouse: fire was kept burning at the top (by slaves, no doubt), and mirrors reflected the light out to sea for the guidance of sailors. The lighthouse finally collapsed in a series of earthquakes sixteen hundred years later; its foundations have recently been rediscovered.

One of the buildings in the palace compound was a Mouseion, a temple to the Muses, the goddesses of culture. The Museum of Alexandria functioned both as a temple of learning and as a residential college for scholars (who doubled as tutors for Ptolemaic princes and their companions), with a particular focus on science, technology, literature, and scholarship. All the expenses of the "cloistered bookworms" who worked in this "chicken-coop of the Muses," as one of Antigonus' acquaintances, Timon of Phleious, called it, were covered by the king, including the development of their major resource, a library, started or expanded by Ptolemy II.

The library was not a separate building: the book-rolls were stored on shelves in the Museum. Ptolemy's intentions in establishing the famous library—apart from enhancing his status—were typically universalist: to collect a copy of every single book ever written in Greek (and colorful stories exist of the extent to which the Ptolemies were prepared to go to achieve this aim), and to translate into Greek the most important books written in other languages. This second aim led, most famously, to the translation within the Museum of the Old Testament into Greek. The work was undertaken by a group of about seventy Alexandrian Jewish scholars; that is why the Greek Old Testament, which is still considered the definitive version, is called the Septuagint, *septuaginta* being the Latin for "seventy." The Septuagint became the body of law for the Greek-speaking Jewish communities of Alexandria and elsewhere.

It is impossible to estimate the number of papyrus rolls the library contained at any given time, and many books occupied more than one roll. If each roll held about thirty thousand words, this book, for instance, would make three rolls. It is possible that it came to hold over one hundred thousand rolls, few enough by today's standards, but an incredible achievement in the ancient world.

The library was not entirely without precedent. Scientific research seems to have become institutionalized in Babylonian temples in the fourth century, and before that there had been libraries both private and royal in Assyrian Mesopotamia and Hittite Asia Minor. Private collectors in Greece had begun to accumulate libraries from the late fifth century onward; Aristotle's was particularly famous, but there were others. What was unprecedented, however, was the sheer scale of the Ptolemies' project. As the Hellenistic period progressed, other cities established great libraries—Antioch and Pergamum, especially—but none compared with the library of Alexandria. The Ptolemies were the only ones who aimed for universal completeness.

The library finally burned to the ground in 642 CE, but by then it had been in decline for eight centuries, and had suffered from neglect, as well as earlier fires and other natural disasters. But, in the third century BCE, it was an integral part of the Ptolemies' program of claiming to represent and encompass all Greeks everywhere. The idea was that all the Greeks' cultural heritage was being preserved and developed in Egypt. Alexandrian scholars even began to edit the texts they received, and produced the first authoritative recensions of poets such as Homer, the foundational figure of Greek culture. Again, the message was plain: if you want to find authentic Greek culture, it resides in Alexandria.

This was the Ptolemaic empire with which Antigonus had to contend. It was a potent and brilliant construct, woven together by military might, economic power, cultural imperialism, and religious symbolism. The fact that Antigonus did successfully resist speaks volumes for his caliber. He did enough to prove to Ptolemy and the world that the Egyptian empire was not, after all, a universal empire. As we shall see, he even challenged its claim to cultural primacy.

PART TWO

Kingship (276–239)

CHAPTER 6

King of Macedon

After Antigonus' defeat at sea by his cousin Ptolemy Ceraunus in 281, he retreated to Boeotia. Many Greeks seemed to think his cause was lost. Within a few months or a couple of years, Areus of Sparta attacked the Aetolians, who were Macedonian allies, though the alliance was perhaps not very secure; the Aetolians annexed Heraclea Trachinia; the Achaean Confederacy began to reform; Argos and Megalopolis expelled their garrisons; the Athenians remained extremely disgruntled by the degree of control Macedon exercised over their lives; and the loyalty of the Boeotians and Megarians became doubtful. Antigonus' fortunes were at a low ebb; in Greece, he could be sure of only Corinth and a scatter of other towns in the Peloponnese, Euboea, Phocis, Piraeus and the other Attic fortresses, and Demetrias. The Aegean harbors were largely in Ptolemaic or Seleucid hands.

The defeat of Antigonus' first attempt to recover his kingdom was clearly severe enough for him to have to regroup, rather than make another immediate attempt. Still, he did not stay inactive for long, though he probably waited until he was sure that Areus had been defeated by the Aetolians before returning to the northern Aegean. First, however, he placed his half brother Craterus in Corinth as his viceroy in the Peloponnese; he would govern the southern Greeks, with the garrisons of Corinth and Chalcis under his command, while Antigonus focused on his primary responsibility, Macedon. Craterus' position was more or less the one Antigonus himself had held under Demetrius Poliorcetes.

The history of the next few years is very poorly documented, but enough remains for us to be certain that, so far from treating his defeat as in any way decisive, Antigonus spent considerable time and effort trying to secure his place in Macedon. After Ptolemy Ceraunus' death, there were, as we have seen, a number of claimants to the Macedonian kingdom. One of them, it now appeared, was Antiochus I of Syria. By killing Lysimachus, Seleucus had, by the standards of these lawless days, legitimated his claim to Macedon (though he had not lived to take it up), and, as Seleucus' son and heir, Antiochus felt that the kingdom belonged to him, or at least that it was worth the attempt. As a preliminary, he tried to win over some important Greek states—the Aetolians, Athenians, and Spartans. He also entered into an alliance with Apollodorus, the tyrant of Cassandrea, who was already on good terms with the Spartans himself. On the principle that attack is the best form of defense, late in 280 Antigonus went to war with Antiochus.

Although the Syrian king could, given time, muster mighty forces from his vast empire, he was in a very difficult position. In the almost two years that had passed since his father's murder, large chunks of Asia Minor had slipped from his grasp. Cappadocia was poised to become an independent kingdom, and Thracian Bithynia already was; the powerful Greek cities of Heraclea Pontica and Byzantium had joined with others in the region to form a confederacy whose Lysimachean coinage showed that they rejected the legitimacy of Seleucid authority; and much of the rest of the southern Black Sea coastline had been taken over by the new kingdom of Pontus. Most of the southern cities around the coastline up to Caria, and for some way inland up the river valleys, were part of Greater Egypt.

Finally, there was Pergamum: in return for his defection from Lysimachus, a man called Philetaerus, the governor of this wealthy and impregnable city in northwestern Asia Minor, and the guardian of its ample treasury, had been allowed a measure of independence by Seleucus. Philetaerus' successors would turn semi-independence into full independence, and Pergamum would become one of the great Hellenistic kingdoms.

A WORLD-CHANGING AGREEMENT

Naturally, none of these new states and kingdoms was going to help Antiochus against Antigonus. Even the Byzantine-Heracleote confederacy, which had previously let Ptolemy Ceraunus use its fleet to defeat Antigonus, preferred an Antigonid to a Seleucid. Antigonus also found a ready ally in the Bithynian king, Nicomedes. He made good use of his allies. In the first place, it seems that the people of Lysimachea gave him permission to establish a long-term camp nearby, as a headquarters during the war. More importantly, in terms of the strategy of the war, by their very existence, his allies blocked Antiochus' overland route into Thrace and Macedon, and their fleets would prohibit any naval ventures.

That was their primary role in the war: to keep Antiochus away from Europe—to act as a shield to protect Antigonus to the west. Hence, when they confronted Antiochus' fleet at sea, they did not actually engage it, but just halted its progress. And while they were protecting Antigonus in this way, he would attack Macedon. He was never making a serious attempt on Asia Minor; he did not have the forces to take a kingdom there for himself. His object was always the recovery of Macedon, and he fought Antiochus only to stop him from making good *his* claim to the Macedonian throne.

The war with Antiochus lasted from 280 until 278, but there was a truce for the campaigning season of 279, while both Antigonus and Antiochus sent small forces to join the other Greeks in blocking the pass at Thermopylae against the Celts. Then, shielded by his allies, in 278 Antigonus launched his second attempt on Macedon. It was unsuccessful. That might have been Sosthenes' doing, though it is also possible that Sosthenes, were he alive, would have welcomed Antigonus as a legitimate king, since he had refused the kingship himself. But we hear no more of Sosthenes; he may have died, and there were others in Macedon who had good reasons to resist Antigonus' invasion.

Meanwhile, Antiochus remained blocked by Antigonus' allies. Seeing the futility of the war, the kings brought it to an end, late in 278, with a world-changing agreement whereby neither would interfere in the other's territory. Antiochus and his successors therefore largely removed themselves from the Aegean basin; their vast empire forced them to have other priorities, chiefly recovering Coele Syria from the Ptolemies and holding it, attempting to halt the fragmentation of Asia Minor, and securing the frequently rebellious eastern provinces of the empire.

What was astonishing about this pact between Antigonus and Antiochus was not that it took place, but that it stayed in place. In the forty-five years since the death of Alexander the Great, the Successors had often entered into treaties with one another, but these were invariably regarded as temporary measures, not as permanent friendships. The ethos of the kings was unremittingly belligerent. Royal status was gained by war and maintained by war. In a never-ending, bloody cycle, military success brought wealth (from plunder and indemnities), fame, and increased territory, which enabled a king to create more revenue, bind his courtiers to him with gifts of land, pay for more troops, and hence gain more military successes. The only international law was that might was right.

It took about forty years for this destructive cycle to be broken, and it was Antigonus and Antiochus who broke it. It was a major concession on both their parts, since it restricted their fields of endeavor and expansion (and Ptolemy, now the natural target of both these dynasties, must have been worried). I wonder whether Stratonice, Antigonus' sister and Antiochus' wife played a part in brokering the pact. Antigonus was fond of his sister—he named a town after her and founded a festival in her name after her death—and Antiochus was famously in love with her. Be that as it may, now, with the second generation after Alexander the Great, more realistic and less destructive means of interaction became possible. Belligerence was still all too common, especially in the series of wars fought between the Ptolemies and the Seleucids over possession of Coele Syria, but it was of a more restricted form. The kings felt their first duty was to retain or claim what was rightfully theirs, rather than conquer the world.

The deal was sealed by Antigonus' promising to take Antiochus' half sister, Phila, as his wife. Since Phila was the daughter of Stratonice (when she had been married to Seleucus), she was Antigonus' niece, but uncle-niece marriages were not considered incestuous. Antiochus' bid for the Macedonian throne was over, never to be resuscitated; Antigonus had neatly neutralized the man who could have become his most formidable rival for the kingdom. He was free to focus all his energies on making Macedon his own. He is revealed as a man of resolution and diplomatic skill, and one who was sure that his destiny lay in ruling Macedon.

THE BATTLE OF LYSIMACHEA

After their defeat at Delphi, two formidable bands of Celts remained, but they both gave up on Greece. One enormous horde settled for a while in Thrace, before being invited into Asia Minor by Nicomedes of Bithynia to serve as mercenaries in his conflict with his brother Zipoetes, who had taken a good portion of the kingdom for himself. These Celts eventually settled in central Asia Minor, and the land they occupied came to be called Galatia, the "land of the Celts," otherwise known as the Galatae (as in Saint Paul's letter to the Galatians). A kind of Celtic was still being spoken there in the late fourth century CE.

When Brennus had marched on Delphi, he had left all the women and children in northern Greece, along with thousands of soldiers to guard them. This group, joined no doubt by survivors from Brennus' party, now left Greece and made their way to Thrace, pillaging and fighting as they went. Eventually, they drew close to Antigonus' position near Lysimachea. Justin tells us that Antigonus was on his way back to Macedon—in other words, for his third attempt to take the throne by force:

> Meanwhile, the two kings, Antigonus and Antiochus, had made peace, and Antigonus was on his way back to Macedon, when a new enemy suddenly arose against him: the Celts Brennus had left behind to guard their frontiers while he marched into Greece. . . . They sent envoys to the king to offer him peace, provided he paid

for it, and at the same time to spy out his camp. In keeping with the generosity befitting a king, Antigonus invited them to dine with him, and he put on a magnificent banquet. But the Celts, impressed by the masses of gold and silver they could see, and tempted by the richness of the booty, left more eager for war than when they had arrived.

The Celtic delegation returned to their camp and aroused their comrades' enthusiasm for attacking Antigonus and looting his camp. But Antigonus guessed or got word of what they were up to, and had his men clear themselves and their valuables out of the camp and hide in the nearby woods. The Celts seized the unoccupied camp and then turned in frustration to plunder and burn the ships of Antigonus' fleet, which were beached close by. That was when Antigonus had his men emerge from their ambush and attack. For the Celts, trapped between soldiers and the sea, the slaughter was immense.

After the battle, Antigonus' friend, the philosopher Menedemus of Eretria, decreed a vote of thanks for the victory. Menedemus was politically influential in Eretria, although not all his fellow citizens were happy with his closeness to the Macedonian king, and the decree was an indirect way of reaffirming the city's allegiance. The decree started: "Seeing that King Antigonus, having defeated the barbarians in battle, is returning to his own country . . ." It treats Antigonus as an exile, finally recovering what was his all along. This is undoubtedly a true reflection of Antigonus' primary policy in these years; he felt that Macedon was his by right, and he just had to find a way to get the Macedonians, and the rest of the world, to recognize it. The battle of Lysimachea did the trick.

THE PRETENDER WARS

Sosthenes had managed to check the Celts to a certain extent, but it was Antigonus who finally freed the Macedonians from the years of terror, anarchy, and hardship they had endured. Benefaction was at the heart of kingship. A king was expected to do good to his people, and Antigonus now fitted the bill perfectly. He also had a legitimate claim to the kingdom, as the heir of a former king, who had abdicated in his favor, but it was his victory at Lysimachea that tipped the scales and made him acceptable to the Macedonians as their ruler. It might have helped if his father had made him joint king, which was common practice in the early Hellenistic period; but it would be a mistake to read more into Demetrius' failure to do so than that he was still young and was not expecting to die in his early fifties. And Antigonus was also the grandson of Antipater and the nephew of Cassander, both of whom had been rulers of Macedon.

When Antigonus arrived in Macedon in 277, flush from his victory, he had to fight to gain the entirety of the country. Others were still contending for the throne, but Antigonus had the upper hand. By now, he had probably been presented by his noble friends to an assembly of the Macedonians (made up mostly of the troops he had just led to profitable victory) in order to receive their noisy acclamation and oath of allegiance, making him the officially approved king. This gave him moral authority to wield against the other pretenders, as well as access to the royal army, or as much of it as remained after the years of trouble.

Antipater Etesias had taken over a part of Macedon; Antigonus defeated him with the help of a large force of Celtic mercenaries, and Antipater took refuge in Egypt. Polyaenus informs us that Antigonus paid these mercenaries "one Macedonian gold coin" each, at a total cost to him of thirty talents. That might represent about two months' pay for five thousand men, or one month's pay for ten thousand, since the standard rate of pay for mercenaries was one drachma a day. Generally, Antigonus did not mint gold coins, but he ordered up a special issue for this purpose; very few of them survive. He must already have occupied enough of Macedon to include the mints at Amphipolis and Pella. After the fighting was over, these Celts were probably settled on Macedonian land; henceforth, they would be available to Antigonus if required, as all landowning Macedonians were obliged, since the time of Philip II, to make their menfolk available for service in the armed forces.

Ptolemy, the son of Lysimachus and Arsinoe, was finally driven out of the region, and he too sought the protection of his uncle in Egypt, who was now married to his mother, and in any case was always prepared to give shelter to an enemy of Antigonus. There are too many men in this epoch called Ptolemy for us to be certain as to this one's future, but he is either the Ptolemy who was co-ruler of Egypt with Ptolemy II in the 260s, or the Ptolemy who was responsible for the city of Telmessus in Lycia, part of the Egyptian empire—or possibly both.

There may have been more pretenders, an Alexander and an Arrhidaeus; Alexander might be another son of Lysimachus, but we know nothing of this Arrhidaeus. They might be the same person, an Arrhidaeus who took the royal name Alexander, as Alexander the Great's brother Arrhidaeus took the royal name Philip. At any rate, it is clear that Antigonus had a lot to do before he could make good his claim to the Macedonian throne. But no doubt every victory over these pretenders boosted his prestige and gained him further loyalty among the war-weary Macedonians, as they saw the country gradually being reunited, rather than partitioned among various warlords.

The final problem Antigonus faced in Macedon was the tyrant Apollodorus, who held the fortress town of Cassandrea and controlled its many commercial interests. He was allegedly a demagogue who had ascended to power by redistributing the property of the rich among the poor, but this was a standard slur against tyrants, perpetuated by the landowning class when they wanted to arouse hostility. Probably all Apollodorus did was confiscate the property of his political enemies, whom he killed or sent into exile, so that he would have the money to win the venal loyalty of his Celtic mercenaries.

Cassandrea controlled a large territory, so that Apollodorus not only occupied an important and productive part of Macedon, but he also needed to be punished for his alliance with Antiochus. Antigonus' agreement with Antiochus left Apollodorus bereft of allies who were in a position to help, but he still promised to make a formidable opponent, and indeed Antigonus had Cassandrea under siege for ten months without dislodging him. He had to resort to cunning instead; specifically, he made use of a man called Ameinias, a Phocian. We are told that Ameinias was a "pirate," but one man's freebooter is another man's freedom fighter. He was a condottiere: he owed allegiance to no one and commanded a militia that was for hire.

Antigonus pretended that he had given up, and withdrew his army from Cassandrea as if to give space for negotiations; the negotiations were conducted by Ameinias, who was claiming to be a neutral mediator. Apollodorus put his trust in him and, seeing that Antigonus was absent, grew careless in his posting of sentries. Ameinias had secreted a force of two thousand men nearby, and had ordered them to prepare ladders of the right height; at dawn one day he gave the signal for them to scale the walls. They gained possession of the city and Apollodorus, and summoned Antigonus. Antigonus was apparently pleased enough with Ameinias to give him and his men more permanent employment; we have already met him as the commander of the mercenaries stationed at Corinth in 272.

THE RESTORATION OF MACEDON

So by the end of 276 Antigonus had gained Macedon; he was in his early forties. He had recovered Thessaly as well, probably during the months when he had Cassandrea under siege, since his full army would not have been required for the siege. The recovery of Thessaly was largely a matter of diplomacy, however, not force; he entered into alliances with the Thessalian cities.

There were certainly still factions in Macedon that did not favor Antigonus, especially in the west where Pyrrhus had influence, but he had achieved a great deal in a short time. Some of his internal enemies must have fled, or been killed in the pretender wars. In any case, Antigonus had made the transition from stateless pretender to legitimate king. He had been a king in waiting since his father's abdication seven years earlier, and he had never stopped plotting and planning his return to Macedon. His determination is impressive, and must have been one of the factors that endeared him to the Macedonian power-possessors and convinced them to accept his rule. Qualities such as virility, bravery, and strategic intelligence were expected of Hellenistic kings.

It was a time-honored practice for the hostile tribes of Illyris and the Central Balkans to seize the opportunity created by Macedonian weakness or an awkward succession to launch plundering raids. Some of these tribes had been dispersed or moved on by the Celts, but the Dardanians remained a menace, and one of the Celtic peoples, the Scordisci, an offshoot of Brennus' expedition, had settled in what is now Serbia (after massacring and subduing the local inhabitants), and were not averse to raiding Macedon from there. They would later give the Romans a great deal of trouble, attacking them year after year in the province of Macedonia.

It was invariably the first priority of every new Macedonian king to deal with these threats, and it was very likely Antigonus' too. We do not know how he did it—by warfare, bribery, or a combination of the two—but Macedon's northern borders seem to have remained remarkably quiet for much of his reign. Raiding no doubt continued, but no major incursions seem to have taken place for many years. He may have been lucky: it is possible that two of the main hostile peoples, the Thracian Triballi and the Celtic Scordisci, were distracted by fighting each other, and the Dardanians needed some years to recover from the passage of the Celts through their territory. The Celts who had occupied much of Thrace were probably kept quiet by regular payments and gifts.

As part of the program of sealing his northern borders, Antigonus recovered Paeonia, a useful buffer where the king had sporadically been a vassal of Macedon since the time of Philip II; it had seized the opportunity created by the Celtic chaos to go independent. By taking Paeonia, Antigonus denied it to the Dardanians, who would have become very dangerous neighbors. In territorial terms, he had given Macedon back the extensive borders it had enjoyed under Philip II.

MARRIAGE

The Macedon that Antigonus had gained was impoverished. Crops, seed, and livestock had been stolen by the Celts; houses and farmsteads destroyed; commercial relations in the entire northern Aegean had been disrupted. A surviving inscription shows that the town of Cyrrhus had to rebuild its economic infrastructure more or less from scratch. The country had the resources to recover, but it would take time, and it required stability. That was what Antigonus intended to give it.

In the winter of 276/5 Antigonus celebrated his marriage to Phila, the daughter of Seleucus I, in fulfillment of the betrothal of 278 and his agreement with Antiochus. He was forty-three, she perhaps twenty-two years old. The ceremony, which was attended by dignitaries from all over Macedon and Greece, and possibly by Antiochus and his retinue as well, was itself part of the process of healing the country. The conspicuous consumption involved was a symbol of the future prosperity that the marriage would bring to the country.

The marriage took place in Pella, the traditional civic capital of Macedon, which Antigonus too chose to make his seat; many of the landowning rich had their townhouses there, and it made sense for Antigonus to make a connection with the Argead dynasty, which had preceded him. Late in 275, Phila would bear him a son, the future king Demetrius II, so that the kingdom would also have the stability of an heir to the throne. Despite the ever-present possibility of early death, Antigonus never fathered another child, perhaps because he had seen, during his takeover of Macedon, the bloodshed that followed when there were too many claimants to the throne.

Antigonus had already started to gather luminaries of the Greek world into his court, and the poet Aratus of Soli composed a hymn to Pan and an epigram for Phila. Neither has survived, but in the hymn he seems to have raised the god Pan to the status of a major deity, whereas previously he had scarcely figured in Macedonian worship, and before long (beginning probably in 271), Antigonus began to strike coins, silver tetradrachms (four-drachma pieces), which prominently featured the head of the god. Pan was in origin a rural deity, worshipped especially in rugged Arcadia; he was the god who, among other things, caused flocks of goats, peacefully grazing one moment, suddenly to take fright and flee. He was the god of "panic" among humans as well, and the prominence given to him by Antigonus makes it plausible to think that he was honoring the god for having caused panic in the ranks of the Celts at Lysimachea. A recently discovered base of a statue of Pan that was erected in Beroea during Antigonus' reign calls the god a "wartime ally" of Macedon. On Antigonus' Pan coins the bust of the god is surrounded by Macedonian shields.

Pan coins were issued throughout Antigonus' reign, and in part they were meant to remind the Greeks of Antigonus' role in freeing them from the Celtic menace. Forever afterward, portraying a king on a coin or statue with a pair of stubby Pan horns on his forehead signified that he had been successful at war. Ptolemy jumped into this propaganda war by issuing coins of his own with the image of a Celtic shield. He had wiped out a force of rebel Celtic mercenaries in 275 (by trapping them on an island and starving them to death), so it was as though he were saying, "I can defeat Celts just as well as Antigonus." In a world without mass media, coins were frequently used for propaganda purposes.

PYRRHUS' CHALLENGE

The wedding ceremony was, however, the calm before a devastating storm. In 275 Pyrrhus returned from Italy to his kingdom of Epirus. He had gone to Italy in 281, in response to an appeal from Taras, which wanted to resist the encroachment of the Romans into southern Italy. His initial successes greatly alarmed the Romans; at one point, he was only about sixty-five kilometers (forty miles) from Rome itself. His war elephants in particular terrified the mounts of the Roman cavalry, which had never come across the creatures before. It was beginning to look as though the Romans could lose southern Italy to a Greek king, and they were contemplating a negotiated end to the war.

But the tide turned in favor of the Romans. Pyrrhus invaded Sicily (at the invitation of the Greek communities there) and achieved considerable success against the Carthaginians, who occupied the west of the island, but his regal ambitions and his failure completely to rid the island of the Carthaginians turned his allies against him.

At the same time, he irritated the Tarentines and his other friends in Italy by focusing on Sicily, and by calling one of his sons the king of Italy. But above all, there was the fact that however often he defeated the Romans, they gathered further armies and returned. His losses were less than those the Romans sustained, but he could not recover from them, whereas they could. "One more victory like that," he is said to have remarked after one of these battles, "and we shall be completely undone." That is why a "Pyrrhic victory" is a futile victory, one that amounts to defeat. And so he returned to Greece, abandoning the southern Italian cities to the mercy of the Romans, and the Sicilians to a Carthaginian revival.

Pyrrhus brought a sizable army back to Epirus, and he had more forces already there, which had guarded the country in his absence. He had his people to look after and a substantial army to maintain, but he did not have enough money. While still in Italy, he had asked Antigonus for reinforcements, adding the warning that if Antigonus refused and he was forced to leave Italy, he would seek to expand his kingdom at Antigonus' expense. And that is exactly what he did. In 274, he joined forces with a large band of Celts, who were still on the loose nearby, and set out with them to invade Macedon.

Antigonus' position turned out to be frighteningly insecure. Garrisons in the north and west of the country, where Pyrrhus had always had supporters, surrendered, leaving the towns they were supposed to be protecting for Antigonus no choice but to open their gates to the enemy. Flushed with success and laden with booty, Pyrrhus returned to Epirus to prepare for a proper invasion the following year, having arranged to be subsidized by Egyptian gold. He left his eldest son, Ptolemy, an extremely talented general, to protect his new acquisitions in Macedon; Antigonus came out against Ptolemy, but was once again defeated.

When Pyrrhus returned in 273 and the two armies met, Antigonus' outnumbered Macedonian troops broke and ran at the first assault, and his elephant unit was trapped and forced to surrender. His Celtic mercenaries, however, offered stiff resistance, until, in a battle of Celts against Celts, they were slaughtered almost to a man. Pyrrhus then advanced once more against Antigonus—and a large number of Antigonus' troops immediately surrendered and placed themselves at Pyrrhus' disposal. This mass desertion was a replay of what had happened to Antigonus' father, in *his* confrontation with Pyrrhus fourteen years earlier. Pyrrhus' reputation as a general was formidable.

Antigonus fled to the coast, where the cities remained loyal, while the rest of the country, and then Thessaly (except for Demetrias), fell to the invader. Perhaps this was the occasion of Antigonus' hollow joke that he was not retreating, but taking up a more advantageous position in the rear. But he had little territory to count his own, and Pyrrhus poured scorn on him, saying that he should be embarrassed to go on calling himself king.

Pyrrhus crowed about this victory. The most sacred site of northern Greece was Dodona in his native Epirus, with its famous oracle of Zeus. This was where Pyrrhus chose to dedicate some of the shields taken from Antigonus' troops, as was traditional with spoils of war, and the inscription that accompanied the shields read:

> Once these sacked the land of Asia, rich in gold;
> Once, too, they wrought slavery for the Greeks.
> Now they hang in the temple of Zeus Naios,
> Spoils of war reft from the swaggering Macedonians.

Pyrrhus was exploiting Antigonus' unpopularity with the Greeks to present himself as their liberator, and he did the same in another monument, dedicated in Thessaly, that boasted of his defeat of Antigonus' Celts as a Greek victory over barbarians—despite the fact that he employed plenty of Celtic mercenaries himself. But he did not remain king of Macedon for long enough for us to know how he would have treated the Greeks.

Pyrrhus was a better general than king, and he soon lost the favor of the Macedonians. The city of Aegae was almost sacred to them. It was the original capital of the country (before Pella); it was still the site of royal ceremonials and burials, and a splendid palace; and it was considered the "hearth" of the country. When it fell to Pyrrhus,

The Macedonians believed so firmly in an afterlife that they built magnificent and extremely costly tombs, filled with riches and everything the deceased might need. The best artists and architects were employed on such tombs, rather than on temples, as they would have been among their southern Greek neighbors.

he installed a garrison of his Celtic mercenaries. That was his first mistake, to give responsibility for such a place to people who were regarded by Macedonians as barbarians.

Then, when the Celts heard of all the valuables that were customarily buried along with high-ranking Macedonians in their tombs, they broke into some of them and robbed them, in the process scattering the bones of the dead. The Macedonians believed, more than other Greeks, in the continuing existence of a person after death, and tombs were among the most substantial, splendid, and expensive architectural features of Aegae and elsewhere. This was serious desecration, and Pyrrhus' second mistake was not to punish the Celts, "because he needed them for his wars."

A few years later, once Antigonus had recovered Macedon, one of the earliest acts of his reign was to cover (or perhaps re-cover) a cluster of the royal tombs at Aegae with a huge tumulus, to deter further robbery and destruction. Tombstones that had been smashed by the Celts were reverently laid horizontally in the fill. Antigonus had no dynastic predecessor to bury to legitimate his accession to the throne, but he could at least show his respect for the Argead dynasty, which had ruled Macedon for centuries before him. When archaeologists discovered these tombs in the 1970s, they found unmistakable signs of the Celts' depredations in the utter ruination of one of them, the scattering of bones, and the scratches caused by their crowbars.

THE DEATH OF PYRRHUS

But possessing almost the entirety of northern Greece was not enough for the ever-restless Pyrrhus. Cleonymus, the pretender to the Agiad throne of Sparta, had fought alongside Pyrrhus during the invasion of Macedon (he captured Edessa for him), and when in 272 Cleonymus asked him for help, Pyrrhus leaped at the chance. He put together a huge army (probably with financial assistance from Ptolemy of Egypt) and marched south. The crazy seesaw ride that was Antigonus' fate in these years continued, but this time in his favor: while Pyrrhus was preparing his Peloponnesian invasion, and was then bogged down there by unexpectedly robust Spartan resistance, Antigonus recovered Thessaly and Macedon.

He can only have done so with such rapidity if force was hardly required. Pyrrhus had removed the bulk of his army for the Peloponnesian expedition, and his rule was probably unpopular. The Aegae incident would have helped in this respect, but so also would the lack of interest Pyrrhus was showing in being the king of Macedon, rather than some kind of adventurer. That was not the way to give his people the security and stability they so badly wanted. In Antigonus' words, Pyrrhus was like a gambler who makes good dice-rolls, but then has no idea what to do with them. Besides, he was not Macedonian, and many Macedonians would not have been happy with a foreign ruler.

Once Antigonus was satisfied that Macedon and Thessaly would remain his in his absence, he sailed south to the Peloponnese for the final showdown with his greatest rival. He was aware what he was up against: once, when he was asked who was the greatest military commander in the world, he replied: "Pyrrhus, if he makes old age." But things were not going well for Pyrrhus in the Peloponnese, as we have seen. He had been forced to give up on Sparta, and he was marching from there to Argos, where he expected the city to be betrayed to him by his sympathizers. He was harassed all the way by the Spartans, and he lost his son Ptolemy in the fighting.

He avenged his son's death by massacring the Spartan battalion that had killed him, but that was a further delay, and by the time he reached Argos, Antigonus was waiting there for him, with the garrison from Corinth as well as the troops he had brought by ship from Macedon. Pyrrhus challenged Antigonus to a pitched battle, and both men knew that the outcome would decide who occupied the Macedonian throne. The Argives, however, begged the kings not to embroil their city in warfare, and Antigonus withdrew and made camp a little way from the city; but Pyrrhus sneaked inside at night with a substantial force through one of the gates, which was opened for him by friends.

The Argives called on Antigonus for help. Areus of Sparta arrived at the same time with another thousand men. Much of the fighting took place inside the city at night, and it was a messy business. Daylight did not much improve the situation. Pyrrhus was trying to retreat out of the city, while his son Helenus was trying to bring the rest of his army into the city, having misunderstood his father's wishes. Chaos ensued, and with thousands of men and even some elephants crammed into the narrow streets and alleyways, mostly uncertain of what they were supposed to be doing or whether the man they were facing was friend or foe, Pyrrhus' men were killing as many of their own as of the enemy. One Celtic mercenary looked much like another.

Gradually, the battle turned against Pyrrhus' forces, and then Pyrrhus himself died. He could never resist taking revenge, just as he had after his son Ptolemy had been killed. When he was struck in the chest, he turned against his assailant, even though he had been no more than scratched:

> Now, this man was an Argive of no social standing, the son of a poor old woman, who was watching the affray from the rooftops, along with all the other women. When she saw that her son was fighting Pyrrhus, she was terrified for him, and she picked up a roof-tile with both hands and threw it at Pyrrhus. It struck him on the back of the head, just below the helmet, and crushed the vertebrae at the base of his neck. His vision blurred, his hands dropped the reins, and he slid from his horse and fell to the ground.

Since war was an intrinsically male activity, being mortally wounded by a woman counted as an ignominious end. Even so, Pyrrhus was not quite dead, and while he was still conscious one of Antigonus' men cut off his head. Horribly, it took more than the usual single stroke of a sharp blade, because the man missed his aim and hacked through the bone of the jaw before reaching the neck. It was Halcyoneus, Antigonus' son, now aged about eighteen, who presented the head to his father as proof that his rival was dead. But the lack of respect with which Halcyoneus treated the head—he tossed it at his father's feet—distressed Antigonus, and he lashed out at Halcyoneus with both his staff and his tongue.

Magnanimous in victory, he buried Pyrrhus with honor, and allowed his captured son Helenus to return to Epirus, where his brother, Alexander II, had taken over the throne. Nor did he further punish the Epirotes. He did not blame them for Pyrrhus' wildness. In a curious footnote, some people later came to the conclusion—since, as we have already seen, it was possible in Greek religion for a human being to be temporarily possessed by a deity—that the old woman who killed Pyrrhus was none other than the goddess Demeter.

TROUBLES POSTPONED

Antigonus returned to Macedon in 272 as its one and only king, and also with his influence in Greece much improved. He had secured the Peloponnese (including regaining Argos) and recovered Megara. In Euboea, either now or within a year or two, he recovered Chalcis, which had seized the opportunity presented by Pyrrhus' invasion of Macedon to rebel (it had joined the Boeotian Confederacy), and added a new garrison in Eretria, but Oreus/Histiaea, an extremely useful harbor on the north coast, seems to have remained out of his direct control. He needed to safeguard his throne, renew his attempt to stabilize the country, and keep the Greeks quiescent. Hieronymus of Cardia, a courtier of Antigonus, chose the death of Pyrrhus as the point at which to end his history (lost to us) of the early Hellenistic period, because now his patron was in far less danger than he had faced before. It was a fitting conclusion artistically—"the return of the king"—but there were still troubles looming.

Above all, there were already hints of renewed trouble from the Aetolians after their brief rapprochement. They had recently granted all the citizens of Egyptian Alexandria the right to jump the queue if they ever came to consult the Delphic oracle. When Pyrrhus marched south into the Peloponnese, the Aetolians must have granted him passage through their territory and allowed him to sail from their harbors. These were not good signs, and over the next few years the Aetolians continued to provoke the Macedonian king.

One of Antigonus' first tasks, as I have mentioned, had been to secure Thessaly and return it to its usual status as a satellite of Macedon. The Aetolians felt they had to respond to this. They already had Heraclea Trachinia, which commanded the two best passes south from Thessaly, and before long they incorporated mountainous Dolopia, on the southwestern border of Thessaly, into their confederacy, which gave them the ability to block a number of other routes south, should they choose to. Aenis and Doris, neighbors of Dolopia, followed within a few years. These were poor, upland regions, of little use to the Aetolians except as buffers. The Aetolians were making it plain that they were the people small states could turn to for protection. Previously, this cluster of states had been largely within the Macedonian orbit.

Antigonus seems to have let them get away with it. He did nothing in military or diplomatic terms, and as the confederacy expanded and the Aetolians came to wield more and more votes on the Amphictyonic Council, Antigonus refrained from using his seven votes to oppose them; in fact, he or his delegates hardly attended the council at all, seemingly as a result of a deliberate boycott. Perhaps he chose not to antagonize the Aetolians because he hoped to stay on reasonable terms with them—or because he wanted to pick the time and context for confronting them.

In 272, however, the Aetolian problem merely loomed for Antigonus; the Aetolians made it plain that, for the foreseeable future, they would remain neutral but unfriendly, and the rest of Greece was quiescent enough. So Antigonus turned to defusing other potential sources of trouble. Cassandrea was incorporated into the state more fully than it had been before. Earlier, the Cassandreans had given their own local names to the months of the year; now they began to employ the names that were common throughout Macedon. This was not just a superficial matter of changing the names of the months, because a calendar was largely made up of the festivals that constituted the core of public religious devotion; Cassandrea was now a fully Macedonian town. Antigonus may have done the same for other towns, such as Philippi, but the evidence is too poor to be certain.

Anyway, Cassandrea was a special case, and Antigonus was to make doubly sure of it not just by keeping a garrison there, but by building two fortified towns nearby and populating them with Macedonian colonists. One of these towns was called Antigonea, and the other Stratonicea, after his sister. He built two other Antigoneas as well, one on the border with Paeonia and the other on the border with Illyris; these too were fortress towns, keeping an eye on potential trouble spots. There were to be no loose ends. The

Thessalian cities had alliances with him; Thrace east of Amphipolis and west of the Nestus River had a military governor who was appointed by him (with eastern Thrace a kind of no-man's-land between him and Antiochus); the northern peoples and the Illyrians had been paid off or subdued.

THE KING AND HIS COUNCIL

Antigonus turned to reforming and modernizing the administrative structures of his country. There is, as usual, a large element of guesswork in deciding what it was that he did—and, in addition, I am guessing that it was this early in his reign that he undertook his reforms. But it must have been a priority for him, and it may even be the case that he had long been dangling promises of reform as a way to win over elements of the country that were insufficiently enthusiastic about the prospect of his kingship. As we have seen, he had to fight to gain his kingdom, but once he had eliminated the pretenders, there is no sign that the barons and the civic authorities did anything but acquiesce to his rule.

Macedonian kingship before Antigonus was not quite unfettered. A king was constrained to a great extent by custom (as all monarchs are) and to a lesser extent by his counselors. He was advised by a group made up of the most privileged of his "Friends," as they were called, who served as his chief ministers, ambassadors, priests, military commanders, bodyguards, flatterers, intellectual companions, and friends; not a few of them had grown up at court alongside the future king. The members of this council were concerned with all important matters of strategy, policy, religious practice, and administration, and these were in effect collective decisions, though they were usually signed off by the king alone, who had the final say in everything. Like all premodern monarchs, Antigonus ruled his kingdom by means of an oligarchy of trusted men, who were bound to him by ritualized friendship.

On public occasions, such as one of the many sacrifices the king was obliged to perform, he would appear magnificently attired and surrounded by his scarcely less impressive Friends. In many ways, their job was to enhance his majesty, "like stars around the sun." Another important function of theirs was to represent the king outside the court, and act as channels of communication between the peripheries and the center; both Ammonius of Alexandria, a courtier of Antigonus, and Dorotheus of Seleucia, a member of Queen Phila's retinue, are thanked in extant inscriptions for acting as channels to central government for petitions from Cassandrea. The Friends were the means by which the king's power reached his subjects.

A Macedonian king selected many members of this council himself, unless he inherited some from a dynastic predecessor, and he bound them to himself with generous gifts (especially of land, which was then taxed), by promoting them to high office, and by leading them to profitable victory. It was a delicate matter: the choice of the right or wrong Friends could make the difference between the success or failure of his rule. He had to be careful not to surround himself just with yes-men; in forming his council he needed to avoid fomenting dissidence in the kingdom.

Many were members ex officio, just because their families had high rank in the kingdom, with their own networks of dependents. Antigonus elevated quite a few non-Macedonians to high positions within his court, perhaps to undermine the assumption by noble Macedonians that they would naturally inherit their fathers' status. He once famously refused to honor a son who lacked the caliber of his father. To his credit, although royal courts generally swirl with rivalries (personal or political), jealousies, and conspiracies, Antigonus' court seems to have remained free of intrigue.

Macedonian kings before Antigonus always preferred this personal style of monarchy, through friendship and ties of loyalty, over anything more constrained by institutions; they liked to establish relationships with individuals and get business done that way. Those who were accounted the king's friends, in both Macedon and the Greek states, tended to be the ones who were in positions of power, and so the whole system ran on friendship. In Macedon, the king and those who were close to him hunted together, dined together, and got drunk together. Council meetings were as likely to take place during a symposium as in a more sober setting. The Macedonian nobility were a cavalry elite, some of them considered royal in their own cantons, and they were allowed to speak freely to the king. A Macedonian king had no constitutional restraints, but without the goodwill of these Friends, he could hardly function.

In official documents, Macedon was regularly said to consist of "the king and the Macedonians." But before Antigonus, administration was largely the responsibility of the king and his Friends. "The Macedonians" in the formula had the right to petition the king, and even to assemble, but such assemblies only acclaimed decisions already taken at the higher level. When a king felt the need of such acclaim, especially to preempt disagreement, he might convene an assembly out of whichever Macedonians were available at the time, enough to be able to claim that he had the approval of his people. There were festivals in the spring and autumn that were attended by large numbers of Macedonians, making them a good time for the king to call an assembly if he wanted.

At home, he might want such an assembly to confirm his accession to the throne, for instance. It was fairly common for a king's Friends to present him to the assembled people, whose acceptance came in the form of swearing an oath of personal loyalty to him. When out on campaign, the "Macedonian assembly" was made up of the Macedonian troops he had with him, and he convened them if, say, he wanted them to approve a stratagem that would risk their lives. During the disturbed years of Alexander the Great's eastern campaigns and the wars of the Successors, the army occasionally took on a more active role, even calling their own assemblies to protest about something, but that was a thing of the past by Antigonus' time. Receiving the approval of the Macedonians delivered obvious practical benefits, but there was no regulation or tradition that such approval was required before the king could act.

ANTIGONUS THE REFORMER

The best way for Antigonus to stabilize his position, and the country, was to make a display of care for his people. He remembered how his father had been treated when he lost the favor of his subjects. Antigonus' military victories over the pretenders and Pyrrhus helped in this context, because they allowed normal life to resume. We know, for instance, of an inscription from Demetrias (the stone is now lost, but not before its text had been transcribed) in which Antigonus is praised for his general care for the city, and in particular for making it possible for its citizens to resume their calendar of festivals after a period of disruption, plausibly the Celtic invasion or the time of the pretenders. Thessalonica, which increased greatly in size during Antigonus' reign, named one of the tribes into which citizens were divided for administrative purposes Antigonis, and perhaps that was a token of gratitude. He was also, as we shall see later, worshipped in the east of Macedon as a Savior, a title that was generally reserved for those who had delivered a town or country from an enemy by military means, so this too was probably a way of thanking Antigonus for his victories.

But Antigonus had been defeated as often as he had been victorious, and military prowess alone was not going to be enough for him to win the lasting loyalty of his people. Macedonian kings who were unsuccessful on the battlefield had a habit of losing their thrones rather quickly, or being deserted by their more competent generals. The main way that Antigonus showed his concern for his people was to give them more power, delegating some of the responsibilities that had previously been the province of the crown, and further developing the blend of monarchic and traditional institutions that had been instigated by Philip II. Specifically, Antigonus went some way toward separating the Macedonian state from the king and allowing it an independent existence. He retained the essential institutions of the council of Friends (and the occasional general Macedonian assembly), but added further administrative layers.

This was a good move, a way for him to overcome lingering prejudice against him because of the unpopularity of his father's autocratic style of kingship. In effect, Antigonus turned Macedon into a hierarchical federal state. At the pinnacle of the pyramid was the king, and then his Friends; the next level consisted of the four main regions or administrative districts into which he divided the entire country, each under the command of a general, who was a member of the council of Friends. The precise boundaries of these districts are controversial, but their main cities give some idea of their location; they were Amphipolis, Thessalonica, Pella, and possibly Pelagonia. The final level was made up of the towns and cities (or ethnically based federations of villages, in Upper Macedon), each of which was now made responsible, as a mini-federation in its own right, for its local villages. Each of these levels performed regularly repeated rituals that helped to bind the new communities together.

We know little about the administration of these levels, and nothing about how the relationship between the levels worked; they must have had developed bureaucracies, but there is little trace of them. It is likely that the districts each minted their own coins, because an ME monogram occurs on a number of coins, which is presumably short for *meris*, or "division." Even this minor detail indicates the delegation of responsibility, since the minting of coins had traditionally been a prerogative of the crown. In the past, the Friends had been responsible for the various regions where their baronial lands lay; it was they who recruited troops, made sure taxes were collected, and kept the peace. Now Antigonus delegated at least some of this work to the district and civic authorities themselves.

THE NEW DISPENSATION

Where the towns were concerned, Antigonus seems to have extended all over the country the structure that the major cities already had, so that they had considerable powers of self-determination, and the institutions to put those powers to work. That is, they had an assembly, an advisory council, a board of generals, and magistrates, often called "politarchs" ("civic leaders"), whose elections (probably annual) were free and not subject to the king's will. The assemblies made decisions that were recommended to them by their councils, and ordered the magistrates to execute those decisions. They were responsible for their own revenues, once they had paid what they owed to the crown; they made their own arrangements as to how those revenues were raised; and they were responsible for their own citizenship rolls.

They were not, however, being granted unadulterated autonomy. The major cities, at any rate, in both Macedon and Thessaly, also had chief magistrates called "overseers." These were local men who were either royal appointees or, after election by their native state, had on their own initiative worked their way into the king's favor, but in either case they were answerable to the king and were the conduits of his instructions for the city. They were probably annually elected, unless they were put in place by the king. Even so, under Antigonus, the Macedonians enjoyed more self-determination than they had before. Antigonus might issue orders, but they did not become valid until incorporated into the local legislation of towns and federations.

The majority of the Macedonian population still lived in villages rather than towns, and clusters of these villages, as I have said, were now made to depend on the towns; the villages or village clusters had representatives on the town council, and the town council could direct its officers to raise some matter with the king or one of his Friends, once it had been approved by the common assembly of its citizens. Even at the village level, Macedonians now had an institution that could gain them the ear of the king—and vice versa: the system also made it easier for the king quickly to call up however many troops the villages were required to supply (there was no standing citizen army in Antigonus' Macedon), and to tax his subjects.

Even if the king had nothing directly to do with the decisions taken by town councils, it of course made sense for them not to annoy him. If they did, they received a sharp reprimand. In 248, Demetrius, Antigonus' son, who by then was joint king, wrote to the chief magistrate of the town of Beroea: "Demetrius to Harpalus, greetings. The priests of Heracles have informed me that some of the god's revenues have been incorporated into those of the city. See to it that they are returned to the god. Farewell." Harpalus was probably one of the overseers I have just mentioned; they were the ones the kings wrote to. Antigonus may have devolved some power to the towns, but his monarchy was still well short of a constitutional monarchy, and he could intervene if he felt it necessary.

Seleucus I of Syria is reported to have said that the most tedious aspect of kingship was the endless letters he had to read and write. Antigonus certainly had a busy chancery, but only one letter survives from his pen. It is addressed to one of the overseers, the man in charge of Dium, and was first published only about twenty-five years ago. The subject of the letter is relatively trivial, but it shows the same peremptory tone: "King Antigonus to Agasicles, greetings. Numenius has settled his sons between Asicum and Lake Pyrrolia, and has called the estate Mysia. See to it, then, that everyone is aware of the situation and that no one undertakes any commercial transactions with them without Numenius' knowledge, by having our letter inscribed in the sanctuary." It was so inscribed, and that is how it has survived.

We have a series of four decrees from the year 242 that reflect the new dispensation. Various cities in Macedon were visited by a delegation from the island of Cos, which wanted recognition that its famous festival honoring the healing god Asclepius had *asylia*, "inviolability." This was a grand tour: the Coans were diplomatically starting in Macedon, but they would then travel south through Thessaly to Greece. Recognition of *asylia* by the Greek states would mean not just that none of them was allowed to involve the sanctuary of Asclepius in warfare, but also that a truce would be in place such that anyone traveling to the festival from anywhere in the Greek world should not be impeded or harmed.

What is striking about these inscriptions is that Cos, an independent Greek city, clearly regarded these Macedonian cities as capable of dealing with a foreign state on their own. It is apparent that the delegates had first had an audience with Antigonus himself, and three of the inscriptions acknowledge that *asylia* for the Coan sanctuary is what Antigonus wanted as well; Antigonus may even have expressed his will in a letter to the town councils. But the matter did not end with the king's wishes: the Coans still had to visit the towns themselves and gather the decision of the town councils. Macedonian cities were now part of the international network of autonomous or relatively autonomous Greek cities. By the same token, within the span of Antigonus' reign, we find Cassandreans being used as impartial judges to assess boundary disputes in Greece, and various Macedonian cities granting honors to individuals from all over the Greek world.

Naturally, Antigonus remained responsible for foreign policy and declarations of war and peace, and he remained the sole beneficiary of war indemnities, a large range of taxes, and so on. As the supreme judicial authority, he resolved disputes among the towns that threatened disorder, such as boundary disputes; as the supreme religious authority, he would make his will known in such matters as well. But he added layers to the hierarchy, and allowed his subjects greater self-determination. That this was a popular move is shown by the longevity of his reign and by the fact that he died of natural causes, not by an assassin's knife. Over the past fifty or sixty years, Macedonian kings and dynasts had been primarily military commanders, who owed their power and authority to the fact that they led the armed forces. Antigonus changed the dynamic and showed that kings could be good peacetime leaders too. He inaugurated an annual festival called the Basileia, a celebration of kingship, to commemorate the new dispensation.

ANTIGONUS' FINANCES

It is impossible to assess Antigonus' financial situation with any degree of precision. We know the main sources of his revenues—mines, timber, agriculture, taxes, war booty, fines imposed by courts, the minting of coins—but we have little idea of how much they produced. We know his main expenditures—the defense of Macedon, making war, equipping and paying troops, building towns and fortresses, maintaining garrisons, putting on religious festivals, making dedications at international sanctuaries such as Delos and Delphi, other forms of magnificence, maintaining his court, giving gifts—but, again, we cannot sensibly guess their levels. At any rate, while it may be impossible to estimate his revenues, it is clear from his expenses that they must have been very healthy. He also inherited a great deal of capital from his father, who had inherited even more of it from *his* father, whose wealth, in today's terms, would be measured in many billions of dollars.

It is safe to assume that as soon as he had restored a degree of stability to Macedon, he made sure not just that internal trade and local coastal trade revived, but that foreign trade in the country's two major assets, minerals and timber, did so as well. The number of Antigonus' coins found in Asia Minor and elsewhere suggests that trade was healthy. The importance of these resources to Macedon may be measured by the fact that when the Romans wanted to reduce the country in the second century, among the measures they took was the banning of the sale of timber and the closure of the precious-metal mines.

Despite the necessary vagueness, it is clear that Antigonus did succeed in stabilizing his financial situation. He was able to build up a large war fleet, consisting of perhaps two hundred ships, mainly triremes and quinqueremes, with a sprinkling of larger vessels. The construction and maintenance of a large fleet was an incredibly costly business. Macedon was blessed with most of the natural resources needed, but thousands of men must have been employed in the preparation of materials and construction of ships and shipyards. Then there were crews to pay: up to four hundred for a quinquereme and two hundred for a trireme.

The king owned all the forests, but he often rented out the right to exploit them to his Friends. In Classical Athens, long-distance trade in commodities such as grain and timber was the main stimulus to the development of a simple banking system, but we have no evidence for banks in Antigonus' Macedon. Of course, there were men who assayed coins and exchanged foreign coins for legal tender, but we know of no sophisticated lending systems. Loans were probably made by friends, at low rates of interest—by individuals or groups of friends who were rich enough to have the money in the first place and to absorb any losses that might arise from piracy or shipwreck.

Taxation was of course fundamental, though the shortage of evidence leaves us only guessing what Antigonus' regime was. We know that states all over the Greek world were very creative about finding ways to tax their citizens, and Antigonus probably did likewise, while falling short of the Ptolemaic total of over fifteen hundred forms of taxation. Some of his taxes on agricultural produce were paid in kind rather than cash, as was normal; the king then resold the commodity, or gave it away to deserving beneficiaries.

A 2 percent tax on imports and exports was widespread in the Greek world; harbor dues, market dues, and road tolls were another important source of income, though some of these were normally given to the king's associates as a benefaction. Taxes on herds and flocks over a certain size are likely, as well as on vineyards, other forms of agriculture, the ownership of land and property, the exchange of foreign coinage, and the exploitation of Macedon's natural resources. As a satellite of Macedon, Thessaly provided some tax revenues to the king's coffers.

In Macedon, as elsewhere, there was no regular income tax, but rich men were expected to help out financially in emergencies, such as warfare. Once, when Ptolemy V of Egypt was asked how he was planning to finance a campaign against the Seleucids, he pointed to his courtiers and said: "See? There are my money-bags, walking about." It was more a form of gift-giving than taxation: the king had enriched them, or allowed them to stay rich, and he expected gifts in return.

Given Antigonus' transformation of Macedonian society, as outlined earlier in this chapter, he must have put in place efficient systems whereby all the revenues raised by his various taxes arrived in his central treasury from the outlying towns. Tax-farming was the most widely used such system all over the Mediterranean; it was popular because it saved the state, or in this case the crown, the bother of looking after the matter itself. Rich men bid for the right to collect taxes, and as long as they gave the state treasury what they had contracted to provide, they were free to keep anything extra for themselves, to compensate them for their work.

We have no direct evidence that Antigonus demanded tribute from the Greek cities, but it is hard to see what was in it for him if he did not. His father was said to have a total annual revenue of

1,200 talents, raised largely from the Greeks; the sum, the equivalent, perhaps, of about $400 million today, is an exaggeration, but only an exaggeration. When the Romans declared the Greeks free of Macedonian dominion in 196, they said that they were to be "free, ungarrisoned, untaxed, and autonomous," so some of them were certainly being taxed by then. Antigonus was spending large amounts of money on maintaining garrisons in the Greek cities, and must have expected some return. One of the chief conveniences of cities for Hellenistic kings was precisely that they already had infrastructures for the collection of taxes. It is likely, then, that Antigonus demanded tribute where he could, and he certainly expected valuable gifts once in a while, as it were of the city's own free will.

There is no firm evidence even that those Greek states that were garrisoned by Antigonus were required to pay, in whole or in part, for the upkeep of the garrison, though this certainly happened elsewhere in the Greek world. But if it was a commercial port that was garrisoned, he probably took a portion of its harbor dues and import/export taxes; and if he had paid for some building work in a city—such as the stoa he built in Corinth—he may have taken all or some of the rent the buildings produced. He probably found other ways to extract money from them on an occasional basis. His father, Demetrius, was said to have once required the Athenians to raise 250 talents for him.

Antigonus issued coins in both precious metals and base metals for the lower denominations. The main mints were at Pella and Amphipolis. The coins were on the Attic weight standard, which had been introduced into Macedon by Philip II and then perpetuated around the world by Alexander. The highest-value coins, the gold issues and some of the silver, were minted for the primary purpose of paying mercenaries, and Antigonus' three main minting periods coincided with times of warfare. The smaller silver and base-metal issues were for daily use, such as wages, shopping, and the payment of taxes.

There were never enough coins in circulation for the country to count as fully monetized, and coins dating back to the reign of Philip II, and coins from other countries, were acceptable, given how widespread the Attic weight standard was. At all levels of society, barter continued, and so did the use of bullion (including coins not on the Attic standard, which could simply be assayed and weighed); there was also a flourishing credit economy. Antigonus never had to debase his coinage, which suggests economic stability.

He needed a strong economy. We have already seen that the Aetolians and others were threatening to make trouble. Warfare was the most expensive of his commitments, and under the circumstances of an impoverished Macedon, in the process of slow recovery, it made perfect sense for him to ensure that the Greek states were quiescent. Hegemony is the subordination of others by political and economic means, and by the real or implied threat of military intervention. Antigonus' next job was to see that he had hegemony over the Greeks.

CHAPTER 7

Antigonus and the Greeks

At much the same time that Alexander the Great was taking over the Achaemenid empire, another young man was carving out an empire in India. Chandragupta of Maurya, Sandrokottos to the Greeks, came to rule one of the largest empires the Indian subcontinent has seen. At its height, all India except for the far southern states made up the Mauryan empire, and in the north Pakistan and southern Afghanistan were included as well.

In the final years of the fourth century, probably in 304, a great battle was fought between Chandragupta and Seleucus, the Macedonian ruler of Syria and the eastern satrapies of the former Achaemenid empire. No account of the battle survives, but the outcome seems to have been a kind of draw. Chandragupta had already taken over the provinces and kingdoms that Alexander had left in place in Pakistan, and now he forced Seleucus to cede all the parts of his empire that bordered Pakistan, an enormous swath of territory comprising eastern Arachosia, Gandaris, Paropanisadae, and parts of Areia and Gedrosia. In return, Seleucus was given a large number of war elephants straightaway (of which he made good use, especially at the critical battle of Ipsus) and an ongoing supply over the years. He was probably satisfied not to have the trouble of governing these remote provinces of his empire.

The third king of the Mauryan empire was Chandragupta's grandson, Ashoka, who ruled from 268 until 232. A few years into his reign, he converted to Buddhism, and like new converts the world over, whatever their religion, he wanted to spread the word. One way in which he did this was to publish a large number of "edicts," as

A typical edict that Ashoka had carved on rocks throughout his empire, as a way of preaching Buddhism. This one is from the mountains in what is now the northwest frontier of Pakistan. Photo © Niskhan65 / Wikimedia Commons. CC BY 3.0 (Unported).

they are known. More than thirty of these inscriptions survive, on stone pillars or rocks or cave walls. They served various purposes, but were designed fundamentally to perpetuate Dhamma, meaning simultaneously cosmic law and the teachings of the Buddha.

Antigonus was one of a number of Greek rulers to whom Ashoka reached out, in the first phase of the long and ongoing conversation between Buddhism and the West. The edict known as Major Rock Edict 13 was written in Greek sometime in the 250s and set up in Arachosia, the farthest extent of Ashoka's kingdom, where it abutted Greek lands. It includes the following information:

> The Beloved of the Gods [Ashoka] considers victory by Dhamma to be the supreme victory. And the Beloved of the Gods has gained this victory on all his frontiers to a distance of six hundred yojanas, where is the kingdom of the Greek king named Amtiyaka, and beyond the realm of Amtiyaka in the lands of the four kings named Tulamaya, Antekina, Maka, and Alikyashudala.

"Amtiyaka" is Antiochus II, who came to the Syrian throne in 261; "Tulamaya" is Ptolemy II; "Antekina" is Antigonus; "Maka" is Magas, who ruled an independent Cyrenaica from 276 to 250; and "Alikyashudala" is an Alexander, probably Alexander II, the ruler of Epirus from 272 until 232.

So it appears that these five kings received envoys from Ashoka, and that his "victory by Dhamma" consisted in persuading them to enter into a bilateral treaty of nonaggression. His envoys would have presented this as the core Buddhist teaching of *ahimsa*, nonviolence toward all creatures, so that in agreeing to peace, the kings were, in Ashoka's terms, won over by Dhamma. Ashoka is said to have converted to Buddhism in part because of his horror at the number of deaths he had caused in imperialist warfare. In Antigonus' case, his acquaintance with Stoicism would have made living and ruling in accord with cosmic law a familiar concept. It was not one he chose to follow, however, and he was no convert to *ahimsa* either. Where his Greek dependents were concerned, he expected them not to make trouble for him, and to know the consequences of doing so.

A PRECARIOUS POSITION

At the start of his reign, Antigonus' relations with the Greeks were uncertain. Even though the Antigonid garrisons in Greece had not been affected by the chaos and anarchy that beset Macedon in the early 270s, the Greeks as a whole had seen that Macedon was vulnerable. But Antigonus had grown up with the presumption that the Greeks would cooperate with him—that they would be a resource for him, in terms of revenues, manpower, facilities, and expertise, more than for the other kings. Without the cooperation of the Greeks, Macedon's status as a world power would be precarious. If the Greeks united to throw off the Macedonian yoke, it would be hard for Antigonus to suppress the uprising. Like his predecessors, he had to find a way to keep the Greeks disunited, and even to set them against one another if necessary.

The overall bargain, since the time of Philip II, was that the

Macedonian king would keep the peace and protect the Greeks from enemies, while the Greeks would go about their business without interference from Pella as long as they made no trouble by taking up arms against the king or by treating with one of his enemies or by disturbing the status quo in Greece. They were self-governing, but they were accountable to the Macedonian king, and they would support him in a time of need. But the king needed a strong Macedon in order to impress the Greeks with his power and his ability to protect them. At the start of his reign, Antigonus was faced with a dilemma: he needed the Greek states to be obedient in order to secure Macedon, and he needed a strong and secure Macedon in order for the Greeks to be willing to obey him.

The problem was that he lacked an institution that would enable him to deal with the Greeks as a whole. He had to treat separately with each state, and if there were few who were willing to be his open enemies, there were also few who were willing to be his friends. His predecessors had formalized their relationship with the Greeks. Philip II, Alexander III, and Demetrius Poliorcetes were all presidents of the League of Corinth. Polyperchon and Ptolemy I would probably have organized the Greek states into similar leagues if they had succeeded in gaining the allegiance of enough of them; and, following Antigonus, his successor Antigonus III Doson did so, forming the Greeks into a Common Alliance, which was then inherited by Philip V. These hegemonial leagues were a way of recognizing the autonomy of the Greeks, while making it easier to control them as a whole, and they were usually instituted after warfare had netted the relevant Macedonian a sufficient number of Greek subjects.

Antigonus, however, apparently did not create any such institution. Clearly, he was not confident that he had the authority to impose a league on the Greeks by royal fiat, and he certainly did not want to do so by conquest. He felt—probably rightly—that too many of them would refuse to join, as Sparta had in the time of Philip II and Alexander the Great. Since perhaps 335, some Greek states had formed themselves into a quasi league based in Plataea; by Antigonus' time, it was explicitly anti-Macedonian, it made Greek freedom its rallying cry, it was backed by the Ptolemies, and it had the support of known opponents of Macedon such as Glaucon of Athens, the brother of Chremonides, as we shall shortly see. Although we do not know how many Greek states were involved, if Antigonus tried to impose his own league on the Greeks, there was a good chance that war might break out, which was the last thing he wanted. In short, he simply had too few friends in Greece.

Moreover, Antigonus had seen how the Greeks lost no time in defecting from his father's league after the battle of Ipsus, as soon as the Antigonids lost power. It was clear that the Greeks were only going to respond to a display of power anyway, so that is what Antigonus gave them, even if not in the guise of a league. Given the strong likelihood that at least some Greeks would be restive—and that Ptolemy would be fanning those embers—Antigonus resorted to repressive means to make sure that the Greeks kept to their side of the bargain, so that he could focus on the recovery of Macedon. In the background were his experiences as a younger man. After Ipsus, he and his father had been left, in Greece, with only four towns in their possession: Demetrias, Corinth, Piraeus, and Chalcis. By the mid-280s, after their expulsion from Macedon and Demetrius' departure for Asia, they were not much better off. Holding on to these places had been absolutely critical and had required a heavy hand. It had worked, and Antigonus saw no reason not to continue and even expand the same approach.

THE FREEDOM OF THE GREEKS

The rise of the Successor kingdoms sounded the death knell of the independent Greek city-state as a major power-player. They were simply no longer the most powerful political entities in the eastern Mediterranean. The daily reality of this could be stark: some towns had permanent garrisons of foreign mercenaries; some had governors appointed by the king and answerable only to him; many had men in power who were known to be favored by the king; all prioritized the king's business in their assembly meetings. Sometimes kings did drastic things, such as ordering two neighbors to form a single community or moving a city's population to a new location; sometimes they specified the type of constitution a city was to have. In return for a king granting certain privileges or immunities, a city might hail him as its Savior and Benefactor, and grant him honors, up to and including status as a god.

These generalizations need to be offset by the reminder that every city was different, and was differently treated by the kings. A number of factors, such as military and commercial considerations, perceived hostility, and prestige, determined how bluntly or diplomatically a king intervened in a city's affairs. But however close or remote the king's presence was, it was a fact of life that had to be acknowledged and responded to. It was a good tactic for a city to ask for and receive a written guarantee of its autonomy as a foundation for its future dealings with the king.

The slogan of Greek freedom had been bandied about for a long time. Each time a potentate proclaimed that he would "free the Greeks," it was little more than cynical propaganda, a way to gain the goodwill of people who were, strictly, not his subjects. Every promise of freedom could realistically be read as a veiled threat from an overlord, a reminder that their freedom was in his hands. The clear-sighted historian Polybius wrote: "All kings mouth platitudes about freedom at the beginning of their reigns, but once they have gained their ends they soon treat those who believed them as slaves, not as allies."

But the Greeks were locally self-governing, so citizen loyalty did not change. Everywhere, citizens still met and determined their relations with both their neighbors (up to and including going to war with them) and the local kings, elected officers, hired public doctors, ratified treaties, worried about their food supply, employed citizens of neutral states to arbitrate their disputes, decided who were and who were not citizens, passed laws and decrees, organized festivals, tried to increase revenues and spend them wisely, and administered justice. Large-scale foreign policy was out of their hands, unless they rebelled, but they were self-governing as regards domestic policy.

The Greek states acted as though they were independent, and the pace of local political life scarcely slackened in the Hellenistic period. Kings too pretended that cities were independent, and generally disguised their commands as polite requests, or praised certain behaviors as a way of showing how they should behave in the future. When democracy returned briefly to Athens in 319, Philip III of Macedon (prompted, no doubt, by Polyperchon) wrote to express his view of the leaders of the previous oligarchy; the gist of his letter was "that while he had no doubt of the men's treachery, he left it up to the Athenians, as free and autonomous agents, to reach a verdict." The "free and autonomous agents" duly put the men to death. The pretense in public documents was that relations between kings and cities were cordial, even if they were strained; the pretense was that the kings were not being manipulative, even if they were. And the overall pretense, in Antigonus' case, was that he was merely "protecting" the Greeks against control by an overseas enemy such as Egypt.

There was another factor in the third century that forced the Greeks states further into dependency. A great many of them were very poorly off, chiefly as a result of the almost continuous warfare that had followed the death of Alexander the Great, and their need to respond to modern siege capabilities by spending enormous sums on well-made rural fortresses, and even more on urban fortifications. A not-insignificant number of places had been ruined, in economic terms, as a result of occupation by hostile forces or the need to supply a friendly army. All sources of income had been interrupted, pirates swarmed the seas, and brigands came down from the hills, many of them impoverished former farmers. Doctors had to be hired to treat the wounded, and money found to ransom citizens who had become prisoners of war, pay a militia, build or repair fortifications, and perhaps maintain a small fleet. Food shortages, natural or caused by war, were frequent, with the price of grain fluctuating accordingly. Even without all this, agriculture was always an uncertain business in ancient Greece, and society was founded on agriculture. Cities commonly took out loans from other cities as a temporary solution to their problems.

Kings were obliged to help their dependents; that was expected. If the city was lucky—if it suited a king's military plans—he might even pay for its fortifications. And kings frequently donated necessaries such as money, grain, or timber. But these benefactions were not free gifts; they were paid for by subservience. "The hand that gives is above the hand that receives," as Napoleon is reputed to have said. This is one reason why many Greek cities chose to become members of confederacies: they preferred to lose a degree of independence by joining as equals with other Greeks than to be subservient to kings.

THE RULE OF THE LANDOWNERS

On a day-to-day basis, there were more immediate restrictions on Greek freedom than those imposed by distant kings; these restrictions stemmed above all from the increasing power of the rich in their towns. We find the same families holding office generation after generation, often through what we would call nepotism. They had to be rich because they were expected to pay for some of the city's functions themselves; even generals often had to supply arms and armor for their men. The trend had begun in the fourth century, but it accelerated in the third. Typically, these men would be called on to perform public duties, or relieve poverty and hunger among their fellow citizens, or fund a festival, or embellish the city in some way—precisely the same kinds of roles, but on a lesser scale, as those that were played by kings. The practice is not dissimilar to the expectation today that billionaires such as Bill Gates and Richard Branson will contribute toward solving problems—except that today they are not usually rewarded with political power.

The gap between rich and poor widened considerably in the Hellenistic period. There were inevitable economic forces at play: when population growth is low, productivity growth is low, and inflation is low—all of which were the case in third-century Greece—income derived from capital is bound to do better than income derived from labor; ownership of land was a safeguard against risk. As former smallholders abandoned their farms and became the urban poor, they increased the demand for produce from remaining, larger farms, thus raising the value of the land. So, for instance, archaeologists find an increasing gap at this time between the sizes and furnishings of the houses of the rich compared with the poor. Research also reveals a prosperous middle class, but in the major states, for the first time in the Hellenistic period, everyone was directly taxed in various ways by the civic authorities—a tax on produce, for instance, and a poll tax—and the poor suffered.

Many small farmers went under, and their land began to be absorbed by their more prosperous neighbors, paving the way for the large, slave-run estates of the Roman period. Dispossessed farmers tended to sell their labor instead, and the more of them there were, the cheaper labor became, while the price of food and other commodities fluctuated, but steadily rose. Meanwhile, the rich were living increasingly ostentatious and luxurious lives. There were murmurings in the Greek world about a more equitable redistribution of land, taking from the rich to give to the poor. Usually, such rumbles were firmly quashed by the landowners, or appeased by the sop of temporary relief.

The rule of the rich was not generally resented, however, since they were genuinely doing their fellow citizens good, and, given increasing social inequalities, they were the only ones with the time to devote to politics. Moreover, they were the only ones with the necessary access to the kings. Kings, as I have said, did business primarily through and with individuals, who thereby gained enormous authority in their states, and formed an elite group. But they were, of course, useful to a king and to their city only as long as they had authority at home. The king was rarely a direct presence in a Greek state; he relied on his friends.

These men might initiate the contact themselves, or inherit access to the court from their fathers, or come to the king's attention because of something they had done. The best-case scenario was if a fellow citizen was actually a Friend of a king, one of the inner circle of his court, but at least he had to be rich and politically experienced enough to be able to gain access to the king or someone close to him. One successful mission often led to another. In the last third of the fourth century, whenever the Athenians needed someone to talk to a Macedonian ruler, they chose the statesman Demades, and he passed the job on to his son.

The petitions these men brought to the ears of kings could mean the difference between starvation and plenty, war and peace, decay and modernization, and whereas previously there had been a tendency for the Greeks to denigrate a king's friends as lickspittles and parasites, over the course of the third century they came to be accorded more respect. Under such circumstances, it was easy for them to gain or perpetuate political power at home, and, generally speaking, they prioritized their state's interests over those of the king. In fact, quite a few of them had contacts with more than one king, and might exploit the rivalry between them to get the best result for their state.

It was a common practice in the Hellenistic period for assemblies to vote effusive thanks and honors for these men, whose goodwill they needed to retain. Naturally, they did the same for kings too, when they received a royal benefaction. They might erect a bronze statue, or make a gift of a valuable golden crown, and inscribe the decree giving the reasons for the honor on a stone so that future generations too would know his virtues. The practice was in part a way to try to control the behavior of great men: we will continue to honor you if you continue to behave like this toward us. But the people (insofar as they were still attending assemblies) sacrificed political rights for charity, and the attitudes available to Greek politicians toward kings usually occupied a small range, from polite diplomacy to obsequiousness.

TYRANNY IN THE PELOPONNESE

This was normal practice, and if we had any letters from Antigonus to the Greeks, they would undoubtedly reveal the polite, high-handed benevolence that is the counterpart to obsequiousness. But he also went further. Because of his urgent need for peace from the Greeks, to give Macedon the many years it needed to recover, he did not just employ the kind of remote control I have been describing, but ran the risk of escalating Greek resentment by more direct means of control, especially by installing garrisons and supporting tyrants.

Polybius claims that Antigonus imposed more tyrants on the Greeks than any of his predecessors. When Pyrrhus dedicated some of Antigonus' shields as spoils of war after his victory in 273, he too accused Antigonus of enslaving the Greeks, as we have seen. "Slavery" is typical exaggeration, but the fact remains that Antigonus was liberal in his use of means of control. When so much about his reign has been lost, this was the one fact that was remembered for centuries, even by superficial chroniclers. Eusebius, writing in the early fourth century CE, recorded the view that under Antigonus "Greece was thoroughly oppressed."

At the time in question, the early years of Antigonus' reign, Thessaly was a satellite of Macedon, central Greece was largely in the hands of the Aetolians, and Athens was at least partially garrisoned. So the region where Antigonus intervened more directly in the political lives of the Greeks was the Peloponnese, which, as Pyrrhus' invasion had shown, was critical to the security of Macedon. Almost all of the third-century tyrants we know of in the Peloponnese came to power between the 290s and the 240s—precisely the decades when Antigonus was either the governor of southern Greece or occupied the Macedonian throne. We need to remember that "tyrant" was often, in this period, a tendentious way of describing the power of a man who was less like a king and more like a governor or overseer of a town.

There were a number of reasons why Antigonus wanted control of the Peloponnese. It would make it easier for him to impede Ptolemy's encroachment. With Pyrrhus dead, Ptolemy had lost his chief ally in Greece and would certainly be casting around for a replacement, as well as continuing to support the Spartans (with whom he now had an alliance) and others. Just as importantly, the Achaean Confederacy had recently re-formed, and although there was no hint yet of its future importance, the process was disturbing from a Macedonian point of view. Many of the Achaean towns had been garrisoned by Antigonus in the 280s following his father's departure from Greece, and the ten original members of the confederacy all ejected their garrisons, and their tyrants if they had one (at least one was killed), in order to join. It is not certain that these tyrants had originally been imposed by any Macedonian ruler—they may have been homegrown—but they did have Macedonian support. Their loss certainly harmed Antigonus' interests in the Peloponnese, and so, right from the start, the Achaeans were expressly anti-Macedonian.

The fundamental element of Antigonus' control of the Peloponnese was his possession of Corinth. This was the seat of his brother Craterus, his viceroy in southern Greece, and the headquarters of a strong garrison with a competent commander, such as Ameinias of Phocis. But Antigonus took advantage of the chaotic situation in the Peloponnese after Pyrrhus' death; he may have lost the Achaean towns, but he responded by increasing his grip elsewhere.

In Sicyon, Antigonus inherited a friendly or at least nonhostile tyrant. At the time of Pyrrhus' invasion of the Peloponnese, Cleinias, the father of Aratus, gained power in the city, following a series of sole rulers, most of whom had been on reasonable terms with the Macedonian king. Cleinias kept the city neutral, until he was assassinated and replaced in 264 by a man called Abantidas, when seven-year-old Aratus was taken out of the city and into exile in Argos. But Abantidas too was pro-Macedonian; he killed Cleinias for personal, not political, reasons.

Elis had sided with Pyrrhus when he arrived in the Peloponnese. After Pyrrhus' defeat and death, a man called Aristotimus seized power in the city. He carried out his coup with Antigonus' help and remained in power with his support. Even after Aristotimus had banished his opponents, however, the city remained troubled, and there were some unpleasant incidents involving the foreign mercenaries he had hired. At the time of his assassination a few months later, during an Aetolian-backed rebellion by members of the Elean elite, Craterus had dispatched a force to help him quell resistance. But on hearing that Aristotimus had already been killed, Craterus returned to Corinth, and Elis returned to its normal state of government by an oligarchy of rich landowners, supported by the Aetolians, but also leaning toward Sparta. Antigonus cannot have been pleased to lose his authority in the northwest Peloponnese.

Megalopolis too had supported Pyrrhus, but now a man called Aristodamus seized power. He ruled for a long time—he was assassinated in 252—and was remembered as having been good for the city (despite the fact that his assassin subsequently received cult as a hero), which he embellished with public buildings and successfully defended against the Spartans. Aristodamus' connection with Antigonus is uncertain, but, as an enemy of Sparta and as ruler of the town that was best placed to restrict Sparta, he must have enjoyed at least his tacit support.

In Argos, which had been directly and tragically involved in the fighting, the chief pro-Macedonian politician at the time of Pyrrhus' invasion was Aristippus. With Antigonus' approval, he set himself up as sole ruler of the city, and he ruled until 251, passing the tyranny on to his son, Aristomachus, who in due course would pass it on to his two sons, one named after his father and one after his grandfather. This was obviously a popular tyranny, since it generated a dynasty, and it was certainly pro-Macedonian. Aristippus was a friend of Antigonus; his son Aristomachus was honored at Athens at a time when Athens was securely under Macedonian rule; and his grandson Aristippus plotted against Aratus with Antigonus' help. In short, the whole dynasty of tyrants at Argos was pro-Macedonian, just as the city had usually been for many decades before them. Hence, when Aratus was resident there and was planning his return to Sicyon, a move that would undermine Antigonus' influence in the Peloponnese, he had to conceal his intentions.

These are all the Peloponnesian tyrants we know of, but there were probably more. There were certainly more later in Antigonus' reign. Not all of them were Antigonus' men right from the start, but once they had seized power they naturally looked to Macedon for support. This was not ideology, but practical politics. In any case, the numbers do not tell the whole story. Antigonus did not need to have a friendly tyrant and/or garrison in every Peloponnesian town.

He could easily exercise sufficient control of the Peloponnese as a whole with the garrisons that he had, given that a number of important places were ruled by friendly tyrants and that most of the other states were at least neutral, and only a few openly hostile. He made no systematic attempt to change political cultures to versions that suited him better. Tyrants were installed or supported as opportunities arose, not as a result of a blanket policy.

None of the tyrants were Antigonus' puppets; they were his friends and allies. The career of Demetrius of Phalerum at Athens, who ruled Athens for Cassander between 317 and 307, and about whom we are better informed, suggests that they acted of their own accord in ways that they felt would be good for their subjects, while suppressing anti-Macedonian sentiments among the populace, maintaining a broadly pro-Macedonian political leadership, and avoiding too many measures that might displease the Macedonian king. These men were focused on helping their cities, and if they were in Antigonus' favor and had his ear, that was all to the good, because the king would be more likely to channel money or supplies their way. In return, they would see to it that their cities took Antigonus' part.

THE FIRST OFFENSIVE AGAINST PTOLEMY

No sooner was Antigonus established on his throne—no sooner had his great rival, Pyrrhus, been removed, and the Peloponnese secured—than he turned to the defense of Macedon. Once again, as he had with Antiochus, he followed the principle that attack is the best form of defense, making use of the formidable fleet he had built up. In general, Antigonus' focus on the security of Macedon made him rather cautious in his foreign policy, and disinclined to act aggressively, but he had taken the war to Antiochus in order to win Macedon, and now he attacked Ptolemy in Asia Minor, seeking to curb his encroachment on the Aegean. The evidence for this campaign is slight, but two newly discovered inscriptions—one that has not yet been published—allow us for the first time to see a new side of Antigonus.

First, before embarking on any overseas adventures, he secured Euboea, as we have seen, and in particular installed a garrison in Eretria for the first time. Eretria was a neighbor of Chalcis, and the two ports, which lay close to Ptolemaic possessions in the Aegean, would provide him with excellent facilities for his fleet. And then he set out overseas, probably in 270, with the campaign lasting until 269. We have a unique inscription from Caunus in Caria that starts: "In the fifteenth year of King Antigonus' reign . . ." But why should the people of Caunus, on the southwest coast of Asia Minor, date anything by Antigonus' regnal years unless they were his subjects or allies? It seems, then, that sometime before 268 (his fifteenth year, since he dated his reign from the abdication of his father), Antigonus had taken Caunus from Ptolemy.

This Carian campaign is confirmed by an unpublished inscription from Rhamnous in Attica, which honors an Athenian called Aristides of Lamptrae, who served in the 260s as the general of both Rhamnous and Eleusis, vital Athenian fortresses. Among his other achievements was a successful mission to Antigonus "in Asia." We have no idea what this mission was, so no new light is cast on what Antigonus was doing. How did he take Caunus? Was it conceivably a joint operation with Antiochus? How long did he hold it? Did he take other Carian cities at the same time? Were some of the Aegean islands targeted as well?

There are plenty of unanswered questions, and they will not be answered until more inscriptions or usable chunks of a lost historian turn up. But it seems safe to say that Antigonus was concerned to turn the tables on Ptolemy—to use against Ptolemy much the same policy of interference that the Egyptian king was employing against him in Greece. Ptolemy was bound to respond.

THE OUTBREAK OF THE CHREMONIDEAN WAR

Despite the relatively benign nature of Antigonus' hegemony, the Greeks were clearly being denied autonomy, and resentment built up, especially in Athens and the Peloponnese. By the Athenian year 269/8, Ptolemy had seen his opportunity. He was already allied with

Areus of Sparta, and now he allied himself also with the Athenians. The Athenians and Spartans naturally took the next step, and formed an alliance between themselves, to complete the circle. The Athenian decree that confirmed this alliance and took Athens into its last great war for many decades shows how far the Athenians had traveled since the rebellion of 286; they were again ready to play a major role in international affairs.

The proposal came from Chremonides, a man of means who was one of the leaders of the Athenian democracy; hence the name of the war, though it was really Ptolemy's doing. It is likely that the name was invented by Antigonus' court historian, Hieronymus of Cardia, as a way of downplaying the panhellenic nature of the Greek alliance and implying that the war was due to the will of just one politician. We are fortunate to have an outline of Chremonides' proposal, preserved on stone:

> Chremonides, son of Eteocles, of the deme Aethalidae, introduced the motion: whereas in former times the Athenians and the Lacedaemonians [Spartans] and the allies of each, after making friendship and common alliance with one another, fought many glorious battles alongside one another against those who were trying to enslave the cities, as a result of which they both won fame for themselves and wrought freedom for the rest of the Greeks; and whereas now, when similar circumstances have overtaken all Greece on account of those who are trying to overthrow the laws and the ancestral constitutions of each of the cities, King Ptolemy, in accordance with the policy of his ancestors and his sister, is displaying his concern for the common freedom of the Greeks, and the Athenian people, having made an alliance with him, have voted to urge the rest of the Greeks to adopt the same policy; and whereas, likewise, the Lacedaemonians, being friends and allies of King Ptolemy, have voted an alliance with the Athenian people, along with the Eleans, Achaeans, Tegeans, Mantineans, Orchomenians, Phigaleans and Caphyans, and as many of the Cretans as are in alliance with the Lacedaemonians and Areus and the other allies, and have sent as ambassadors to

> the Athenian people some of their councilors, and they, on their arrival have both made known the zealous regard that the Lacedaemonians and Areus and the rest of the allies have toward the Athenian people, and have brought with them the ratification of the alliance; and in order that, now that there is common concord among the Greeks, the Greeks may, along with King Ptolemy and one another, commit themselves to fighting against those who have wronged the cities and broken faith with them, and may in the future save the cities with the help of their mutual concord; with good fortune, be it resolved by the people: That the friendship and alliance of the Athenians with the Lacedaemonians and the kings of the Lacedaemonians, and the Eleans, Achaeans, Tegeans, Mantineans, Orchomenians, Phigaleans and Caphyans, and as many of the Cretans as are in alliance with the Lacedaemonians and Areus and the other allies, be valid for all time.

In the speech he delivered in August 269, Chremonides clearly harped, in a jingoistic vein, on the great Spartan-Athenian alliance of the early fifth century, over two hundred years earlier, which had driven the Persians from Greece. His stance ignored the many times Athens and Sparta had been on the opposite sides of conflicts—in the world-changing Peloponnesian War, for instance—and glossed over the fact that whereas the Persians had invaded Greece, Antigonus was showing no signs of wanting war. Probably at much the same time as this speech by Chremonides, his younger brother Glaucon helped to fund—at Plataea, where the decisive battle against the Persians had been fought—the establishment of a cult to Zeus the Bringer of Freedom and to Concord. And the town of Troezen, at a time when it was out of Antigonus' control, published or republished a decree purporting to date from the time in 480 when Troezen had given refuge to the women and children of Athens after their evacuation in the face of the city's certain destruction by the Persians.

Panhellenism, the idea that Greeks should unite against a common, non-Greek enemy, was in the air. Although Antigonus is not explicitly named, he is obviously the enemy Chremonides had in mind, the violator of Greek autonomy, and the implication is that he is just as non-Greek as those Persians of long ago. He is not charged with any specific wrongs; it was just general resentment of his repressive policies that inflamed the Greeks. Talk of his "trying to overthrow the laws and the ancestral constitutions of each of the cities" must be a reference to his installation or support of tyrants in the Peloponnese.

Making Macedonians out not to be Greek was a rhetorical commonplace, frequently voiced by those Greeks who loathed them, and throughout his life Antigonus responded by underlining his Greek credentials: he put images of Greek gods on his coins, made dedications at the important Greek sanctuaries, and so on. The slur was not true, because the Macedonians were Greek, even if they belonged to an obscure branch, but given Greek supremacist attitudes toward non-Greeks, it was a useful piece of vilification. The Greeks' ally, Ptolemy, was of course as Macedonian as Antigonus, but that awkward fact was ignored.

The Aetolians played no active part, despite being on good terms with Athens. The comings and goings of votes in the Amphictyonic Council suggest that they might have been preoccupied by some turmoil and conflict among the member states. In any case, their major consideration was the condition of wary neutrality that existed between them and Antigonus. The leadership was probably divided, because they did try at this time (ineffectually, as it turned out) to persuade the communities of the island of Euboea to join their confederacy, and if that had been successful it would have mightily helped the anti-Antigonid cause. And at the end of the war, the Aetolians honored the Ptolemies by recognizing the international festival they were promoting, the Ptolemaia. On the other hand, they appear not to have helped the Greek allies logistically, or by offering to allow them passage through their territory. They were looking out for their own interests, which meant treading a narrow path between supporting their friends in the war and not antagonizing Antigonus.

THE ALLIES' INTENTIONS

What did the main allies, Areus, Ptolemy, and the Athenians, hope to gain from making war on Antigonus? In the first place, both the Athenians and the Spartans wanted Egyptian money and military support; they could not hope to defeat Antigonus on their own. The Spartans certainly seem to have received money, because a relatively large number of Egyptian coins of the period have been discovered during excavations in and around Sparta.

Beyond that, Areus had both personal and state reasons for belligerence. It is noticeable in the Chremonides decree that he is the only one of the two Spartan kings who is named, eclipsing his Eurypontid colleague, Eudamidas II. Areus is almost treated as though he were the sole king of Sparta, and that is certainly a true reflection of his personal ambitions. He was in his midfifties, he had been on the throne since childhood and had garnered considerable international prestige, and he was bidding for recognition as the equal of other Hellenistic kings. He patronized the arts, just like the other kings, and had recently minted Sparta's first-ever issue of silver coins; they bore the legend "of King Areus," with no mention of his co-king, and they looked just like the Alexanders that were still current in every Hellenistic kingdom. But Hellenistic kings were made by their achievements, not their words, and Areus needed a war of liberation to confirm his status.

Areus' other ambition was to resurrect Spartan hegemony in the Peloponnese, so what he hoped to gain from the war was the expulsion of Macedonian influence there, leaving a vacuum that Sparta could fill. He had already taken a giant step in this direction by arranging the extensive Peloponnesian (and Cretan) alliance that is twice mentioned in the Chremonides decree, though it may have been the Athenians who persuaded some of these places to join the coalition. There was still lingering suspicion of Spartan hegemony in the Peloponnese, and we know that Chremonides' brother Glaucon had toured the Peloponnese to whip up support. The only important towns to stay out of this new alliance were Argos, Corinth, Megalopolis, and Messene—the usual Macedonian friends.

A four-drachma coin issued by Areus, a sign of his bid to be recognized as equal to the other Hellenistic kings of the Mediterranean. Note the legend "of King Areus," with no mention at all of his co-king. Photo: Bibliothèque nationale de France.

The Athenians wanted their freedom. They had evicted the Macedonian garrison in the city itself during the rebellion of 286, and had recovered some of the outlying fortresses, but Antigonus still had strong garrisons in Piraeus and Sunium, which interrupted the Athenians' commercial and agricultural activities and denied them a proper war fleet. They had remained consistently hostile to Antigonus and on good terms with Ptolemy; they had hoped that Pyrrhus would emerge the victor in the Peloponnesian conflict of 272. In the years immediately leading up to the war they had provocatively honored famous opponents of Macedon, such as Demosthenes and those who had helped to evict the garrisons of Antigonus' father.

Ptolemy had both aggressive and defensive aims. He wanted to continue to undermine Antigonus' influence in Greece in favor of his own, and he wanted to make sure that his naval bases in the Aegean and Asia Minor were safe. A major step toward the latter goal would be if he could evict Antigonus from Piraeus in the first instance, and then Chalcis and Eretria. He urgently needed a positive response to Antigonus' recent foray in Caria. If the long-term

Ptolemaic policy of gradual expansion in the Aegean was to stand a chance of success, he needed at least to check Antigonus.

Lurking in the background, there may have been another, perhaps far-fetched aspiration. The mention of Ptolemy's sister-wife Arsinoe in the document is fascinating—and not just because it was extremely rare for women to be credited with initiatives in any public field, let alone foreign policy. She was dead by the time of the war, but it is possible that she had wanted to see her and Lysimachus' son Ptolemy placed on the Macedonian throne. He had a good claim to it, and, as we have seen, it was only defeat by Antigonus that had thwarted his ambitions in the 270s. But in order for that to happen, the victory of Ptolemy and his allies would have to be total.

THE STRATEGY OF THE WAR

The first campaign took place in 268, and the war went on until 262, so it was clearly a major effort by the Greeks. The Ptolemaic forces and Antigonus' army and navy arrived in southern Greece more or less simultaneously. Antigonus made Euboea and Corinth his bases for attacks on Athens, but he also occupied the countryside near the city and blockaded the city by sea. Under these siege conditions, Athens remained essentially passive for the entirety of the war; its job was simply to hold out, as it endured the longest siege in its history.

An inscription from the first year of the war, from Rhamnous, the fortress town on the northeast coast of Attica that the Athenians held, reveals something of Antigonus' tactics. The commander of the fortress, Epichares, is praised for having defended the people of Rhamnous, and especially for having deployed guerrilla forces to enable them to gather in all their harvests from the countryside even at some distance from the town. Similarly, an Athenian decree from a few years later thanks the Archon for the year, the titular head of state, for having looked after the countryside and its produce. Antigonus' intention was not to take the city by storm (which would have been time-consuming and bloody), but to deny the Athenians their crops and starve them into submission. History had proved more than once that this was the way to bring the Athenians to their knees.

The Epichares decree also reveals that pirates were active in Attica, adding to the Athenians' woes; the Athenian fleet, such as it was, appears to have been ineffective. These pirates may have been employed by Antigonus—they may even, once more, have been Ameinias and his men—or they may have been self-employed opportunists. At any rate, Epichares is thanked for having ransomed captives out of his own pocket, so that "not one of the citizens was carried off, nor did any of the slaves disappear." We are afforded a glimpse of one of the terrible effects of ancient warfare on the civilian population.

It is unlikely that the Athenians could have held out against the blockade for as long as they did on their own resources. The Egyptian forces, commanded by a Macedonian called Patroclus, must have been able to get grain and supplies into the city from time to time, by devious routes. It is likely that they even got some men into the city, because during the war Athens minted coins that were compatible with the Ptolemaic weight standard, presumably to pay Egyptian mercenaries.

Patroclus' basic tactic for countering the siege of Athens was to impede Antigonus' forces. As soon as he arrived, he had his men occupy a number of places around Attica, building or reinforcing hill forts where necessary. Antigonus had a strong garrison in Sunium, so Patroclus occupied a small island just off the cape (the island is still sometimes called "the Camp of Patroclus") and a lookout post at nearby Atene. Apart from the places that we can identify as having been Ptolemaic strongholds at the time (chiefly by the discovery of Egyptian coins of the period), there are other camps and fieldworks in Attica that may also have been manned by Egyptian troops. Patroclus also had his men reinforce Epichares' garrison at Rhamnous, where the fortified headland guarded the town's two harbors, and where there is evidence of the cult of Arsinoe. Patroclus staked out a strong position in Attica.

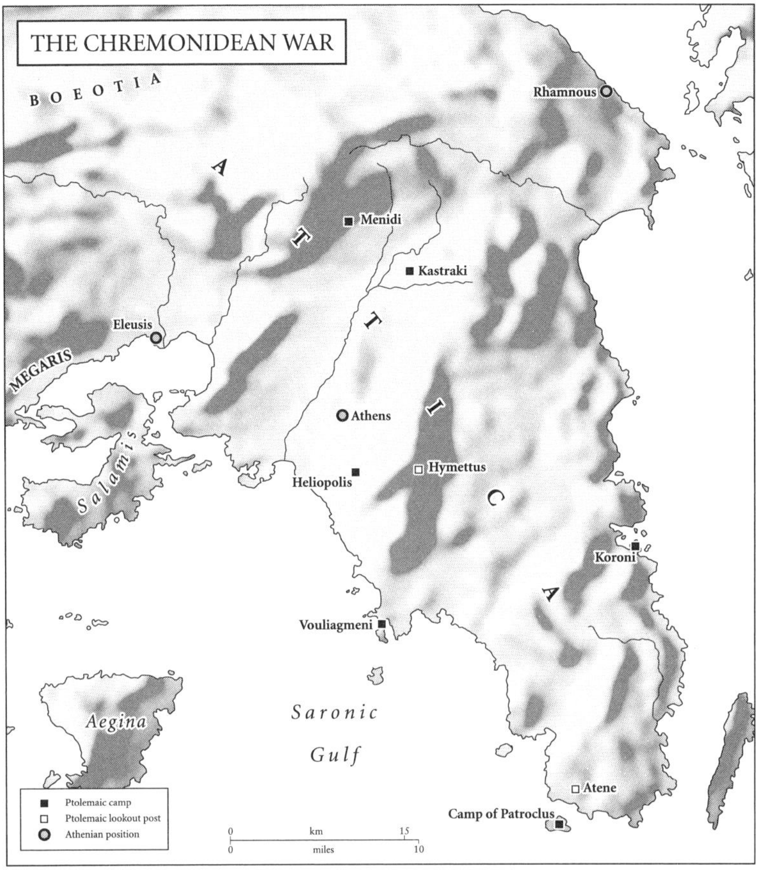

The Ptolemaic camps were hastily erected affairs, protected by rubble walls rather than dressed masonry, and with a limited number of asymmetrical, rubble-built buildings inside the wall. They were made by soldiers rather than professional builders. But, apart from lack of drinking water (which, where necessary, was imported by sea in amphoras), they were good, defensible sites, with nearby beaches for the ships that supplied them. The steep-sided Koroni headland, for instance, which closes the south of the bay of Porto Rafti, was approachable only by sea or by a relatively narrow peninsula, which was well defended by two sets of walls.

Meanwhile, Patroclus' officers were occupying other islets in

The Koroni headland of Porto Rafti is so difficult to access that some of the walls hastily thrown up by Ptolemaic troops during the Chremonidean War are still standing. Photo by author.

the Saronic Gulf, and possibly even Hydrea. The coastal positions would allow the Egyptian troops not just to respond rapidly to any land-based operations by Antigonus' men, but also to impede Antigonus' shipping from Piraeus, Salamis, and Cenchreae, the port of Corinth on the Saronic Gulf. They could hope to get supplies into Athens, while being supplied themselves by the rest of their Aegean fleet, which was based at Samos, Thera, and Ceos. The more inland sites allowed Patroclus to monitor the movements of the Antigonid forces in Attica.

Patroclus' greatest coup was to seize and wall off the volcanic peninsula of Methana in Argolis, actually on the Peloponnesian mainland. It too commanded the sea lanes of the Saronic Gulf. This was a bold stroke, since the most recent eruption of the volcano had occurred only a dozen or so years earlier, but the place was therefore scarcely inhabited and easy to take. It was an excellent harbor, and Patroclus renamed it Arsinoe; the name endured until Roman times.

THE COURSE OF THE WAR

Since, as the Chremonides decree reveals, this was in some sense Arsinoe's war, Patroclus' renaming of Methana (as also at this time of Coressus on Ceos) was appropriate. Ptolemy's attribution of the war to his sister was, of course, gratuitous: Ptolemaic interest in Greece stemmed from his father's time. Arsinoe's role was probably limited to passing on to her brother the pleas of Greek exiles in the Egyptian court that he commit to war against Antigonus. But the mention of Arsinoe reminded the Greeks of his religious propaganda: that he and she were the Sibling Deities, two beings with a single will, and that what they willed was that the Greeks should be free. But we will never know if Ptolemaic control of southern Greece would in fact have been more benign than the Macedonian version.

In Attica, the war was mostly locked in a stalemate. Unless or until the situation changed, Antigonus could not secure the fall of Athens, but Patroclus could not drive the Macedonian army out of Attica either. This helps to explain why so little action is recounted in our sources, and yet why the war went on for so many years. There was probably less action than the threat of action; standoffs and skirmishing were the norm, as the Athenians attempted to sow or harvest their crops, rather than large-scale battles.

But of course Patroclus wanted a decisive battle. This is where the Peloponnesians came in. Patroclus could not simply ship Areus' men across the Saronic Gulf from Methana/Arsinoe, because Antigonus had a sizable fleet in the area. Perhaps they could have crossed the Gulf of Corinth and then come at Attica from the north, but, as I have said, the Aetolians' studied neutrality denied them that route. So Areus' formidable job was to march through the Peloponnese, break through the Macedonian lines at the Corinthian isthmus, defeat the Antigonid garrison at Megara as well, and then proceed into Attica, where he could link up with the Athenian troops at Eleusis. Between them, he and Patroclus could trap Antigonus, coming at him simultaneously from front and rear.

Patroclus needed Areus to bear the brunt of the fighting because the men he had with him were primarily sailors rather than soldiers, sent ahead to prepare positions for later reinforcements. But these reinforcements were unable to get through. Antigonus had a large fleet, and he needed only a proportion of it to guard the Saronic Gulf; the rest was presumably being used to patrol the Aegean against further Ptolemaic initiatives.

It was never going to be easy for Areus to reach Attica. The first time he tried, in 267—the previous year having been spent in recruiting more allies—the plan almost worked. Areus succeeded in reaching the borders of Attica. He made camp on the Thriasian Plain and advanced to a forward position closer to Athens, but he was unable to make further progress, because Antigonus tightened his defenses. When Patroclus urged Areus to engage the Macedonian army, he was unable to comply because, he claimed, he was low on provisions. It is more likely that he did not like his chances against the Macedonians; he must have left large numbers of men in his rear to contain the garrisons in Megara and Corinth.

Areus led his men home, and the war in Attica reverted to stalemate. The Athenians were ready to try anything: it was in the year 266/5 that they erected the stele thanking the Macedonian officer Strombichus and honoring him for his help in the rebellion of 286 against Demetrius. Perhaps they expected word of this to reach Piraeus, so that it was an attempt to get Macedonians there to change sides. Areus tried again in 266 to reach Attica, but to no avail. The chaos that these movements of large armies around southern Greece caused is reflected in a decree issued by the Amphictyonic Council of Delphi, calling impartially on both Ptolemy and Antigonus to protect delegates traveling to Delphi for council meetings. Then in 265 Areus was killed in a battle outside Corinth, still trying to link up with Patroclus' forces in Attica.

Thus the weakness of the Ptolemaic alliance's strategy was exposed; it depended too crucially on the Peloponnesians and Ptolemaic reinforcements being able to reach Attica. Not everything, however, was going Antigonus' way. His son Halcyoneus died in a battle at about this time, and it may have been the same battle in which Areus died. Antigonus was said to have borne Halcyoneus' death stoically.

ANTIGONUS TRIUMPHANT

In 264, the Megarians suborned the Celtic mercenaries Antigonus had installed in their city as a garrison and raised a rebellion. This was a very serious matter for Antigonus; if Megara was friendly to his enemies, or even neutral, it would be that much harder for him to prevent a Peloponnesian army from entering Attica. He had to deal with the issue, and quickly. He marched from Athens at full strength, leaving only a token force in Attica, and no doubt making it possible for the Athenians to stock up on supplies.

Antigonus put down the rebellion by brutally massacring the Celts and the dissident Megarians, and he then resumed his encirclement of Athens. But Areus' death left the Peloponnesians dispirited, and after the Megarian rebellion failed, they confined their activities to the Peloponnese. It did not go well for them there either: perhaps only a few years later, Areus' son, Acrotatus II, who inherited his throne, died in a battle against Aristodamus, the tyrant of Megalopolis, who was obviously working in Antigonus' interests.

The withdrawal of the Peloponnesians confirmed the stalemate in Attica. Seeing that the war could no longer be won, Patroclus seems soon to have withdrawn as well (perhaps at the end of the campaigning season of 264), at least back to his garrisons among the Aegean islands. Justin tells us that the Egyptians as well as the Spartans "retired to safer territory," and no Egyptian coins have been found in their forts that postdate 264. It may be that Antigonus had stirred up trouble in the Ptolemaic possessions of Asia Minor, which demanded Patroclus' attention.

No doubt Patroclus discussed his retirement with the Athenian authorities, and promised to continue to supply them as best he could from the islands. But the Athenians must have known that it was only a matter of time before they were forced to capitulate. Pausanias remarks that the Egyptian contribution to saving Athens was inadequate, and that must have been a common feeling among the Athenians at the time. But, even from a distance, Ptolemy had one last trick up his sleeve. He was not a military man, but he was a good diplomat, and he helped Athens to hang on by persuading Alexander of Epirus to invade Macedon.

By the time Antigonus could respond, in the late summer of 263, some of the northern cantons of Macedon had been overrun and plundered. Antigonus had to grant the Athenians a truce, and they seized the opportunity to sow their grain crops, which would be ready for harvesting in the early summer of the following year. Antigonus made his way north with the bulk of his army, and before long he had contained the situation enough to be able to leave the final defeat of Alexander to his generals. He even recovered the cantons of Macedon that had been in Epirote hands for over thirty years, ever since Pyrrhus gained them as the price of his help to Alexander V. As a way of honoring his son, Demetrius, and of showing the world that he was the heir apparent, he placed the mopping-up operation under the nominal command of the boy, who was only twelve or thirteen years old. The Macedonians drove Alexander not only out of Macedon, but out of Epirus as well. He was soon restored, with Aetolian help, but this was a major success for Antigonus.

The Athenians had enjoyed a respite, but the game was coming to an end. Antigonus was not always successful in war, but he had just convincingly defeated the king of Epirus and was able to get back to Athens in time to prevent the Athenians from harvesting the crops they had sown the previous autumn. The Athenians' will to resist was sapped as they watched Antigonus' troops plunder and burn their fields. The situation was evidently hopeless, and in the summer of 262 they surrendered. Chremonides and his brother Glaucon fled to Egypt and joined Ptolemy's court; Chremonides worked for Ptolemy as a general and Glaucon as a priest of the cult of Alexander the Great.

This was the last attempt by the last two great city-states of Greece to win independence from Macedon, and it showed that, even with Ptolemaic help, they were no longer up to the task. Greek fortunes were in the hands of the great confederacies; Aetolia was now conspicuous in the way that Athens and Sparta had been in the past.

THE BATTLE OF COS

At some point during the war, Patroclus sent Antigonus a cryptic message, a basket containing fish and green figs. Antigonus' interpretation was that "we must either be masters of the sea, or be content to eat green figs." Before long he was ready to crown his great success in the war with a further challenge to Ptolemy's long-standing mastery of the Aegean. The recovery of Athens was perhaps reward enough for Antigonus' efforts, but victory would be sweeter if he increased the area in the Aegean where his traders could find markets, and drove Ptolemy out of the island havens that acted as the forward bases for his fleet.

He met Patroclus and the Egyptians off the southeastern cape of the island of Cos. Since this part of the Aegean was not a theater of the Chremonidean War, and since the date of the battle is uncertain, it is best to treat it as a coda to the war—and probably to relate it to Antigonus' activities in neighboring Caria a few years earlier. Perhaps Antigonus was responding to an attempt by Ptolemy to recover his position there. But all we know about the battle is that it was a victory for Antigonus.

The battle was the occasion of a famous quip by Antigonus. When one of his officers expressed dismay at the number of enemy ships they were facing, Antigonus said: "But how many ships do you think *I* count for?" In part, this was a jab at Ptolemy, who preferred to have his generals do his fighting for him. After the battle, when Ptolemy sent Sostratus to negotiate terms, and Antigonus was inclining to be harsh, Sostratus won him over with an apt quotation from Homer's *Iliad*. Likening Antigonus to Poseidon for his victory at sea, and himself to Iris, the messenger of the gods, who had been tasked by Zeus (Ptolemy) to get terms from Poseidon, he quoted the lines "Dark-haired encircler of the earth, is this then the grim and unyielding message that I am to take back to Zeus? Will you not change your mind, just a little? It is a sign of goodness for a mind to be swayed." Antigonus was swayed. Only some Ptolemaic garrisons were removed (for instance, from Coressus on Ceos), but he allowed other Egyptian forces to remain in the Aegean basin.

There was still an Egyptian fleet in the area a couple of years later, based at Ephesus and commanded by Chremonides, but a defeat in 258 by the powerful navy of Rhodes further undermined Ptolemaic influence in southeastern Asia Minor and the Aegean. The Rhodians were in alliance with Antiochus II of Syria for this affair—surprisingly, since they were usually allied with Egypt—and it was Antiochus who gained Ephesus from Ptolemy. The action was part of the Second Syrian War between Antiochus and Ptolemy, which lasted from 260 to 253 and resulted in considerable gains for Antiochus in Asia Minor.

Antigonus and the Rhodians had severely dented Ptolemaic influence in the Cyclades. A number of inscriptions from the islands refer to "King Antigonus." This may not in every case be our Antigonus, but there is also evidence of Antigonid presence on the island of Samos and in Miletus in or around 260. Both of these last two places had been important Ptolemaic naval bases. Moreover, Ptolemaic dedications and the inauguration of festivals on the sacred island of Delos, at the heart of the Cyclades, stop around this time and do not resume for a dozen or so years, while Antigonus founded two festivals there in 253, an Antigoneia, dedicated to the triad of Delian deities (Apollo, Artemis, and Leto), and a Stratonikeia, in commemoration of his sister, Stratonice, who had recently died. The founding and funding of festivals was a common way for kings to glorify their regimes.

Antigonus also built at this time a magnificent and extremely costly stoa on the island—a marble, open-fronted colonnade, 120 meters long and with projecting wings, as a place to take shelter from the elements, meet friends, do business, spectate festivals and sacrifices, admire the artwork on the walls, and shop. Money raised by renting space in the stoa went directly to the Delian authorities. In front of the stoa there was an imposing monument, with a base about twenty meters long, made of blue marble. The dedication survives, and reads: “King Antigonus, son of King Demetrius, the Macedonian, erected these statues of his forebears, dedicated to Apollo.” There was room for about twenty statues, and Antigonus included among his forebears (who were not necessarily his ancestors) Heracles and Alexander the Great.

Forever after, frequenters of this popular stoa, which was always known as the Stoa of Antigonus, would be reminded of the greatness of the king. This was not in itself a celebration of victory in battle, but just a way of advertising his greatness and the longevity of his royal line; it stretched back to Heracles and would carry on for just as long. Hellenistic kings frequently competed with one another in the building of stoas and other monuments, and Delos, constantly visited by delegations from all over the Greek world, was a good location for a royal display by Antigonus.

It might be argued that Delos, as a sacred island, was open to all the kings; any of them could make dedications and found festivals there, at any rate at this time of the island’s independence from Athens. But a sacred place is not the same as a neutral place; Samothrace, for instance, a sacred island far closer to Macedon,

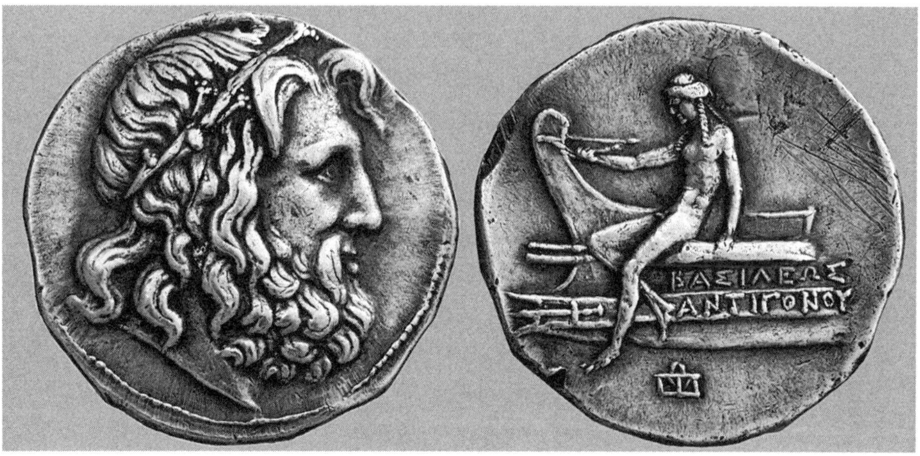

A coin issued by Antigonus in the 240s in celebration of his naval victories in the Aegean. The god Apollo, holding a bow, sits on the prow of a warship (note the ram), which is inscribed “of King Antigonus.” The obverse shows the head of Poseidon. Photo: Athens, Alpha Bank Numismatic Collection 5681.

was effectively closed to Antigonus by prolific Ptolemaic patronage there. At one time or another, all the major religious centers of Greece were influenced by politics: the Delphic oracle urged the Spartans at the end of the sixth century to help the Athenians expel their tyrants; the Eleans banned the Spartans from the Olympic Games of 420. Likewise, the Delians were, for a time, more inclined to accept Antigonus' gifts than those of Ptolemy.

In commemoration of his great victory at Cos, Antigonus also made a more unusual dedication on Delos: he found space somewhere (we do not know where) to make a commemorative monument out of his entire flagship, the *Isthmia* (named after the location of Corinth on the isthmus between central Greece and the Peloponnese). He also minted a celebratory issue of gold coins, and a new silver tetradrachm showed Apollo of Delos sitting on the prow of a warship, indicating his dominance at sea.

Antigonus had greatly weakened Ptolemy. But he did not follow up his victory, as his father would have done, with a mad scheme of further conquest. He rested content with what he had done, winning the goodwill of his people by proving that his overriding aim was the security of Macedon.

CHAPTER 8

The Wheel of Fortune

The Chremonidean War and the battle of Cos swept Antigonus to the height of his power. The war was a disaster for the Greeks. Antigonus' victory changed the whole dynamic in Greece, and not least because he made sure that neither Athens nor Sparta could rise up again for the foreseeable future. He had no remaining rivals on the mainland; there was no new Pyrrhus to whom the Greeks could turn. Pyrrhus' son, Alexander II, had tried, but turned out not to be the man his father was.

But, along with his power, Antigonus had increased his unpopularity in Greece. Winning the Chremonidean War ushered in almost twenty years of relative peace and prosperity for Macedon, but the Greeks, and especially the Aetolians and Achaeans, spent those years building themselves up until they were in a position of strength. By the late 240s, Antigonus' carefully constructed system for Greece was starting to unravel, as the wheel of fortune turned to favor his enemies. This was not his fault, though he was getting on in years and appears to have been less inclined to go to war. It was due partly to his nephew's treachery, partly to the increasing strength and preparedness of the confederacies, and partly to the fact that Fortune gives her hand to the bold man—in this case, Aratus of Sicyon.

Not only had peace been hard won; it was secured by tough measures. In the Peloponnese, Antigonus continued to tolerate sole rulers who were loyal to him, but he also increased his control of as much of Greece as he could. There were Antigonid garrisons in Demetrias, Chalcis, Eretria, Corinth, Piraeus, Eleusis, Salamis,

Sunium, Rhamnous, Athens, Megara, Troezen, Epidaurus, and Ambracia. Much of Greece effectively became occupied territory, and even ungarrisoned towns were likely to be close to an Antigonid force of some size, so that he could control them by the threat of armed retaliation if they went against his wishes. Some of the islands, such as Andros, were garrisoned as well.

A few years after the war, Antigonus made his son Demetrius joint king. This was a common practice in the Hellenistic world: it divided the heavy duties of kingship, formally announced the heir to the throne, and let him gain experience of kingship before he ruled alone. Demetrius' elevation to kingship probably took place in 257, on his eighteenth birthday. A decree from Beroea in Macedon starts: "In the twenty-seventh year of the reign of King Demetrius . . ." Our Demetrius is the only so-named ruler whose reign lasted twenty-seven years—but then only if he had joint kingship. He died in 229, after a sole reign of ten years.

In Demetrius' honor, the Confederacy of Islanders instituted a festival called the Demetrieia, to be held every two years, between celebrations of an already existing Antigoneia. Sacrifices were carried out at "the altars of the kings." The Antigoneia must have started after the battle of Cos, when Antigonus' authority replaced that of Ptolemy. Similar celebrations no doubt went on all over Greece. One way and another, Fortune seemed to be smiling on all Antigonus' endeavors.

ATHENS UNDER DIRECT RULE

Athens was heavily penalized after the Chremonidean War. Antigonus already had garrisons in Piraeus and Sunium and on Salamis, and he now took over the Athenian fortresses at Rhamnous, Aphidna, and Eleusis, and installed his own men. The northern frontier posts of Phyle and Panactum were also now guarded by Macedonian troops, if they had not been before. During the war, Antigonus had destroyed the sanctuary of Poseidon Hippios at Colonus (just outside Athens), which was the spiritual headquarters of the cavalry, and now he crowned this symbolic victory by severely reducing the size of the unit. And the garrisons in Megara, Troezen, and Epidaurus cut the Athenians off from potential friends in the Peloponnese. In military terms, Athens was toothless.

But the greatest blow to Athens was the reinstallation of the garrison on the Museum Hill, actually in the city itself. The Athenians had been free of that immediate a presence for over twenty-five years. They had been wanting to unite the city and the port once again, and in a perverse sense that is what happened; it was all under Macedonian control, and the city was less free than it had ever been. There were thousands of Macedonian troops on Athenian soil, a constant reminder of their humiliation. And Antigonus himself paid his prized possession a visit more than once. He used to stay in Piraeus, the guest of his military commander. It was a morale-boosting tour for his troops—we know that on one occasion he visited the garrison at Eleusis—and a reminder to the Athenians that he was their king.

Military control of Athens, however, was not enough for Antigonus, and for a while he intervened personally in Athenian politics. A fragment of the historian Apollodorus of Athens, written more than a hundred years after the event, says: "The offices were abolished and everything was done by the will of one man." This is an exaggeration: no offices were abolished, but Antigonus certainly made sure that his will was done and that enough of the offices were filled by his friends. He also made sure that his enemies were suppressed or eliminated. Philochorus, active in politics as well as being a famous historian, was executed on the charge of collaboration with Egypt, and he may not have been the only one to die or take himself off into exile—probably adding to the growing presence in Alexandria of Greek exiles urging Ptolemy to take further action against Antigonus.

Antigonus even took it upon himself personally to appoint officers in Athens, as his father had in at least one instance (Adeimantus of Lampsacus), and as Cassander had chosen Demetrius of Phalerum as his governor of Athens. Naturally, the commanders of the most important garrisons in Attica, Piraeus and now Rhamnous, were royal appointees, even though the relevant generalships had previously (a long time previously, in the case of Piraeus) been filled by election by the Athenian people. Sunium, the third in the triangle of coastal fortresses, was, along with Salamis, the responsibility of the Piraeus commander, and although we have no evidence for the Museum Hill commander, the importance of the position makes it likely that he too was a royal appointee.

But there is a curious twist. The decree recording the appointment of the Athenian Apollodorus of Otryne to the Generalship of the Coastline, a position that included Rhamnous, says that he was "appointed by King Antigonus and elected by the people of Athens" to the generalship. Either Antigonus made the appointment and the Athenians ratified it, in a parody of the democratic process, or Antigonus chose Apollodorus as general and the Athenians chose his jurisdiction, the coastline. The latter possibility is both more likely and more disturbing, because it means that every time we read in an inscription dating from these years that the Athenian people elected so-and-so a general, there may have been a prior intervention by Antigonus, which out of pride the Athenians omitted from the inscribed decree.

If Antigonus could do it once, he could do it again. There is a badly preserved inscription, concerning another general for Rhamnous, which might again contain the wording of dual royal appointment and Athenian election, but there is one other certain case. It is troubling, because it concerns the same-named grandson of Demetrius of Phalerum, the dictator of Athens for Cassander between 317 and 307. After the first Demetrius' exile, his family disappeared from view, but now, under Antigonus, they were back in power.

Demetrius was given to extravagant and costly gestures, and abused his position as Cavalry Commander of Athens (he would later go on to serve three times as General) by displaying his mistress at religious festivals almost as though she were the embodiment of divine womanhood. For this impropriety, he was questioned by the Areopagus Council of Athens, which was responsible for the moral behavior of Athenian officials. But when he appeared before the council, he is supposed to have said: "But I am living as becomes a gentleman. I have a very beautiful partner; I am harming no one; I drink Chian wine and have a sufficiency of everything else, since my income is ample enough for this. Unlike some of you, my life does not involve taking bribes or committing adultery." When Antigonus heard of this reply, the story goes, he appointed him a thesmothete.

The story may not be strictly true, in the sense that Antigonus' elevation of Demetrius was surely not due to a single bold gesture by the Athenian at his hearing. But if it is true that he made him a thesmothete, that is shocking enough. However, Antigonus was also having a joke at the Athenians' expense, because once Demetrius' year of office as a thesmothete was over, he would automatically join the Areopagus Council, as all ex-archons did—the very council that had seen fit to question his lifestyle.

The most senior Athenian officials, alongside the board of generals, were the annually appointed nine archons. One, the Eponymous Archon (who gave his name to the Athenian year for dating purposes) was the head of state for the year, responsible for all civic matters; a second, the King Archon, was chiefly responsible for religious matters; a third, the Polemarch, chaired the board of generals. The other six were called "thesmothetes" ("regulators"), and had various jobs, including reviewing the legal code for anomalies. By the third century, the office of archon did not carry much power, but it brought a man authority, and in appointing any member of the board of archons, the oldest office of Athens, Antigonus was trampling on the Athenian constitution, which at that time required archons to be elected by the people from a short list drawn up by the Council. Besides, it is not impossible that Demetrius was merely called a thesmothete, but that in his case the position carried wider-ranging administrative powers. Perhaps that is what the historian Apollodorus was getting at when he said that "the offices were abolished."

Many Athenians would have been appalled by even the slightest interference by a king in their selection of officers. And they would have been no less appalled by the loyal Athenians who abetted him. Most of the royal appointees in Piraeus and Rhamnous were Athenian. For Antigonus, it was perhaps a way to mitigate the fact that in reality they were being ruled from outside, but many would have seen these men as quislings. The traditional democratic way of doing politics in Athens was in any case under threat in a number of ways. Men could now serve on the Council more than twice in a lifetime, and the Council increasingly presented decisions to the Assembly merely for ratification, not for prior debate; the authorities were less strict about the egalitarian rotation of offices through the ten civic tribes.

Within a few years, however, Antigonus came to realize that he had broken the spirit of this generation of Athenians, and in the Athenian year 256/5, he formally freed them from his direct control. He felt he could now rely on the Athenians themselves to choose men who would meet his approval, so his personal appointments came to an end, and he restored the hostages he had taken at the end of the war. The past few years had also been a time of austerity for the Athenians, not least because, after the war, Antigonus had deprived them of the islands of Lemnos, Imbros, and Scyros, which were important breadbaskets for the city. Now he returned the islands and donated a large amount of cash toward the city's recovery. The grateful Athenians voted for the construction and erection of a statue of the king, but they were not really free. Antigonus merely relaxed his control. The garrisons were removed from the Museum Hill, and also from Rhamnous, Eleusis, and the northern fortresses, but Antigonus' retention of Piraeus, Sunium, and Salamis made this no more than a generous gesture.

ATHENIAN SUBSERVIENCE

Athens had no fleet to speak of; the silver and lead mines at Laurium, the source of much of the city's wealth in times past, were not functioning at full capacity; it was unable to extract revenues from Piraeus; piracy was so rampant that harvesting crops was hazardous; and it was probably having to pay some kind of tribute or taxes to Antigonus. In short, the city's humiliation after the war was matched by economic decline.

It is no coincidence that a popular form of history-writing, which

Zeno of Citium, the first Stoic. Although born on Cyprus, he founded his school in Athens, which was the intellectual center of the Greek world, and it was there that Antigonus met him and formed a respectful, lifelong friendship. Photo © Biblioteca europea di informazione e cultura / Fondo Paolo Monti / Wikimedia Commons. CC BY 4.0 International.

celebrated the glorious past of Athens, came to an end with the execution of Philochorus; the contrast between past and present was now too depressing. Philochorus was not the only cultural light in Athens who died at this time. Timaeus of Sicilian Tauromenium, the great historian of the western Greeks, who had long lived in the city and studied in its libraries, had recently died, and so had the philosopher Epicurus. Philemon of Syracuse, one of the most popular playwrights of the era (a specialist in light comedies), passed away, and so did Zeno of Citium. Zeno was buried at public expense in the Cerameicus graveyard of Athens, which was a signal honor, usually reserved for Athenian citizens (which Zeno was not). But it was Antigonus himself who arranged this privilege for his friend, using an Athenian called Thrason of Anacaea as his agent. Thrason employed the proper political channels to see that it was done, and the Athenians were probably happy to commemorate the sage; after all, they had already honored him by letting him hire rooms in the Painted Stoa, in the Agora, as his school. Nevertheless, in a small way, it shows Athenian willingness to do Antigonus' bidding.

Numerous inscriptions attest to Athenian subservience in the years after the Chremonidean War. Immediately after the war, they were quick to send an embassy to Antigonus, renewing their friendship with him. The majority of the resolutions passed by the Assembly took into account Antigonus' desires, expressions of loyalty to the Macedonian king were frequent, and his and his father's friends were honored. Heraclitus of Athmonon, for instance, the king's general in Piraeus, was thanked in 250 or thereabouts for various measures, including proposing a decree that praised Antigonus for his defeat of the Celts in 277 at the battle of Lysimachea. He was awarded a gold crown and commended "for the goodwill and zealous regard that he continues to have for King Antigonus and the Council."

This linking of "King Antigonus and the Council" as the two effective rulers of Athens was pervasive. Before the start of every assembly meeting, it was traditional to offer a sacrifice for the health and prosperity of the Athenian Council and People, and now the king and his family were added to the formula: "Antigonus and Phila and their offspring," or some such wording. This was a sacrifice *for* Antigonus, not *to* him—but both Athens and the Athenian deme of Rhamnous also instituted his worship as a god, as we shall see.

Something of this subservience is revealed by the contrast between two inscriptions, one published just before the war, and one just afterward. The contrast is heightened by the fact that the recipients of Athenian thanks and praise were the brothers Callias and Phaedrus of Sphettus. The Callias decree, published in 270/69, commended him for his help in freeing the city in 286 from the dominion of Demetrius, Antigonus' father, while the Phaedrus decree, published a few years after the end of the war, downplayed Phaedrus' role in 286 and focused instead on the strength of his relationship with Antigonus' father.

A small-scale festival was instituted in Athens to remember Halcyoneus, Antigonus' son, on the anniversary of his death. It seems to have been a private affair, and was perhaps instigated by Hieronymus of Rhodes, the Peripatetic philosopher who hosted the commemorative party at his home. Antigonus covered the costs. As a private celebration, it perhaps should not be added to the list of signs of Athenian subservience, but it must have been galling to some, especially if Halcyoneus died during the Chremonidean War, fighting against Athens' allies. And it therefore affords us a glimpse into the divided nature of Athenian postwar society; there were bitter undercurrents.

However, those who disliked having Antigonus as their king could do little about it. Athens had failed to reassert its independence and reprise its role as a leader of the Greeks. Naturally, Ptolemy brought his subventions to an end. The city became a satellite of Macedon, and the Athenians learned that they would never again play a lead role in the affairs of Greece. In the 240s, Aratus of Sicyon tried time and again to persuade the Athenians to throw off their Macedonian shackles, but the Athenians were just not interested—or, at least, they were not interested in replacing Macedonian with Achaean shackles. Several decades would pass before, at the very end of the century, they took steps to repudiate their Antigonid past.

SPARTA AND THE PELOPONNESE AFTER THE WAR

Where international affairs were concerned, the Spartans largely lay low for the next couple of decades. The deaths of two Agiad kings within a few short years had dealt them a severe blow and, as we shall see, they were consumed by internal issues. The senior king was now the Eurypontid, Eudamidas II, and the Agiad throne was inherited by Areus II, the grandson of the elder Areus. Eudamidas was a nonentity, and Areus died in 254 after a short reign, with no memorable achievements to his name.

Antigonus did not bother to punish Sparta as he had Athens, with garrisons and direct control. The city was not as critical as Athens and Piraeus for his dominance of Greece, or for commercial reasons. It remained ringed by hostile cities—Mantinea, Megalopolis, and Messene—and by pro-Antigonid tyrants elsewhere in the Peloponnese. And, of course, there was the great Macedonian garrison in Corinth, which had already seen to the death of Areus.

In Sicyon, further tyrants had come and gone since Abantidas, the killer of Aratus' father, Cleinias; the current ruler was Nicocles. All of them were pro-Macedonian. During Nicocles' regime, Antigonus stabled horses at Sicyon, which proves the tyrant's sympathies. The Aetolians had recently tried to oust Nicocles and take the city for themselves, but it was Aratus who succeeded where they failed, in the bloodless coup he launched late in 252 or early in 251. When the Macedonians in Corinth heard of the trouble in Sicyon and saw the flames rising from Nicocles' mansion, which the Sicyonians had set on fire, they were preparing to send a force to relieve him, until they found he had already fled. When Aratus called on his fellow citizens to seize their freedom, he was talking about getting rid of not just Nicocles, but also Macedonian affiliation. This was probably also one of the arguments he used a few months later to persuade the Sicyonians to join the Achaean Confederacy: if they felt they needed protection, there was an alternative to Antigonus.

It was never Antigonus' policy to reduce Sparta's power further, because he needed it to counterbalance the growing Achaean Confederacy, which had declared its hostility by joining his enemies' alliance in the Chremonidean War. He could count on Spartan pride to make them reluctant to join the confederacy. His overriding concern was that the Peloponnese should remain undisturbed. He monitored the situation there, and responded to emerging situations on an ad hoc basis, within the overall aim of maintaining stability and a balance of weak powers.

DEMETRIUS THE FAIR

An opportunity arose for Antigonus to make considerable trouble for Ptolemy; naturally, he seized it. Since the 270s, fertile Cyrenaica in North Africa had been independent of Egypt, ruled by a man called Magas, a half brother of Ptolemy, with Seleucid support. At least once, Ptolemy had tried and failed to recover this fertile region for Egypt. Magas' high international status as a king is demonstrated by the fact that he was one of the few who were approached by Ashoka's emissaries, as we have seen.

When Magas died in 250, in his will he betrothed his daughter Berenice to the future Ptolemy III, as a way of reconciling the two kingdoms. This did not please the pro-Seleucid faction in Cyrenaica, which was led by Magas' widow, Apama. As a Seleucid herself—she was a daughter of Antiochus I—she did not want to see Cyrenaica return to Egypt. No doubt, if there had been a suitable Seleucid candidate, she would have chosen him as Berenice's husband, but instead she offered her daughter to Demetrius the Fair, Antigonus' brother. Knowing Antigonus' long hatred for the Ptolemies and rapport with Antiochus II (recently reaffirmed by the wedding of his son Demetrius to Stratonice, a daughter of Antiochus I), she hoped to add Macedonian support to what she already received from Syria.

Antigonus was, of course, involved in all the negotiations, so it was with his blessing that Demetrius set sail for Cyrene to marry Berenice. But after taking up the throne there, Demetrius began an affair with Apama, now his mother-in-law. Berenice responded by leading a coup against the lovers, in the course of which Demetrius was killed—in Apama's arms, according to legend. Over the next few years, the pressure from Egypt grew more intense, until Berenice gave up and agreed to marry the Egyptian prince, perhaps because his father, Ptolemy II, was dying, so that she would immediately become queen. So, in 246, Cyrenaica rejoined the Egyptian empire. Antigonus' oblique offensive against Ptolemy was ruined by Demetrius' unchecked desires.

THE REBELLION OF ALEXANDER OF CORINTH

Perhaps in the early 250s, Craterus died. He had served his half brother loyally as his viceroy in southern Greece, where his military responsibilities included the garrisons at Corinth, Chalcis, and Eretria, and Antigonus saw no reason not to replace him with his son, Alexander. For some years Alexander gave his uncle no cause for complaint. But Antigonus was elderly, and Alexander began to wonder if the Macedonians might not prefer a younger Antigonid king.

Aratus returned from Egypt in the early summer of 250 with plenty of money from Ptolemy and the promise of more. Perhaps it was part of his deal with Ptolemy that he should intrigue against Antigonus by attacking Alexander, Antigonus' viceroy, and the pressure he exerted—not that much was needed, since Alexander was already contemplating rebellion—forced Alexander into alliance with the Achaeans. At this point, Aratus brought his attacks to an end. Even though not yet an officer of the confederacy, he was already working in its interests.

As Antigonus' viceroy, Alexander had the right to make such agreements on the king's behalf, so Antigonus may not have thought twice about it. In fact, he would have been delighted by the apparent taming of the Achaeans. A few months later, however, in the autumn of 249, Alexander translated the semi-independence he had enjoyed as Antigonus' viceroy into full independence. The Macedonian troops and officers under his command proclaimed him king. In the short term, he was king of his southern Greek possessions, but in the longer term he probably saw himself as king of Macedon as well. His plan was to unite southern Greece under his banner, and use it as a springboard to take Macedon.

It was not difficult for Alexander to go independent, since most of his troops were mercenaries. He probably offered them a better rate of pay, as well as the opportunity for profitable warfare (since Antigonus was bound to retaliate), rather than the routine of garrison duty. It made little difference to the civilian populations of the cities who their ruler was. Those few who were, for one reason or another, not in favor of the new regime made themselves scarce. We perhaps find traces of them elsewhere during the war. When the Athenians needed urgently to raise money a few years later to ensure their survival, one of the voluntary donors was a Corinthian called Philocles, resident at the time in Athens.

Did Antigonus have any advance warning? It seems not. He was in Corinth for a visit early in 249, after Aratus returned from Egypt (the episode that is the focus of the introduction to this book), but there is no suggestion that he was there to reprimand or keep an eye on Alexander. He might even have been there to ratify the treaty that Alexander had made with the Achaeans; that would make sense of the remark he made at the time about Aratus—that "he has come over entirely to our side." Alexander was certainly present when Antigonus delivered this speech, probably seated at his right hand, so it must have given him a kind of ironic pleasure to be planning to go independent with the help of Aratus and the Achaeans. Ptolemy's aid to Alexander was limited to money, as far as we know, but it would be surprising if the Ptolemaic garrison at Methana/Arsinoe were not involved.

Fortunately for Antigonus, Alexander did not take the entirety of southern Greece with him. His primary responsibilities were Corinth and Euboea, and they were persuaded to stay with him—along with the considerable proportion of Antigonus' fleet that he found in their harbors—but no one else did. No doubt he approached Antigonus' man in Piraeus, Heraclitus of Athmonon, but Heraclitus resisted his blandishments. An inscription from Eretria thanks a Macedonian called Arrhidaeus for working with Alexander for the removal of Antigonus' garrisons from Euboea, and that prospect was presumably what attracted the Euboeans to Alexander's camp. Alexander also seems to have reinvigorated the loose federal structure that the Euboean cities had earlier enjoyed, but which Antigonus had broken up.

Alexander's defection was a terrible shock for Antigonus. He could be forgiven for thinking that he had everything sewn up tight, and then suddenly he lost two of the Fetters of Greece and saw his ability to control the Greeks vanish. He had Athens and Argos (where Aristomachus had just inherited his father's tyranny), but not much else of value. His friend Aristodamus of Megalopolis had recently been assassinated by associates of Aratus, and it was clear that Aratus wanted to incorporate Athens and Argos into the confederacy as well.

It is a credit to the way Antigonus had won the loyalty of the

Macedonians that troubling ripples did not spread north, despite his age. If the Aetolians had been openly hostile at the time, he would have been in real trouble. Perhaps it was his need to keep them peaceable that prompted him to ignore their ongoing expansion, without taking steps to impede it even when they came close to his own interests. Later events suggest that he was even wondering whether they might not be allies in the future, now that the Achaeans were proving so troublesome.

THE WAR WITH ALEXANDER

Antigonus sent a force down south and bulked up his garrisons in Attica. His generals made Athens and Argos their headquarters. Alexander had plenty of money at his disposal, some of it a gift from Ptolemy. He had increased the size of his army, and he and his allies launched attacks on the two enemy cities. Since both sides were able to move armies through Megarian territory, it seems likely that Antigonus had removed his garrison from there, perhaps to reinforce Argos and Athens, and that the city remained neutral behind its walls. It had already shown, by its rebellion during the Chremonidean War, that its loyalty was suspect—and it would not be long before Antigonus received definitive proof that his suspicions were justified.

Not untypically for this era, Alexander also employed pirates to raid the coastline of Attica. The loss of Euboea made Rhamnous, just across the narrow strait from the island, particularly important for Antigonus, and therefore a particular target for Alexander's men. At one point the situation there was so dire that the general had to put every adult to work, not just his troops. It must have seemed unjust to many Athenians that they were suffering just because they were part of Antigonus' realm, but the main reason Alexander concentrated his efforts on Athens was that if he took it, it would provide him with an invaluable link between Corinth and Euboea. With the Achaeans as his allies, he would effectively have all of southern Greece.

The Athenians were so hard pressed that in 247 they had to

The main entrance to the fortified headland of the town of Rhamnous. Built in the fifth century, the walls made the place virtually impregnable, so that it played an important part in the Athenian defense of the Attic countryside. Photo by author.

appeal for donations from everyone in the city, citizens and foreigners, so that they could defend the countryside and pay their mercenaries to protect the collection of the harvests. The decree was passed in April, and the situation was so urgent that the Athenians were given only a month to come up with the money (between 50 and 200 drachmas per donor), in order for the crops to be harvested in May and June. Most contributors paid the maximum. Both money and food, then, were the issues; as in the Chremonidean War, Athens was on the verge of real hardship.

Alexander constantly had the upper hand in the war, short of actually being able to take Athens or Argos. There is no evidence that Corinth, Eretria, and Chalcis even came under attack, but that might say more about the state of our evidence than the course of the war. Alexander's forces consisted largely of mercenaries and the ships of his uncle's that he had stolen, but he presumably received help in some form from the Achaeans and from the Egyptians at

Methana. A truce was arranged in 245, though it cost Aristomachus fifty talents to secure it for both Argos and Athens, as a kind of indemnity. Perhaps he was subsidized by Antigonus. He was later publicly thanked and honored in Athens for having refused to negotiate with Alexander unless Athens were included in the truce along with Argos. But, as it happened, the truce turned into the end of the war because Alexander died—so conveniently that it is hard not to suppose that Antigonus had something to do with it. Rumors of poisoning sprang up immediately.

ANTIGONUS IN THE AEGEAN

Antigonus' involvement in the war was minimal. He could not commit more troops, because, not coincidentally, a Ptolemaic war fleet returned to the Aegean. A letter written by Apollonius, Ptolemy's prime minister, dated January 250, passes on Ptolemy's orders for the construction of warships. Given that Antigonus had to divide his forces and that Alexander had appropriated a good proportion of his fleet, it is little surprise that he was unable to defeat the Egyptians on this occasion, in 249.

Ptolemy subsequently boasted of this victory, but little seems to have come of it. It was probably not a fully fledged attempt to recover the Cyclades, but more a way of aiding Alexander by keeping Antigonus away from Greece. A few years later, however, Ptolemy III, who inherited the Egyptian throne in 246, was in an expansive mood. Not only was he sweeping all before him (at least temporarily) in Syria and Mesopotamia, in the Third Syrian War against Seleucus II (246–241), but he was also making gains in the Aegean. The strategic port city of Ephesus returned to Ptolemaic hands, and when the northern Aegean towns of Aenus and Maronea fell to Egyptian mercenary forces commanded by an illegitimate son of Ptolemy II called Ptolemy Andromachus, Antigonus became alarmed. The Egyptians were not only regaining some of the ground they had lost in the Aegean, but were now impinging directly on the northern Aegean trade routes that, since the time of Philip II, had been dominated by Macedon.

In 246, Antigonus defeated Ptolemy's admiral Sophron off the island of Andros. That is all we know about the battle. It seems possible that Sophron had been trying to retake the island from Antigonus. It is likely that, despite his age, Antigonus was present, the commander in chief for the battle. Plutarch tells the same story about Andros as about Cos—that Antigonus, who prided himself on his skills at naval warfare, expected his skill to compensate for the fact that his fleet was outnumbered.

Just as he had after the battle of Cos, Antigonus celebrated and offered thanks to the gods on Delos. In a decree honoring an envoy of his, the people of Delos acknowledged that they had long been especially favored by Antigonus. As after Cos, the alternation of Ptolemaic and Antigonid dedications on the island is significant. In 246, Ptolemy III had inaugurated a Ptolemaia there, but in 245 it was Antigonus who was able to use the island for display. Antigonus founded two festivals on the island that year, a Paneia and a Soteria, by establishing funds to cover the ongoing costs. We have already seen how important the god Pan was to him in representing military victory, so this helps us to date his victory at Andros. The same goes for the Soteria. It was sacred to "the Savior Gods," probably Zeus and Athena, and like all Soteria festivals it celebrated and commemorated liberation. Antigonus wanted the Greek world to join him in celebrating his final liberation of the Aegean from Ptolemaic influence.

Only the Egyptian garrison on the island of Thera (modern Santorini) remained in the central and southern Aegean. This was the third defeat of the Ptolemaic fleet in the Aegean in fifteen years, and Antigonus could hope that it was decisive. He secured some of the islands nearest Greece with garrisons (Andros, Ceos, Syros, and probably Cythnos), but he still did not establish political dominion over the majority of the islands, and neither did the Rhodians; it was enough for them both that the islands were free of Ptolemaic control, so that their merchant ships could safely go about their business. Antigonus acted merely as their benefactor, protecting some of them with garrisons and supplying them with expertise, as he sent one of his men to Syros to help resolve a judicial issue, and another to do the same job on Cimolos. He had restored Macedonian authority in the Aegean.

CORINTH RECOVERED AND LOST AGAIN

Corinth was critical to Antigonus' control of the Greeks. In Plutarch's metaphor, he desired the city as a lover does his beloved. At any rate, he was not going to let it remain in others' hands if he could help it. In 245, after Alexander's death, it was his widow, Nicaea, with whom he had to deal. He concocted an elaborate scheme:

> Antigonus immediately sent his son Demetrius to her, flattering her with the prospect of a royal wedding and of marriage with a young man who would make a pleasant companion for an older woman. Although this use of his son as common bait netted him Nicaea, however, she would not give up the Acrocorinth, but kept it under a strong guard. Antigonus continued to feign indifference: he set about celebrating their marriage in Corinth, and put on shows and arranged symposia every day, for all the world as though he were so pleased and happy that he had nothing more on his mind than amusement and relaxation. But then his moment came. Amoebus was due to sing in the theater, and Antigonus personally escorted Nicaea to the show in a litter, decorated with royal trappings. Preening herself on this high honor, she had no idea what was in store. When they reached the point in the road where there was a turning up to the citadel, Antigonus gave orders that Nicaea was to be taken on to the theater, but he turned his back on Amoebus and the wedding celebrations, and raced up to the Acrocorinth with a speed that belied his years. Finding the gate locked, he knocked on it with his staff and ordered it to be opened, and the guards inside were so intimidated that they did so. That is how he gained control of the place.

Polyaenus adds that at least some of the garrison had made the wedding ceremony a holiday. Perhaps Antigonus had made sure that all the senior officers were invited, so he could intimidate the ordinary soldiers who remained in the citadel. The disappointed Nicaea was allowed to leave, husbandless, and Antigonus reclaimed Euboea as well, where he dissolved the newly revived confederacy and reinstalled his garrisons.

Antigonus was having a brilliant few years, but he was sensibly cautious. After his experience with Alexander, he abandoned the policy of having a member of his family as his viceroy in southern Greece, and installed instead reliable men whose heads were less likely to be filled with dynastic dreams. He also divided what had been one man's responsibilities into three. He made a certain Archelaus the military commander; another senior officer, perhaps responsible for finances, was called Theophrastus; and as civic governor he chose the philosopher Persaeus, the former protégé of Zeno and tutor of Halcyoneus.

Antigonus reactivated the network of tyrants and garrisons in the Peloponnese. Megalopolis had enjoyed a few tyrant-free years after the assassination of Aristodamus, but now Antigonus helped a man called Lydiadas to become tyrant, in order to both keep Sparta down and resist the encroachment of the Achaeans. In Argos, the tyrants were friends of Antigonus, as we have seen. Troezen and Epidaurus still had Antigonid garrisons. Orchomenus, Hermion, and Phleious all gained tyrants, now or within a few years. We know nothing about Nearchus of Orchomenus, but Xenon of Hermion and Cleonymus of Phleious seem to have been pro-Macedonian in their orientation, because they both abdicated in 229, when Macedonian fortunes were at a low ebb, suggesting that they had enjoyed the favor of the Macedonian kings.

The situation in the Peloponnese had changed, however, since the war. The main difference was that the Achaeans were now far more confident and far more belligerent. Aratus became General of the confederacy for the first time in 245, and he intended to turn the entire Peloponnese into a single Achaean state, eliminating Antigonus' tyrants in the process. Antigonus' recovery of Corinth in that same year had been the result of a bold scheme, but only two years later Aratus matched him. He desired Corinth as much as Antigonus did.

Four Greek brothers from Syria were among Antigonus' mercenaries on the Acrocorinth. They were senior enough to have access to the mercenaries' pay. Three of them chose to abscond with some of the money, which they deposited with a banker in Sicyon. Aratus got to hear about this, and the Syrians told him about a particular stretch of the Acrocorinth wall that was relatively easy to scale.

One midsummer night, under a full moon, Aratus and an advance force of four hundred approached the city. He and a quarter of his men scaled the city wall, barely avoiding discovery, while the rest went around to one of the gates, where they broke in with the help of the Syrians. By now, the alarm had been sounded, but the three hundred were able to scatter the troops, commanded by Archelaus, who had set out after Aratus. They then joined Aratus and the rest for the assault on the Acrocorinth itself. At dawn, with the arrival of a larger force of Achaean troops from Sicyon, Antigonus' dispirited garrison surrendered. The Corinthians welcomed the Achaeans as their liberators. Aratus "gave them back the keys to the city gates, which had been denied to them since the time of Philip II," and the process was set in motion for the incorporation of the city into the confederacy. It was another great leap forward for the Achaeans.

Theophrastus was executed, but Archelaus was allowed to go free. Persaeus' fate is unclear. Athenaeus records a scurrilous story that Aratus was able to take Corinth in part because Persaeus was incapacitated by drink. Whatever the truth of that, some writers tell us that he escaped to Cenchreae, the southern port of Corinth, and traveled from there to Antigonus in Macedon, but others tell us that he was killed, fighting bravely, in the course of Aratus' assault. But whatever the fate of Persaeus, Aratus had undone Antigonus' position in southern Greece. Its weakness had always been its dependency on Corinth. It had always been assumed that the Acrocorinth was all but impregnable, but Antigonus himself had proved that false two years earlier.

ALLIANCE WITH THE AETOLIANS

The capture of Corinth in 243 was the single act that made the Achaean Confederacy a major force in the Greek world. Mainland Greece was now effectively divided between Macedon, Aetolia, and Achaea. Twenty-five of Antigonus' warships and several hundred horses were captured by Aratus. The Achaeans were now strong enough to take on the role of protectors of any southern Greeks who chose to resist Macedonian dominion—the same role that the Aetolians had been playing in central Greece. The domino effect was startling, and exposed the unpopularity of Macedonian hegemony: within just a few weeks Epidaurus, Megara, and Troezen had expelled their garrisons and joined the confederacy. The Achaeans could now command the Saronic Gulf.

Antigonus was bound to respond, but he did so in an unexpected fashion, by making use of the Aetolians, rather than committing men and matériel himself. The Aetolian Confederacy had continued to grow. Malis was incorporated in the late 260s, and by the 240s the Aetolians had for commercial reasons (such as the gaining of friendly ports) even sought and established good relations with a number of states in and around the Aegean. They demonstrated their complete control of the Amphictyonic Council by giving Chios a seat on the council, even though the island scarcely counted as a "neighbor" of Delphi. They had maintained the state of uneasy neutrality that existed between them and Antigonus.

They were preoccupied in these years with adapting their federal state to accommodate all the recently added non-Aetolian members, especially by creating enough posts to see to the increased volume of business and to disperse power among the elites of the new member states as well as the original ones. The state was now divided into seven districts, with financial and military officers appointed for each district. The Aetolians were also trying to build up a federal reserve, so they did not want to exhaust all their funds on warfare. The exercise was successful; before long they were minting fine coins in gold, silver, and bronze, and in general behaving like a normal, high-status Greek state. In 246 they declared their new standing to the world by refounding the Delphic Soteria as a panhellenic festival to be celebrated every four years, equal to the other great athletic festivals of the Greek world, such as the Olympic Games. Now the Greeks would regularly be reminded of the Aetolians' role in saving Greece from the Celts.

The flourishing of the Aetolians frightened the Epirotes. The Aetolians and Epirotes had earlier divided Acarnania between them, and now the Epirotes became concerned, with good reason, that the Aetolians wanted to take over their half as well, despite the fact that the two states had been on good terms for over a hundred years. The Epirotes found a good defense. The kingdom was currently ruled by Olympias, the half sister and widow of Alexander II. She approached Antigonus and was granted an alliance, sealed by the marriage of Antigonus' son Demetrius to her daughter Phthia.

Antigonus leaped at the opportunity to keep Epirus peaceable for the foreseeable future, but Demetrius' marriage to Phthia had an unfortunate consequence. He already had a Seleucid wife, Stratonice, whom he had married in 253 when Antigonus and Antiochus II renewed the friendship between their two states. Despite the fact that polygamy was far from unknown in the royal courts, Stratonice took offense. She had failed to produce a son, and rightly felt that she was being ousted by Phthia. She returned to the Seleucid court, where she was later executed for stirring rebellion against her nephew, Seleucus II. This weakening of the ties between Syria and Macedon was particularly disturbing to Antigonus because Syria and Egypt were drawing closer—making it likely that Stratonice was, in fact, acting as a Seleucid and merely pretending to be offended, to give her brother a reason for coldness toward Antigonus.

Meanwhile, tension built up between the Aetolians and the Achaeans, particularly as the Aetolians strengthened their relations with the Messenians and helped the Eleans not only to recover dependencies that had been lost to them for over a hundred years, but also to expand into northwest Arcadia. The Achaeans felt threatened by this Aetolian interference in the Peloponnese. In 245, the year of Aratus' first Generalship, they went on the offensive. There was friction between the Aetolians and their allies, the Boeotians, and Aratus prized the Boeotians loose from the alliance and persuaded them to attack Aetolian Phocis from the east, while the Achaeans crossed the Gulf of Corinth and raided the coastline. They would trap the Aetolians within a pincer.

For all their past prowess, however, the Boeotians were now weak in military terms, and the Aetolians, recognizing an easy target, retaliated by ignoring the Achaeans and invading Boeotia. Aratus and a large force of Achaeans came to help, only to find that the Boeotians had already been devastatingly defeated by the Aetolians at Chaeronea. The Achaeans retreated, and the Aetolians forced the Boeotians back into alliance with their confederacy.

The capture of Corinth in 243 made the Achaeans the common enemy for Antigonus and the Aetolians, and they acknowledged this fact by setting aside their simmering hostility, recently exacerbated by Antigonus' alliance with the Epirotes, and entering into an agreement to try to break up the Achaean Confederacy. No doubt some of this offensive was diplomatic, but in military terms Antigonus left it all up to the Aetolians. He effectively bribed them to do his fighting in Greece for him, by conniving at their further encroachment on the Peloponnese. Without Corinth, he himself could no longer control events in central and southern Greece, so he set the two protagonists there against each other. Aratus responded by forming an alliance with the Spartans, now dominated by Agis IV, the forceful young king who had inherited the Eurypontid throne of Sparta the year before.

Allying himself with the Aetolians was an extraordinary move for Antigonus. Why would he deliberately have allowed the Aetolians to grow stronger, knowing that this would only lay up trouble for himself (or, since he was elderly, for his successors)? I doubt that it was an impulsive move, dictated simply by a desire for revenge on the Achaeans. He was about seventy-five years old, and he may have been ill, but the agreement with the Aetolians suggests considerable Macedonian weakness, and I can only think there was trouble on Macedon's northern borders, so that Antigonus was preoccupied in the last years of the 240s with repelling raids by the Dardanians and other tribes. Within a few years, his successor on the Macedonian throne was to be constantly plagued by the Dardanians, and it is possible that their resurgence started earlier, during the final years of Antigonus' reign. Antigonus always made the security of Macedon his first priority, and under such circumstances he might well have focused his attention and forces there, while hoping to recover his position in Greece at some later date.

ARATUS' ATTEMPTS ON ATHENS AND ARGOS

Aratus remained on the offensive. He was quite prepared to use force to achieve his aims. In 242, the year after his seizure of Corinth, he attacked Athens and plundered the Athenian island of Salamis in an attempt to punish the city for its enforced alignment with Antigonus and compel it to join the confederacy. But any captives he took who were Athenian citizens were released without ransom, because he wanted to demonstrate that the object of his offensive was Antigonus, not the Athenians as such. His message was that the attacks would stop if they joined the confederacy. But the Athenians did not comply then, nor would they ever join the confederacy; in their view, lack of full independence under Macedon was little different from being a member of a confederacy. Besides, until recently the Achaeans had been widely regarded as relatively uncivilized, and the Athenians, who were always aware of their glorious history, felt they could not join forces with such people. In the same year, the Achaeans granted Ptolemy III the honorary leadership of the Achaean forces at war on land and at sea, in gratitude for the money he was sending their way.

But Aratus' schemes were disrupted by the Aetolians. In 241, they marched on the Peloponnese. Aratus took the Achaean army to the Isthmus, and summoned his allies from Sparta. The original plan was to wait there for the Aetolians and stop them from entering the Peloponnese. Agis was ready to give battle, but Aratus, who had overall command, made an extraordinary decision, one that contributed to a reputation he acquired for cowardice. He decided that since the crops had already been harvested, it would be safer to let the Aetolians in than to risk a pitched battle at the Isthmus. He was better at surprise attacks and ambushes than formal battles, and Agis was an untried commander. The Aetolian force might also have been smaller than he expected. At any rate, he felt that the Achaeans alone would be able to cope with whatever fighting needed to be done, and he dismissed Agis and the Spartans back home. The consequences of this dismissal would turn out to be lethal for Agis.

Fortunately for Aratus, this risky scheme turned out well. The Achaeans did manage to contain the Aetolians, who returned home in frustration. But Aetolian raiders kept returning in smaller numbers across the gulf, and late in the summer one such band fell on the Achaean town of Pellene. Aratus had dismissed the Achaean army by then, but he raised a scratch force, marched to Pellene, and caught the Aetolians in disarray, intent on looting and pillaging. Seven hundred Aetolians were killed, the rest fled, and Aratus' fame soared. The internationally famous painter Timanthes of Cythnos was commissioned to depict the scene.

On the back of his success, in 240 Aratus attacked Piraeus, breaking a truce with Antigonus in order to do so. Throughout all this, Antigonus remained in Macedon, dealing, I have suggested, with threats to his northern borders. Then Aratus turned to Argos, the last remaining friend of any importance that Antigonus had in the Peloponnese. For thirteen years, the city and its tyrants had given young Aratus shelter. Nevertheless, such was his hatred of tyranny and his determination to expand the confederacy that he went to work against the Argive tyrants:

> He hated to see the Argives enslaved . . . and he put in motion a plot to kill their tyrant, Aristomachus. . . . Men were found who would dare the deed, and Aeschylus and Charimenes the seer took charge of them, but they had no swords, because it was illegal to own one; the tyrant had stipulated severe penalties for anyone caught in possession of weaponry. Aratus therefore arranged for stilettos to be made in Corinth and sewn up inside saddle-cloths; these cloths were then draped over some mules, part of a train taking some

odds and ends to Argos, and sent on their way. Charimenes, however, recruited a disreputable character for the enterprise, to the annoyance of Aeschylus and the others, who gave up on the seer and proceeded to act on their own. When Charimenes found out, in the heat of the moment he betrayed them just as they were walking up to stab the tyrant.

Despite the failure of this plot, Aristomachus was assassinated a few weeks later, though Aratus seems to have had nothing to do with it, not least because he was unable to take advantage of it. Aristomachus' son Aristippus took over. Aratus marched on Argos with a force of Achaeans, expecting the Argives to join him in overthrowing the tyrant, but they remained loyal, or frightened. Aristippus demanded compensation from the confederacy for an attack on the city at a time of peace. The case was heard before the Mantineans as arbitrators, and Aristippus was awarded a substantial sum of money. Aratus kept up his attacks on Argos, however, and a few years later, in 235, managed to kill Aristippus in an ambush near Mycenae. This time there was no surviving plaintiff to bring a suit against him, but he was still unable to bring the city into the confederacy, because Aristippus' brother Aristomachus secured the city for himself with troops supplied by Macedon.

THE REFORMATION OF SPARTA

We have seen that Sparta had gradually, over the past decades, become more or less identical in many respects to other Greek cities. It had become a city of inequalities, whereas previously all full citizens, the Spartiates, had prided themselves on being "the Similars." The city was effectively being ruled by a small number of wealthy households, and citizen numbers were at a critically low level. In addition, over the past 125 years, Sparta had been repeatedly humbled in war, whereas in earlier times its great success and even greater fame had been largely due to its army.

There were those in Sparta, especially among the younger generation, who were inclined to attribute all their woes to a single cause, the abandonment of their traditional ways and "the laws of Lycurgus." They found a champion in Agis IV, who "took pride in his thin cloak and made a point of adhering to traditional Spartan ways in his diet, bathing, and general way of life; and he used to say that there was no point to his being king unless he could use the position to restore the ancestral constitution and training regime." Graduation, at about the age of eighteen, from the training regime (*agōgē*) had always been a precondition of citizenship; it proved that a young man had what it took to serve the state, especially in the armed forces. But the *agōgē* had lapsed into disuse two or three decades earlier.

Not long after coming to the Eurypontid throne in 245, Agis contrived the exile of his co-king, Leonidas II, and placed a relative of his on the Agiad throne. He deposed the five ephors, one of the most powerful political forces in Sparta, because they were likely to resist him, and replaced them with more amenable men. Then he instituted a package of reforms, claiming that he was restoring the original, Lycurgan constitution of Sparta. This involved, first, the cancellation of all debts, so that poorer Spartiates would not be beholden to the plutocrats to whom they owed money, especially in the form of mortgages on their hereditary farms. The second plank of the reforms was even more radical: Agis confiscated all the farmland of Laconia and divided it into almost twenty thousand lots, which were to be distributed afresh and in equal portions. Since the ownership of land was essential for membership of a mess, which was a precondition of Spartiate citizenship, this move would automatically generate a new and greatly enlarged batch of citizens. The *agōgē* was reinstated for the sons of the new citizens.

Only some of the new landowners were Spartiates; the rest were either Inferiors (of whom there were perhaps two thousand at the time) or deserving and militarily capable non-Spartiate inhabitants of Laconia. But Agis was no socialist; he was trying to create a new ruling class for Sparta, not overall equality. With citizen numbers replenished, the Spartan army would be back up to strength and able to hold its own again. In the long term, Agis hoped that these reforms would enable Sparta to reclaim its position as the leader of the Peloponnese. He believed that Sparta could be great again.

But then in 241, as we have just seen, Aratus summoned Agis and the Spartan army to the Isthmus to confront the Aetolians, only to dismiss them as surplus to requirements. There were two immediate effects. First, it meant that Agis was away from Sparta for long enough for his political enemies to get to work and undermine his reforms; they were aided in this by the obvious corruption of one of Agis' associates, who brought the movement into disrepute. Second, the first outing for Agis' new, reformed army had turned into an inglorious farce.

It may well be that Aratus intended these consequences. He and the rest of the Achaean leadership were wealthy landowners, and felt an affinity with the wealthy landowners of Sparta. Agis' reforms were anathema to them, and they were afraid of a revolutionary movement spreading from Sparta. Nor, in the longer term, did they want to see a reinvigorated Sparta, since they hoped one day to incorporate Sparta into the confederacy. The humiliation of Agis by Aratus served many purposes.

So Agis returned to find his reforms in disarray and his enemies in the ascendant; Leonidas had returned from exile and resumed his kingship. Before long, Agis was forced to take refuge in the sanctuary of Athena of the Bronze House. It was a soft imprisonment, however, and his stature as a king meant that occasional excursions outside of the sanctuary were tolerated—until he was arrested on a trip to the bathhouse. A kangaroo court was convened; he was condemned to death and hanged. But Agis' work was not in vain, because in the 220s another king, the Agiad Cleomenes III, who had married Agis' widow, pushed through a very similar program of reforms. He succeeded, at least for a while, where Agis had failed, because he was more prepared to use violence.

Meanwhile, in 239, the Aetolians invaded Laconia. They claimed that their intention was to restore the men who had been exiled in the aftermath of Agis' failure, but they had no sympathy for Agis' reforms, and rather than tackle the formidable obstacle of Sparta itself, they were content to damage the local economy by kidnapping large numbers of agricultural serfs. It is unlikely that they were acting as Antigonus' agents; this was just a predatory raid, designed to punish the Spartans for having dared to side with the Achaeans against them. If there was more to the offensive, it was to point out, forcefully, that the Spartans' alliance with the Achaeans was no protection. It was clear that, for the foreseeable future, central and southern Greece would be dominated by the Aetolians and the Achaeans, no longer by Macedon.

CHAPTER 9
Court and Culture

Like most premodern kings, Antigonus maintained a mobile court, moving between several royal cities, depending on the season, or on his need to be seen somewhere. He had fabulous, enormous palaces at Pella (the political capital) and Aegae (the ceremonial capital), but could also be found, suitably housed, in Thessalonica, Pydna, Mieza, Cassandrea, Demetrias, Corinth, and Chalcis. Antigonus himself renovated and extended the royal palace in Aegae. When out on campaign, his pavilion became the court, and rivaled in splendor the interior of his palaces.

Wherever he went, the royal residence was simultaneously a place where he could be private and a public presence in the lives of his subjects, a physical representation of his kingship. The palaces, built on sites with commanding views, were designed to overawe spectators, and access to the wonders of the interior was gained by passing through a monumental entrance reminiscent of a temple, and past splendidly attired troops from the household guard. Inside, the size of the rooms and the quality of the furnishings, paintings, tapestries, and sculptures spoke of regal power and boasted of his achievements.

THE COURTIERS

But a royal court is more than a palace or a pavilion; it is also the people in orbit around the king, those who live or work there, or pass through on official business. From this perspective, a palace or a pavilion is merely the location of the court; Antigonus had several residences, but only one court.

The court encompassed, first, Antigonus and his immediate family, including mistresses and illegitimate offspring (we know of one of each), and other relatives. In the unsettled years of the early Hellenistic period, royal Macedonian women (such as Olympias, Eurydice, and Thessalonice) had occasionally come into prominence, and they continued to do so in the Seleucid and Ptolemaic courts, but neither Phila nor any other woman is known to have played a significant role in Antigonus' court or in the courts of later Macedonian kings. In the other kingdoms, they often became prominent because of their involvement in dynastic struggles over the succession, but no such storms disturbed the Antigonid court.

Attached to the immediate family were those who attended them, who in Macedon (again, as distinct from the other kingdoms) were more likely to be drawn from the aristocracy than to be slaves. They were, for instance, the Chamberlain, responsible for managing the household, the Keeper of the King's Seal, the King's Physician, the Master of Hounds. Ushers wielding staffs guarded doorways and limited access to the king. High-ranking attendants either lived in the palace or had accommodation nearby. Their mansions were luxurious as well, and served as mini-courts for their retinues and dependents.

These men were some of the "Friends" of the king, whom I have already described as the effective ruling class of the kingdom. The court was the center for their activities; the court was the seat of government. Financial management of the kingdom as a whole, military planning, delegation of responsibilities to local government—all these kinds of functions were handled in court by the Friends. Then there were the artists and intellectuals patronized by the king (of whom more later), court priests to perform sacrifices, and closely attached personnel such as Antigonus' personal physician, Aristogenes of Cnidus.

If these groups constituted the inner court, those with regular access to the king's person, the outer court was made up of the bureaucrats, secretaries, grooms, bakers, and so on, who saw to the

A beautiful pebble mosaic from the "House of Dionysus" in Pella, the Macedonian capital, showing the god riding a panther. We glimpse the splendor of the houses of the Macedonian elite, who were close to the king. Though built toward the end of the fourth century, the house was still in use in Antigonus' time.

daily running of the kingdom and the palace, along with all the envoys, ambassadors, and emissaries who arrived from other kingdoms, from Macedonian cities and districts, and from Greek states. Envoys were expected to come not just with a request, but with a gift or an offer of services to increase the likelihood of their state's receiving the king's favor.

Plutarch gives us a sketch of a typical Hellenistic king in his court, by contrasting Cleomenes III of Sparta:

> When people approached Cleomenes . . . they were struck by the absence of purple-dyed robes or cloaks, or equipment such as sedan-

> chairs and litters. They found that doing business with him was not a frustrating and laborious experience, impeded by hordes of pages and doorkeepers or the intermediation of secretaries, but that he came to meet his visitors in person, dressed in ordinary clothes, and made time to talk graciously and kindly to his petitioners.

But Plutarch slightly misses the point. It was essential for a king to be aloof. He had to maintain an aura of "otherness," because otherwise he was no different from ordinary men. He had to appear closer to the gods, and all the kings claimed descent from gods—Heracles, in Antigonus' case, and therefore Zeus, Heracles' father. Hence a king was distinguished also by his insignia. A Hellenistic king did not wear a crown, but a diadem—a simple band of white cloth tied around his head and knotted at the back of his neck. In origin, it was the headband awarded to victors in athletic competitions, because victory—the reward given by the gods to those they favored—was the foundation of kingship. He also carried a scepter, the symbol of his authority, and wore a large ring with the royal seal. On ceremonial occasions, he sat on a special chair, a throne, and might wear chased and gilded armor, with an ornate sword at his side.

In any monarch's court, courtiers and visitors are subject to certain regulations, usually unwritten, which govern the behavior of both them and the king. He is expected to act with splendor and dignity, they with deference. Antigonus' court was the point from which he projected his identity as monarch to the outside world, in the audiences he granted and the orders he issued. It was the setting of royal ceremonial (state banquets, for instance, or the reception of ambassadors) and a place where a theatrical display of the king's power was presented to the wider world. From the inner chambers of the palace, the king would appear before his subjects almost like a divine epiphany. Rituals enacted around Antigonus' person took place in the court. The king presented himself as sacred, and as essential to his people. The statues and portraits of himself to which he gave his blessing perpetuated the same ideas of power and divinity.

Luxury and opulence were justified because they were understood to be tokens of a successful kingship. According to Polybius, the Macedonian court a few decades later than Antigonus threw even the Egyptian court into the shade in these respects. Philip II, Alexander the Great, and Antigonus' father, Demetrius Poliorcetes, had taken over many aspects of their kingship styles from the Achaemenids of Persia, but Demetrius' rejection by his people, in part for his oriental style of kingship, held a lesson that Antigonus had securely learned. His subjects did not take kindly to too much trumpery. He reverted to a more traditional version of kingship, in keeping with his devolution of power to the cities and districts of Macedon. He retained only those eastern features that had already become entrenched over the decades: extravagant luxury and generosity; the royal throne; and certain courtly functions and functionaries, such as the Royal Pages.

A COURTIER'S LIFE

It had long been traditional for several dozen sons of high-ranking Macedonians and Greeks to come and live in the royal court in Pella during their teenage years as Royal Pages, to serve as the king's attendants and guards, and to be the friends and, in some cases, the future Friends of the heir apparent, who was educated with them. It is likely that Alexander, the son of Craterus, served as a Royal Page, making his eventual defection even more of a blow. The boys were being trained for high office, but they were also hostages for the loyalty of their fathers and tokens of their fathers' recognition of the supremacy of the royal house. Antigonus formalized the system by age groups: Royal Pages might graduate to become Royal Huntsmen, and then one of the seven Bodyguards, but all the pages, whatever their official duties, were forever the future king's "foster-brothers," a title of high honor in court. They had a lifelong connection to the king, and felt themselves a cut above most other courtiers.

Among other qualities, a good courtier was expected to try to get on with his fellow courtiers. Nevertheless, all royal courts were hotbeds of rivalry, as men vied for the favor of the monarch and the enormous rewards that such favor could bring. It could be a precarious situation, as the historian Polybius recognized:

> The truism that a fleeting opportunity raises a man up or lays him low is nowhere more true than in the courts of kings. Courtiers are indeed just like the counters on an abacus, which according to the will of the person doing the calculating are worth now a fraction of an obol, and a moment later a talent. Just so, courtiers become objects of envy and then of pity at the whim of the king.

Gift-exchange was at the heart of the relationship between king and courtiers: the king massively enriched and entitled those he favored, but he expected something in return—loyalty, services, a poem, a new invention, an educational treatise, a more accurate calendrical system, an antidote to poison, a battle-ready regiment, a particularly beautiful ornament or piece of jewelry.

Kings had various ways of showing their favor and ranking their courtiers, not just by the titles they assigned them. Gift-giving was an easy method, because gifts could be greater or smaller than the recipient expected; or a man might be made to wait longer than he expected for an audience. Certain privileges were significant: riding alongside the king when he went hunting, the right to greet him with a kiss, the right to attend him when he first awoke in the morning. At symposia and banquets the king could demonstrate his partiality by the seating arrangements: who sat with whom, and how close to his personal table or couch. Along with the king's favor, the prestige of a man's family, his wealth, the value of his gifts to the king, and his achievements were the kinds of factors that determined his status in court.

Polybius has given us a famous account of the fall of a high-ranking courtier early in the reign of Philip V, who came to the Macedonian throne in 221. Apelles was (allegedly) involved in a number of plots and schemes to help those courtiers who were his friends and to eliminate his rivals. He had no idea that Philip had turned against him:

> Apelles was sure that at a face-to-face meeting with the king he would steer everything in his desired direction. . . . On arriving, he went straight to the king's quarters. He expected to be let in, as was customary, but one of the ushers, acting under orders, blocked his way, saying that the king was engaged. Apelles was taken aback. After spending quite a while stunned by this unexpected turn of events, he withdrew in utter confusion. All his followers immediately began to slip away, without making any attempt to disguise what they were doing, until by the time he entered his quarters he was left with only his slaves.

Before long, Apelles and his associates had committed suicide. No doubt Antigonus' court was occasionally disturbed by rivalry and ambition, but never enough to have rocked the boat too violently. Antigonus' court was a tight ship, founded on the gratitude of all Macedonians, whatever their rank, for his preservation of their country.

A DELICATE BALANCE

Two common Macedonian court practices, hunting and symposia, reveal the delicacy of the relationship between king and courtiers. On the one hand, anyone who joined the king in these activities had a traditional right to speak and act as an equal, but on the other hand he could not take that assumption too far. Famous stories about Alexander the Great illustrate the point. Anyone who threatened, during a hunt, to reach a quarry before him, or tried to help him, incurred his wrath, because they impugned his virility. The fine line between aiding a king and irritating him might depend on nothing more than his mood or whim. On one notorious occasion, Alexander killed one of his Friends, Cleitus, in the course of a drunken symposium, precisely for having spoken his mind too freely. Antigonus was neither as short-tempered nor as absolute a king as Alexander, but some of the same dynamic survived. A courtier's career could be made or broken during a hunt or symposium.

Heracles the Hunter was an important deity in Antigonid Macedon; the largest sanctuary in the town of Beroea, for instance, belonged to him, and the Royal Huntsmen took him as their personal god. Hunting always remained a central pastime of the Macedonian court, as of many other courts throughout history. It was a ritualized activity, quite different from the daily hunting of the poor for food. Above all, it was one of the main ways for the king to relax, but there were more serious undertones. In Antigonus' time, it was still the custom in Macedon to shame a man by denying him the right to recline on a couch if he had not yet hunted down and killed a boar by himself, without using a net. He was condemned to sit upright at banquets and symposia, while everyone else reclined. Consumptive Cassander was in his thirties before he passed this initiation test.

Hunting, along with warfare, was one of the main ways a man proved his virility, an issue that was important to everyone in the court, and skill in hunting was taken to be the peacetime equivalent of prowess at war. The riding skills and physical fitness it promoted were transferable to war, and the quarry in Macedon might well be a dangerous beast, such as a mountain lion or a wild boar. It was therefore an intense male-bonding experience, but it was also highly competitive, as the Friends pursued the king's favor along with the quarry, by displaying their courage and their skill before him.

Symposia tested courtiers in a different way, on the proverbial principle that "wine reveals a man's mind." Those present had to find a balance between speaking their minds and offending the king. Drunkenness was not uncommon at these symposia, especially since, unlike their southern Greek neighbors, high-ranking Macedonians probably drank their wine undiluted by water and in general used the occasion for a greater degree of self-indulgence. Symposia could therefore get violent, as Cleitus learned at the cost of his life. But that episode was atypical; symposia basically provided the king with good company, binding Friends to him and to one another.

Entertainment was provided by singers, dancers, actors, musicians, jugglers, conjurors, lecturers, and so on, but more importantly by some of the guests themselves. They might be called upon to recite some Homer, for instance, or a poem or philosophical tract, or perform an impromptu scene from a famous play, make up clever stories about famous people of the past, or trade wisecracks of their own composition; they might spontaneously be moved to get up and dance for a while. *Hetairai*—erudite, witty, sexy courtesans—also contributed to the sparkle of a successful symposium.

The object was always to please the king. Banquets were regularly laid on for foreign ambassadors, so they became venues for the display of regal power, from the furnishings and tableware to entertainment by world-famous actors and the generosity of the king's gifts to his guests. The valuable tableware from which they were eating was a typical gift—and the palace at Aegae had nine dining rooms with space for 178 couches, each of which would commonly be occupied by two people.

Since symposia were traditionally venues for frank and free speech, those that were limited to the king and his immediate Friends doubled as council meetings, where policy was debated and decisions taken. Even under these intimate circumstances, however, a courtier had to be careful when pushing his own agenda. A successful courtier's rewards could be very substantial, setting himself and his family up for generations, but it was a hazardous game to play.

MIRRORS FOR PRINCES

Before the Macedonian conquest, kings had not been a major presence in the Greek world within living memory; they hung on in some parts of northern Greece, notably Epirus and Macedon, and in outlying Cyprus, but in civilized central and southern Greece republican forms of government had predominated since the eighth century. Monarchy, on those rare occasions when it occurred, was considered an aberration—the Spartans being an aberration in this respect, as in others.

The conquest of Greece by Philip II, the takeover of the Persian empire by Alexander the Great, and the violence of the Successors sparked Greek interest in the phenomenon of kingship. Fourth-century thinkers paved the way with portraits of ideal rulers, but the earliest Hellenistic statement, dating from the time of the Successors, is based on observation of current reality, not on any ideal: "It is neither descent nor legitimacy which gives monarchies to men, but the ability to command an army and to handle affairs competently." And the unknown author—the fragment perhaps comes from the pen of a lost historian—goes on to cite the case of Philip III: the fact that he was the son of Philip II did not enable him to become king, because he did not have what it took.

According to the Successor ideology, kings made victory and victory made kings. Antigonus' accession to the throne on the strength of his victory over the Celts is just one example of many. But, as I have already said, this belligerent ideology, driven by the economics of endless conquest, was undermined by the agreement between Antigonus and Antiochus in 278. It was possible now for kings to be more than warlords—kings whose first priority was the security of their core territory, not expansion. They could no longer simply treat their subjects as sources of revenue to be spent on warfare to enhance their own glory; they had to demonstrate benevolent care as well, and not just by protecting their subjects from their enemies.

Antigonus and his contemporaries were second-generation kings. Inheritance could now take the place of conquest as the chief factor in succession. Although the army remained the source of a king's power, he needed other ways to demonstrate his superiority. Philosophers stepped up with their ideas, and historians sketched models of kings, good and bad, in their works. The first two theoretical Hellenistic treatises on kingship were written by no less than Aristotle in the court of Philip II, and were addressed to Alexander the Great.

By Antigonus' time, at least a dozen such treatises had been written, and at least two of them—those by Persaeus of Citium and Cleanthes of Assos—were addressed to him. Possibly the one by Euphantus of Olynthus was as well; it was addressed to an Antigonus, but we cannot be certain that this is our Antigonus. The importance of these treatises lay in the fact that although they were addressed to kings, they were not commissioned by them. When Demetrius of Phalerum, after his expulsion from Athens, was living in Alexandria, he advised Ptolemy I to read such treatises "because the advice that their Friends shrink from offering kings is contained in them." They were considered mirrors, in which the king could assess his performance.

None of these treatises survive, but we can infer something of their contents from other sources. They seem to have been rather generalized productions. The philosophers who wrote them came from various schools, but they focused on the same topics, especially the virtues and qualities that a good king should possess to justify his monarchy and, as the representative on earth of the gods, to bring order and harmony to the world. Above all, the good king was educated in the Greek manner, so that he could control his passions (because if a man cannot rule himself he cannot rule others), see what is best for his subjects and put it into effect, and justify his choices. This was important because, in a vigorous debate about the relation of the king to law, it was generally agreed that he was above the law. Hence, Alexander the Great's tame philosopher, Anaxarchus of Abdera, exonerated Alexander from the killing of Cleitus on the grounds that whatever a king does is just.

But if whatever a king did was right, he had to be constrained by a moral code. The chief virtues that a king was urged to acquire were justice, courage, moderation, piety, and benevolence, and these were the qualities that sculptors and artists also tried to express in their representations of kings. It was one of the jobs of a king's Friends to urge him to virtue. Benevolence was stressed above all: *philanthrōpia*, literally "love for humankind," was made specific as the care the king showed, especially in material terms, for his dependents. For this, it was accepted that a king had to be very rich. The king was to be the shepherd of his people, ruling not for his own benefit or that of his clique (which would be tyranny), but for their good.

The constraints that virtue placed on the king, above all the requirement that he care for his subjects, made kingship, in Antigonus' famous words, "a glorious state of slavery." His father, Demetrius, was notorious for having neglected his subjects in favor of foreign conquest, and Antigonus did not intend to repeat the mistake. This is not to say that he did not find the job arduous; on another occasion he is reported to have said that if people knew the trouble it brought, they would treat the royal diadem as no more than a rag, and would not bother to pick it up if they found it lying in a pile of rubbish. But we cannot be sure that we are actually hearing Antigonus' voice here, since a very similar story is also told of Seleucus.

ANTIGONUS THE GOD

I have already explained that, strange though it may seem to our modern minds, it was possible in Greek religion for a living human being to be identified as a god. From the time of Alexander the Great onward, the most common recipients of this form of worship were kings, because they had power that seemed more than human. When Ptolemy I saved Rhodes, or Demetrius Poliorcetes Athens, they achieved something remarkable, even miraculous, and in so doing they proved that they were embodied Savior gods. Deliverance and protection were two of the marks of divinity.

The deification of living rulers, then, was in origin a spontaneous emotional reaction to a lifesaving or otherwise astonishing event. Hence it was not just cities that instituted cults, but certain small-scale statuettes suggest that there was private worship as well. It was a way for the Greeks to accommodate the new phenomenon of mighty kings into their worldview and to express their devotion. Even if the kings did not themselves demand such worship, they did of course recognize its advantages.

Antigonus too counted as a Savior god. An altar has been found in the Strymon valley, in eastern Macedon, inscribed as the altar "of Zeus and Antigonus, King and Savior." It has generally been held that the "Antigonus" here is the later king, Antigonus III Doson, but that is because it was thought that Antigonus Gonatas refused to be deified. Since there is now sufficient other evidence for his cult, we can tentatively add this altar as well. Philip II was an exception, for understandable reasons, but otherwise Macedonians did not normally institute cult of their rulers (though, after Antigonus, Philip V was occasionally deified), but that was because they did not usually need saving; it was the Greek states that were "liberated" by Macedonian kings, as Athens was by Demetrius Poliorcetes, and which therefore instituted their worship as gods. It is noticeable, therefore, that all the inscriptions referring to Antigonus or Philip V as gods come from outlying areas of Macedon (especially Amphipolis), rather than the original Macedonian heartland; in these outlying areas, Greek traditions might occasionally supersede Macedonian ones. But it does seem possible that Antigonus was recognized as divine by at least some of his Macedonian subjects.

He was also worshipped as a god farther south. A decree from Rhamnous reveals that he received sacrifices not just there, but in Athens itself:

> Since King Antigonus, the Savior of the People, continues to be a benefactor of the Athenian People and because of this the People honored him with godlike honors, for good fortune the Rhamnousians have decided to sacrifice to him on the nineteenth of Hecatombaeum, at the gymnastic competition of the Great Nemesia, and to wear crowns, and the market tax shall provide the means for the demesmen to make this sacrifice; the demarch and whoever is appointed treasurer shall see to the sacrifice, and shall inscribe this decree on a stone stele and stand it [by the altar?] of King Antigonus.

This shows that at some time in the past the Athenians had instituted the worship of Antigonus—probably after the Chremonidean War—and that later the Rhamnousians decided to turn the most important festival of their calendar, sacred to Nemesis (a personification of law and order), into a joint festival with Antigonus. The nineteenth of Hecatombaeum (our July, roughly) was perhaps therefore Antigonus' birthday, which was the usual occasion for such a celebration. This step might well have been taken shortly after the war against Alexander of Corinth, when, as we have seen, the Rhamnousians suffered badly. Another preserved decree commemorates the revival of this Rhamnousian cult of Antigonus in the 230s after it had been interrupted by warfare; the proposer, Elpinicus, was the same man who had instigated the cult in the first place. The cult probably did not outlast the 220s, by when Athens was free of Macedonian control.

Antigonus was undoubtedly worshipped elsewhere in Greece as well. We have already seen that the Confederacy of Islanders instituted the joint worship of him and his son Demetrius, and there was another Antigoneia festival in the Euboean town of Oreus/Histiaea. An inscription from the Cycladic island of Ios refers to a King Antigonus and his cult on the island as Savior; this is probably our Antigonus, and the Antigonus who received cult on the island of Cos might also be Gonatas. It is likely that he was worshipped, along with his father, as a "founder" of Iolcus, near Demetrias. He allowed himself to be assimilated to the god Pan on his coins, since the god bears his features, and by his court poet Aratus of Soli in his *Hymn to Pan*. It is safe to think that the recognition of Antigonus' divinity was quite widespread in the Aegean.

Some of this evidence is new, based on inscriptions discovered in the 1990s, and until recently the rest of it was commonly ignored or explained away. The reason was that there exists an anecdote, which was attributed to Antigonus, that seems to pour scorn on the idea of his divinity, and so Antigonus was celebrated as a rationalist, not given to such superstition. The anecdote is delightful: "When a certain Hermodotus proclaimed him to be 'the son of the Sun and a god,' the response from the elder Antigonus was: 'The slave who deals with my chamber pot knows better.'"

Plutarch tells the story on two separate occasions, and both times he attributes it not to our Antigonus, but to his grandfather, Antigonus Monophthalmus, the "elder" Antigonus. We know nothing more about Hermodotus, so we cannot use his dates to decide which Antigonus is meant. It is true that "son of the Sun" fits Gonatas well, since his father, Demetrius Poliorcetes, was famously splendid, and was explicitly likened to the sun in a hymn composed in Athens. But comparing a king to the sun was a commonplace in the Hellenistic period. Hermodotus was merely paying Antigonus an outrageous compliment. Since we now know that Antigonus Gonatas was worshipped as a god, in both Greece and Macedon, we must accept Plutarch's word: it was not Gonatas who denied his divinity, but Monophthalmus.

PATRONAGE IN THE ROYAL COURTS

Kings were expected not just to be rich, but to put their wealth to use. There is a passage in Theocritus' *Encomium of Ptolemy Philadelphus* that illuminates the point:

> Gold is not piled up pointlessly in his rich palace, like the wealth of ants that toil without pause: much do the glorious houses of the gods receive, as Ptolemy ever offers first fruits and other gifts of honor; much too he bestows upon powerful kings, much upon cities, and much upon his brave companions. Nor does any man, skilled in raising aloud tuneful song, enter the sacred contests of Dionysus without receiving a gift worthy of his art. The intermediaries of the Muses sing of Ptolemy in return for his benefactions.

Theocritus here outlines five areas in which kings were expected to be bountiful: gifts to and dedications in the gods' sanctuaries; gift-exchange with other kings; gifts to cities; gifts to his Friends; and the patronage of poets, such as Theocritus himself. One way or another, we have already covered the first four, in Antigonus' case. Now we will consider the fifth, his patronage of deserving artists and intellectuals. Such patronage had a long lineage in Macedon, dating back at least to the time of the king Archelaus, who reigned from 413 until 399; before him, in the seventh and sixth centuries, the Greek tyrants in cities such as Athens and Corinth had patronized artists and poets. It was a monarchical tradition.

All over the Hellenistic world, royal patronage fueled developments in astronomy, mathematics, geography, medicine, technology, engineering, and literature. Almost all the important work in these areas was carried out at the courts of kings. Euclid was a protégé of Ptolemy I of Egypt; Archimedes worked in the Syracusan court. Philosophers sometimes stayed away, expressing horror at the opulence of court life, but for the rest patronage was both necessary and an honor, a sign that a man or woman had won or deserved international renown. Artists and writers (like poets laureate today) were expected to pay for their privileged lifestyles with the occasional work or passage of fulsome praise of the king—such as the poem just cited by Theocritus. These poems were signs of inventiveness as well as obsequiousness; poets were not obliged to write such things, but wanted to, because it was a way of gaining the attention of the king and further distinction.

By stimulating competition among literary and scientific courtiers or would-be courtiers, royal courts were the drivers of innovation and originality, but the court context could also be restrictive. The greatest inventor of the third century, Ctesibius of Alexandria, made an astonishing breakthrough. In a world that was powered by human and animal muscles (and by wind, but only for water-going vessels), he found a way to get compressed air to move objects. However, the discovery was used to create a water organ (the first keyboard musical instrument) for the king's entertainment, and while some of the principles employed in the organ, such as the use of pistons, found practical application elsewhere—especially in the force pump—no one seems to have found more practical uses for compressed air for many centuries. It was enough that it had pleased the king.

Since it was clear that progress depended in large part on the patronage of kings, an ambitious intellectual had to win that patronage, and the way he did so was to win the court over to his side. The courtiers were the peers who reviewed a scientist's or writer's ideas. But the court consisted largely of people who, although well educated (by ancient standards), had little or no interest in pure science or literature, so candidates had to find ways to gain their attention. Entertainment was prominent, but scientists also had to stress the practical applications of their theories, by coming up with technological advances. Ctesibius' force pump is a case in point, the first uses of which were in firefighting and misting theater audiences with perfumed spray. Or again, when Eratosthenes of Cyrene, later in the century, addressed the theoretical problem of the doubling of the cube, he stressed that his solution would help create larger siege catapults, among other practical applications. Catapults were more likely to get the king's attention than abstract theories.

THE LUMINARIES OF ANTIGONUS' COURT

Antigonus had of course always had a court. Even in his wilderness years he had been accompanied by family, friends, advisers, and senior military men; that was one reason why he was able to continue to call himself king, even though at the time he was a king without a country. By the time he came into his kingdom in 276, he had already drawn the poet Aratus of Soli to his court, and it was probably then that Persaeus arrived as well. Persaeus was the adopted son of Zeno of Citium, the founder of the new school of Stoicism, which was attracting many of the brightest stars in the philosophical firmament at the time. Antigonus invited Zeno himself to come to his court; fanciful letters exist, later forgeries, purporting to be those that passed between the two men on this occasion. At least in part, Antigonus was trying to find an eminent tutor for Halcyoneus and any future sons, but as a gracious way of refusing, Zeno sent Persaeus in his stead, along with another of his students, Philonides of Thebes.

Antigonus became close friends with Persaeus, but at first he might have been disappointed. The more famous the intellectuals a king was able to attract to his court, the greater his prestige, and Persaeus, though erudite and clever, was not Zeno. But arguably Zeno was right to refuse: court life was hardly compatible with the sobriety and self-discipline that Stoicism demanded of its students. Persaeus himself seems to have acknowledged this difficulty in his writings, and he was criticized for having chosen the court rather than philosophy. Besides, as Zeno's thought developed, he may have decided that his ideas were more compatible with democracy than monarchy.

Persaeus authored a number of works, none of which sounds much like profound philosophy (except perhaps his critique of Plato's main work of political philosophy, the *Laws*): the treatise on kingship that I have already mentioned, a book on the constitution of Sparta (his fellow Stoic, Sphaerus of Borysthenes, helped Cleomenes III revamp the Spartan *agōgē*), a treatise *On the Gods* (in which he registered his agreement with earlier thinkers who had claimed that the gods were originally human benefactors of mankind), and a few others. But his most famous work, very suitable for Antigonus' court, was a series of dialogues called *Symposium Memoirs*. Whereas his models, Plato and Xenophon, had depicted Socrates at symposia, Persaeus' protagonist was Zeno, who was portrayed as sternly sober amid the drunkenness, as a critic of the misbehavior of his fellow symposiasts, and as able to resist the temptations even of topless dancing girls.

There were other philosophers at Antigonus' court. Epicureans, naturally, stayed away, since they had imbibed loathing for all things Macedonian from the founder of their school. Philonides of Thebes, the other student of Zeno's who arrived with Persaeus, we know nothing about. Menedemus of Eretria, whom we have already met, was banished from his hometown in the late 270s and ended up in Pella, in Antigonus' court, where he died a few years later.

One of the most interesting characters was Bion of Borysthenes. He does not seem to have been a permanent resident of the court, nor should we expect him to have been, since, as a Cynic, he was supposed to reject all social conventions and prick the bubbles of all pretensions. In fact, he had once accused Antigonus of rank cowardice in response to Pyrrhus' invasion of Macedon in 274 and 273. He was best known as an author for his moral diatribes inveighing against conventions such as religion and marriage. "It is ridiculous to take money seriously," he said (for instance), "since it comes by chance, enslaves anyone who wants to hold on to it, and is lost by decent behavior."

A rare surviving fragment of Bion's writings seems to be addressed to Antigonus. He is illustrating the topic, common in Greek thought, that we must each accept the part Fortune has allotted us:

> Sometimes she gives a man a lead role, sometimes a lesser role; sometimes she casts a man as a king, sometimes as a beggar. If you have a minor role, you should not want the lead role; that would be incongruous. You make a good ruler, I make a good subject; you are the guardian of many men, I of just one man, myself. You are rich and give generously, and I am glad to be the recipient of your generosity, without fawning or degrading myself or blaming fate.

Antigonus was fond of Bion; he sent him nurses when he was ill, and once gave him the enormous sum of a silver talent.

Bion was humbly born, his father a fish-seller and his mother a prostitute, and apparently Persaeus and Philonides used to needle him for it. We glimpse a rivalrous undercurrent in the court (insofar as Bion was a temporary courtier). Bion responded by saying that the legend on Persaeus' statue should not read "Persaeus of Citium, son of Zeno," but (it involves only a slight change in the Greek) "Persaeus, slave of Zeno." This seems to be a fairly good-natured exchange, more of a tease than anything else, but there was bad blood between Persaeus and Menedemus. After Menedemus' banishment from Eretria, Antigonus was tempted to use force or his influence to bring about a regime change in the city and the restoration of his friend, but Persaeus persuaded him not to. Later, at a symposium, Menedemus outargued Persaeus on a point of philosophy, and then said: "He may be a philosopher, but as a man there's no one more objectionable in the world, nor will there ever be." Such rancor was not untypical of Macedonian royal symposia; Alexander the Great seems to have deliberately pitted the philosophers of his court against one another.

Other philosophers were supported by Antigonus, though they do not seem to have been regular members of the court: the Stoic Cleanthes of Assos, and the Aristotelians Hieronymus of Rhodes and Lycon of Troas, whose eloquence Antigonus admired. But

Antigonus' court supported many luminaries apart from philosophers, particularly men of letters. The only other prose writer we know of was the important historian Hieronymus of Cardia, who, like Persaeus, was a man of action as well as an intellectual: he served, for instance, as the Antigonid governor of Thebes in the late 290s. But he had retired from active service by the time of Antigonus' reign, and spent his time in the court writing up his history. Pausanias says that Hieronymus "was biased against all the kings except Antigonus, to whom he was unfairly partial"—but that was only to be expected from a courtier.

For poetry, there was Antagoras of Rhodes, who wrote in many genres, but whose most famous work was an epic, *Thebais*. He was also the interlocutor in a fine bantering exchange with Antigonus. The king one day found him preparing conger eels for the kitchen (a very time-consuming business) and teased him by asking whether Homer would have got around to writing the *Iliad* if he had spent all his time cooking congers; Antagoras replied that Agamemnon (the leader of the Greeks in Homer's poem, and so equivalent to Antigonus) would never have performed all *his* glorious deeds if had spent his time nosing around to see who was cooking congers.

The tragedian and poet Alexander of Pleuron, the only known Aetolian poet, joined the court in the 270s, enticed away from Ptolemaic Alexandria—a major coup for Antigonus, since Alexander was considered one of the best poets of the era. Lycophron of Chalcis, another of the "Pleiad"—the seven greatest Alexandrian poets of the third century—perhaps also spent some time in Pella; at any rate, one of his many plays, *Cassandreis*, was set in Macedon and dramatized the founding of Cassandrea. Posidippus of Pella, a wonderful poet who specialized in epigrams, would surely, as a native Macedonian, have been supported by Antigonus. Another epigrammatist, Leonidas of Tarentum, spent his life moving from court to court, including some time spent in Pella.

One-eyed Timon of Phleious spent some time there as well, as he traveled the Greek world from city to city and toured the royal courts. He was famous especially for his "cinaedic" poems on sexual or scatological subjects, to be sung or recited as entertainment at symposia. The genre had been invented by Sotades of Maronea, and since Alexander of Pleuron also wrote such verse, it was clearly popular at Antigonus' symposia. The point was to push the boundaries of good taste, and it was possible to go too far: I have already mentioned how Sotades was first imprisoned and then killed for his obscene criticism of Ptolemy II's incestuous marriage to Arsinoe. Timon even attacked Antigonus' favorites, describing Menedemus, for instance, as "a puffed-up, supercilious producer of bombastic fluff."

But the most famous of Antigonus' literary protégés was undoubtedly Aratus of Soli. Aratus' best-loved work, the *Phaenomena*, was not only composed in Antigonus' court, but might have been undertaken at Antigonus' suggestion. It is largely a versification of the groundbreaking work of the astronomer Eudoxus of Cnidus about a century earlier. The first part of the poem is a description of all the major astronomical phenomena and their usefulness for navigation and so on; the second part covers the forecasting of weather from meteorological and other signs. It was a didactic poem, then, and from one point of view that was its contemporary importance. If the Alexandrian Museum of the Ptolemies could lay claim through their scholarship to Homer, the primary guide to Greek popular thinking, Antigonus could claim to be resurrecting the kind of poetry that Hesiod of Boeotia wrote, and he, more or less contemporary with Homer, was considered to have made as great a contribution to Greek culture as Homer had.

The somewhat dry subject matter of the poem was enlivened by references to mythology and by vivid descriptions, and it became the most widely read poem in the ancient world after Homer's *Iliad* and *Odyssey*. It was translated into Latin by eminent Romans, used as a school text, and read and studied for centuries, until the Middle Ages. It was even quoted in the biblical Acts of the Apostles. Aratus' universe was guided, in a Stoic fashion, by a providential Zeus, and we are undoubtedly meant to think that Antigonus acts as Zeus for his subjects. However, Aratus was also enticed to spend some time in the Seleucid court, before returning in his old age to Pella, where he died around 245.

THIRD-CENTURY CULTURE IN ANTIGONUS' COURT

Clearly, Antigonus' court was making a major contribution to third-century culture. He seems to have indulged his predilections for philosophy and literature, where the Ptolemies, the main driving force of Hellenistic culture, focused on literature, mathematics, science (especially medicine), and scholarship (especially philology), while largely eschewing philosophy. A library is of course the sine qua non for research, and Antigonus founded one in Pella. We know of it chiefly because its later theft by the Romans was remembered. It was certainly a fine library, but in this competition Pella, along with all other centers of culture, was dwarfed by Alexandria.

Our knowledge of the work of all the intellectuals who graced Antigonus' court is severely limited. Only Aratus' *Phaenomena* survives, and a number of Posidippus' epigrams. The rest of their work exists at best in fragments, and otherwise we know only the titles of the books they wrote. Third-century developments in tragedy are more or less lost to us. Comedy we have to assume continued on the path laid down in the last quarter of the fourth century by Menander of Athens and his fellow poets of the so-called New Comedy, who were writing light, soap-operatic plays, with less of the political and social engagement of their predecessors. Epics were being written, but we have only the famous *Argonautica* of Apollonius of Rhodes, the second head of the Alexandrian library. Nevertheless, we can go some way toward putting flesh on the bones.

Poets aimed both high and low—from the elevation of a profound hymn to one of the gods, such as Aratus' *Hymn to Pan*, to the scatological vulgarity of Timon. Notoriously, some of the language and allusions of the more serious varieties of third-century poetry were incredibly opaque. This was deliberate; the poets were not just trying to show off their erudition, but to get the learned courtiers who formed their audience in a symposium to show off *theirs* too, in a competition to decode the allusions. The obscurity of some of these poems also reflects the fact that whereas in the past literature was written to be read aloud, in a performance people now read to themselves as well, so they had time to analyze what they were reading. It was a time of transition for literature as well: a "song culture" was giving way to a "book culture," and there began to be a flourishing book trade.

The epigram, previously used almost entirely for commemorative purposes (on tombstones and votive offerings, especially—the word *epigramma* originally meant just "inscription"), became a popular verse form, with its often poignant focus on ordinary folk and their feelings, as in this one from Posidippus:

> All Nicomache's favorite things, her trinkets and her Sapphic
> conversations with other girls beside the shuttle at dawn,
> Fate took away prematurely. The city of the Argives
> cried aloud in lament for that poor maiden,
> a young shoot reared in Hera's arms. Cold, alas, remain
> the beds of the youths who courted her.

Painters and sculptors too were aiming for a similar kind of everyday realism. They were still sometimes presenting their subjects as civic types—the stern leader, the warrior-king, the modest woman—but in increasing numbers they were also creating portraits of ordinary people doing ordinary things, aiming to arouse a similar range of emotions to that of the epigrammatists.

In prose, there were plenty of histories being written. All are lost, but there was a common characteristic of all Greek history-writing over the centuries, and we can safely say that third-century historians plowed the same furrow. They all felt that their purpose was not just to preserve knowledge of the past for its own sake, but also to spin that information into moral examples for future statesmen and generals to imitate or avoid. Scholars nowadays tend to think that Hieronymus of Cardia, the only historian we know of in Antigonus' court, avoided this "fault" and was a more "modern" historian, but in fact it is likely that he followed his predecessors in this respect. He seems to have stressed the fickleness of Fortune, the good that follows when leaders are benevolent, and the evil consequences of cruelty.

But Antigonus' courtiers were taking part in what was, in a sense, the last gasp of Greek literature: by the end of the century, more nonscientific literature of quality was being written in Rome and Italy than in the Greek courts. Philosophy remained a Greek domain for longer, but it too was in transition in the third century. Antigonus' support of philosophers suggests that he recognized the importance of the revolution that was taking place.

All four of the major new schools—Stoicism, Epicureanism, Cynicism, and Skepticism—climbed down from the abstract realms of Platonic metaphysics and Aristotelian polymathy, which had dominated the fourth century, and learned also to appeal to a wider audience with promises of self-improvement. That is why we can still apply the names of the Hellenistic schools to ordinary people; even though the meanings of the words have altered over the centuries, we still say that people are stoical, epicurean, cynical, or skeptical, but not usually that they are Platonist or Aristotelian.

All the schools, then, set out to demonstrate how individual human beings should live, and provided methods and theoretical contexts for achieving this goal. They all saw philosophy as the remedy for human ills, but differed in what they saw as the fundamental problems and in how to go about attaining peace of mind and fulfilling one's potential as a human being. The three main branches into which philosophy was divided by the schools were logic (understood as the way or ways of discovering the truth of any matter), physics (the nature of the world and the laws that govern it), and ethics (how to achieve happiness).

So philosophy in the third century went in two incompatible directions. High philosophy, as we may call it, was the impersonal presentation of often very subtle ideas and arguments; some of the work of the Stoics, for instance, on logic and epistemology is as challenging as philosophical work of any era. Zeno, and probably Persaeus (in his commentary on Plato's *Laws*), proposed extremely radical and idealistic changes to society. Low philosophy, on the other hand, was the attempt to make philosophy accessible to the common man and woman, and to guide them toward peace of mind in troubled times. Hence philosophers presented a public image that stressed poverty, or at least frugality, as a way of advertising the success of their teaching: they themselves had moved beyond the superficial values of the world, and could teach others to do so as well. Something like this undoubtedly lay behind Zeno's refusal to join Antigonus' court. The royal courts were recognized simultaneously as the mainsprings of cultural development and as places where the souls of courtiers were in danger of corruption.

CHAPTER 10

A Glimpse of the Future

Antigonus died in 239 of natural causes, aged eighty. His tomb, undoubtedly magnificent, awaits discovery. Phila, being much younger, probably outlived him, but we hear no more of her. His son and co-king succeeded him as Demetrius II. Soon after he had come to the throne, the simmering hostility between the Aetolians and the Epirotes flared into warfare, and Demetrius was dragged into it by his alliance with the Epirotes, based on his marriage to Phthia, the daughter of Alexander II. Almost fifty years of uneasy peace between Macedon and Aetolia, carefully fostered by Antigonus, came to an end.

The Aetolians could not hope to resist the combined forces of both Epirus and Macedon. They needed help—and, surprisingly, they were approached by Aratus and formed an alliance with the Achaeans, who simultaneously abandoned their alliance with the Spartans. No doubt both the Aetolians and the Achaeans saw how Antigonus had manipulated them, setting them against each other in the Peloponnese to distract them from their primary purpose: opposition to Macedon.

The Achaean-Aetolian alliance was extremely powerful, with great potential for the future of the Greeks. Almost all of central and southern Greece was united, albeit only for military purposes, for the first time ever. With the help of this alliance, the Greeks could hope to put an end to the hegemony of Macedon and recover their freedom. Not surprisingly, both confederacies were aided financially by Ptolemy III.

THE WAR OF DEMETRIUS

Fighting began in 238 or 237. We know hardly anything about the war; it fizzled out in the late 230s when republican Epirotes assassinated the last members of the Aeacid royal family, and Epirus withdrew. During the war, the Achaean Confederacy expanded into Arcadia, where all the major towns, including Megalopolis (which had for so long been a Macedonian ally), were pressured into joining. They could read the writing on the wall. Lydiadas, the outgoing tyrant of Megalopolis, even became the Achaean General in 234, the year following his abdication, and then on several other occasions.

The Achaeans also continued their attempts to force Argos and Athens into the confederacy, and they caused the Athenians considerable distress, chiefly by destroying crops. Typically, Aratus kept up his assaults even though no war had been declared; unexpected attacks were always his preferred modus operandi. Demetrius sent troops south to help these two cities, the last two Macedonian friends in southern Greece. But in 236 he gained new subjects, when—a great coup—he detached the Boeotian Confederacy from the Aetolians. There was still a powerful pro-Aetolian faction in Boeotia, however, and he could hardly regard it as a secure possession.

When Epirus descended into chaos after the elimination of the royal family, Ambracia, the city that had served as the royal capital, and the district of Amphilochia, split off and joined the Aetolian Confederacy. These are the places that had been annexed by Pyrrhus some sixty-five years previously; they had clearly retained a sense that they did not really belong to Epirus. At the same time, the Aetolians renewed their attempt to take over as much of Acarnania as remained part of the Epirote empire. They started by putting the town of Medion under siege. Demetrius was unable to respond, having recently been defeated, with great loss of life, by the resurgent Dardanians. Instead of sending help himself, he paid King Agron of the Ardiaei, currently the most powerful tribe in Illyris, to relieve the siege.

The Illyrians succeeded against the Aetolians, and next seized the town of Phoenice, the Epirotes' main town since the defection of Ambracia. The Epirotes abandoned Demetrius and turned for help first to the Aetolian-Achaean alliance, and then, when this Greek alliance was defeated by the Illyrians at sea off the Ionian islands of Paxoi in 229, the desperate Epirotes allied themselves with the Illyrians instead, in order to recover Phoenice. For a while, all northern Greece had been united, but now Macedon was isolated again.

RECOVERY UNDER ANTIGONUS DOSON

In 229 Demetrius died fighting the Dardanians and was succeeded by Antigonus III Doson, the son of Demetrius the Fair. Demetrius had a son, the future Philip V, but he was only eight or nine years old, so Doson, his closest relative, was at first regent, but soon became king on the understanding that young Philip was his heir. To confirm the arrangement, he married Chryseis, Philip's mother, who had been Demetrius' mistress. Macedonian authority in Greece was virtually nonexistent. Even some of the Thessalians had turned to Aetolia, and many other towns no longer saw the point in being aligned with a state from which they could expect little support. Aristomachus of Argos stepped down from his tyranny and brought the city into the Achaean Confederacy, and the tyrants of Hermion and Phleious followed suit.

Meanwhile, the Athenians raised 150 talents (twenty of them a personal gift from Aratus), which Diogenes, the commander of the Macedonian garrisons in Attica, used to pay off his mercenaries. Macedonian garrisons now remained only in Euboea; Chalcis was the last of the Fetters of Greece in Doson's hands. For the first time in many decades Athens was genuinely free, and it would never again have to endure Macedonian control. Despite Aratus' pointed generosity and his personal attempts to persuade Diogenes to give up, the Athenians did not join the Achaean Confederacy. They managed to remain neutral for the next three decades, enjoying the greatest degree of independence the city experienced in the entire Hellenistic period.

But the Athenians' belief that membership of a federal state curtailed an individual city's autonomy arguably mistook federalism for imperialism. The era of the independent city-state had passed. Before very long, in 192, Sparta was brought into the Achaean Confederacy for the first time (it came and went over subsequent decades), leaving Athens as the only major city-state on the Greek mainland that was not a member of a federal state. But if Athens was something of a throwback to the past, that suited its role as a university town and a museum of art and architecture.

With the Athenian rebellion on top of everything else, it looked as though Macedonian hegemony in Greece was at an end, though Doson had quickly recovered Thessaly. But Fortune was so dominant a force in the third century that, as the historian Diodorus of Sicily said, "what is strange is not that unexpected things happen, but that not everything that happens is unexpected." Cleomenes III's reformation of Spartan society was successful, and one of the consequences was that he soon had a powerful and enthusiastic citizen army, trained and equipped in the Macedonian manner. Within a very few years, he had annexed most of the central and northeastern Peloponnese, including Arcadia, Corinth, and Argos.

Half of the Peloponnese was in Spartan hands, and the Achaean Confederacy was facing extinction. Lydiadas of Megalopolis, one of the state's most popular and successful generals, had died in battle. Ptolemy III transferred his financial support from the Achaeans to Cleomenes. The Achaeans asked for help from their allies, the Aetolians, but the Aetolians were still suffering from the aftereffects of a resounding defeat Doson had inflicted on them in Thessaly. The consequences of this refusal by the Aetolians were momentous. In desperation, at Aratus' urging (though he was first pushed in that direction by the Megalopolitans), the Achaeans performed a sensational about-face and approached the Macedonian king for an alliance.

There were several things Doson could have done. He could have sat on the sidelines and watched the Spartans destroy his enemies, the Achaeans. He could even have allied himself with the Spartans against the Achaeans. But he agreed to help the Achaeans; he saw it as a way to curtail both them and the Spartans at once. The price he demanded was therefore steep: the Achaeans were to give up their claim to Corinth, which would once again be garrisoned by Macedonian troops and governed by friends of Macedon. They were also to recognize Doson as the leader of the Greeks, send hostages to Macedon, cede Megara to the Boeotians, and pay the costs of the war. In 224 Doson marched south and faced Cleomenes. He was unable to break through Cleomenes' well-prepared defenses at the Corinthian isthmus, but the Spartan king was forced to fall back to Argos by a threat to his garrison there, and Doson was able to drive him back from Argos to Sparta.

Doson was anxious to secure his revived authority in Greece. Where Gonatas had employed a policy of repression, Doson preferred gentler treatment of his subjects. To secure his position in Greece and give it a permanent structure, in the autumn of 224 he formed his Greek allies into a Common Alliance, a renewed League of Corinth with himself as president. It was a sign of the times that not one of the original members was a city-state, but all were confederacies: Achaeans, Thessalians, Epirotes, Acarnanians, Boeotians, and Phocians (Phocis, or its eastern half, had somehow detached itself from the Aetolian Confederacy). Relations with the Aetolians being poor, they were excluded; even if in the short term the target of the alliance was Cleomenes, it looked as though it would soon be the Aetolians. And indeed the alliance between the Aetolians and Achaeans came to an end a few years later, due in part to the Achaean rapprochement with Doson. At a stroke, Doson had brought Macedonian influence in Greece back to the level of the 250s, when Antigonus Gonatas' fortunes were at their zenith.

Despite the fact that Doson had recovered much of Arcadia, Cleomenes continued to fight well, though with his back increasingly against the wall, and in 222 he was decisively defeated near the village of Sellasia, not far north of Sparta. He fled to Egypt, where he died three years later. For the first time in its history, Sparta fell to an invading army. Doson installed a governor, and at least some of Cleomenes' reforms were canceled. Under the protection of Macedon, the landed rich of Sparta resumed their former practices, starting with taking over the property of those who had fallen at Sellasia, so that a few years later the leader of a failed attempt on the throne was again offering the program of debt cancellation and land redistribution, and attempts to reform Spartan society continued for several more decades.

In gratitude for their recovery, the Achaeans showered Doson with honors. But he had to hurry back north to deal with an Illyrian raid into Macedon. He succeeded in repelling the Illyrians, but he was consumptive, and the strain of battle brought on his death in the autumn of 221. The accession to the throne of sixteen-year-old Philip V was uncontested; he would prove to be one of the greatest Macedonian kings, in extremely difficult times.

THE COMING OF ROME

Philip V was an aggressive king. Building on Doson's successes, he intended not only to recover full Macedonian hegemony in Greece, but to expand the Macedonian empire abroad as well. It is quite likely that he would have succeeded, but circumstances conspired to thwart him, because by the time he came to the Macedonian throne, the Romans were beginning to show interest in Greece. And the Romans were only ever interested in places if they could control them and exploit them economically.

In the northwest of Greece, precisely where it is closest to Italy, Illyrian power was growing. The Romans became concerned about the threat to their and their allies' shipping. The Illyrian queen, Teuta (Agron's successor), snubbed the Roman ambassadors who came to her court to convince her to check her pirates, and at least one of them was killed by an Illyrian mob. The Romans went to war. They defeated the Illyrians twice, in 229 and again in 219, and as a result felt that the Greek states on the Illyrian coast were now under their protection.

But this attitude was an affront to Macedon, where the kings had long considered themselves the protectors of the Greeks, and Philip responded by provoking the Romans. First, he entered into an alliance in 215 with Hannibal, the archenemy of Rome who was then bidding fair to defeat the Romans in the Second Punic War in Italy; then he extended Macedonian sway to the Illyrian coast for the first time, replacing Roman influence there with his own. The Romans declared war but left most of the fighting to their allies, the Aetolians, so that they could concentrate on Hannibal in Italy. The Aetolians had been on the losing side—though their defeat had been far from conclusive—in the so-called Social War of 220–217, for which their opponents had been the Macedonian-Greek Common Alliance, so they had no reason not to side with the Romans, and hoped that with Roman help they could gain supreme power in Greece.

The war, known (from the Roman perspective) as the First Macedonian War, ended indecisively in 205, leaving plenty of unfinished business. Philip continued to expand his empire, but now a new factor entered the equation. Knowing Roman interest in Greece and hostility toward Macedon, Greek states from both the mainland and Asia Minor began to turn to Rome to voice their complaints against Macedon and ask for help. In the Second Macedonian War (200–197), the Romans reduced Macedon to its original borders and freed the Greeks forever from Macedonian dominion.

Within these constraints, Philip, and after his death in 179 his son Perseus, still tried to build up Macedon's strength as much as they could, but by then the Romans had expanded their influence into Asia Minor as well, and the Macedonians were effectively isolated. Greek concerns about Macedonian intentions continued to reach the ears of the Senate in Rome, and at the battle of Pydna in 168, Perseus was finally defeated. The kingship was abolished, and Macedon was divided into four small republics under Roman dominion—an easy move because the four republics were not much different from the four districts that Antigonus Gonatas had created. It was the end of both the dynasty he had perpetuated against the odds and the country he had so carefully nurtured.

ANTIGONUS' LEGACY

Antigonus' legacy to the Macedonian kings who followed him was mixed, containing possibilities for both success and failure. His greatest achievement was the reunification and consolidation of Macedon, which made it possible for his dynasty to continue unimpeded, and created a firm foundation for Philip V's attempts to expand farther. His personal conduct, along with the reforms he put in place in Macedon, restored the prestige of the kingship after the neglectful excesses of his father, Ptolemy Ceraunus, and Pyrrhus. After driving out the pretenders who had occupied various cantons of Macedon, he reunited the country, and his recovery of lost territory enabled him to restore its borders to those of the kingdom under Philip II. Moreover, he also managed, at any rate up until the end of his reign (I have suggested), to keep the country safe from further invasions by the tribes of the Central Balkans.

These are important accomplishments, but his focus on Macedon made him incline toward caution in his foreign policy. It was above all his 278 pact with Antiochus that allowed him to be cautious, and this must count as his greatest foreign-policy coup. Nevertheless, cautious or not, he won the Chremonidean War, and was able to keep the Ptolemies at bay and greatly improve Macedon's position in the Aegean, paving the way for Antigonus Doson's and Philip V's further forays in the region. He was better at naval warfare than land battles, and he does not seem to have been blessed with Macedonian generals on whom he could rely to make up this deficiency; hence his recruitment of Ameinias of Phocis. This, along with his desire not to drain Macedon's resources and destabilize it with warfare, made him disinclined to take action, and in the military sphere he was reactive rather than proactive. The Macedonian population was not as robust a resource for Antigonus as it had been for earlier kings, and in order not to shed Macedonian blood, he relied on mercenaries rather than citizens to bear the brunt of any fighting.

Where the Greeks were concerned, Antigonus' legacy was less impressive. His caution allowed the Aetolian Confederacy to grow immensely strong, and his successors would have cause to regret that he had not taken steps to curtail it—first when the Aetolians and Achaeans allied themselves against Demetrius II, then when Philip V had to fight them in the Social War, and finally because they became the Romans' main ally in Greece (until they fell out with Rome and were reduced to their original borders in the early 180s). His reluctance to make war was also a major reason why he depended on garrisons and friendly governments to keep the Greeks quiet. But the resentment that this caused led to the opposite result, and once he had lost the Acrocorinth he had no way to prevent the collapse of his policy in the Peloponnese and stem the vigorous rise of the Achaean Confederacy. By the end of his reign, Macedonian control of Greece was considerably less secure than it had been a couple of decades earlier.

The Athenians had as much reason as any Greek state to hate Antigonus, since they had suffered for so long from his garrisons, and even for a while from his interference in their political processes. Their hatred finally erupted in the year 200, when they instituted a thorough *damnatio memoriae*. For some reason, probably religious, inscriptions on the Acropolis seem to have been spared, but otherwise all extant favorable references to the Antigonids in official documents were erased; either the inscription was entirely destroyed or selected words were chiseled off the stones. Scores of documents were involved, the priesthood of the divine Antigonus was brought to an end, statues were toppled and smashed, and the two civic tribes, Antigonis and Demetrias, instituted in 307 in honor of the first two Antigonids, were abolished. The upshot is that we have a number of inscriptions that commend a man, for instance, for having advised the Athenian People to [. . .], where the blank would have contained a reference to an Antigonid king, and others that start "In the Archonship of so-and-so, in the second prytany, that of [. . .]," where "Antigonis" or "Demetrias" has been erased. But the stones stayed in prominent places in the center of Athens, so that the erasures were daily reminders to passing Athenians of their utter rejection of their Antigonid past.

The immediate trigger for the *damnatio* was that Philip V had been attacking Athens, which was in alliance with Rome (though their contribution to the alliance was passionate rhetoric rather than armed might), but the Athenians had good reason to loathe the rest of the Antigonids as well. The city had been critically

Erected in the early 250s, this decree thanking Phaedrus of Sphettus originally contained references to his good relationship with the Antigonids, which, as one can plainly see on the stone, were subsequently erased as part of the Athenian *damnatio memoriae* of all things Antigonid. (The rights on the depicted monument belong to the Hellenic Ministry of Culture and Sports [Law 3028/2002]. The stele with the honorary decree for Phaidros, son of Thymochares from the deme of Sphettos EM 10546 [= *IG* II 2 682] belongs to the responsibility of the Epigraphic Museum. Hellenic Ministry of Culture and Sports / Archaeological Resources Fund. Copyright © Hellenic Ministry of Culture, Epigraphic Museum.)

destabilized by Demetrius Poliorcetes, acting on the orders of his father, Antigonus Monophthalmus, and Antigonus Gonatas had inflicted a crushing defeat on their last bid for freedom by military means. In 229, his son, Demetrius II, drew the reluctant Athenians into a protracted war against the Aetolians. In the last fifteen years of Antigonus' reign, the Athenians were troubled more by his enemies—Alexander of Corinth and Aratus of Sicyon, especially—than by Antigonus himself, but there would have been no such trouble if they had not been subject to the Macedonian throne. I doubt that the Athenians were inclined to attribute their relatively high degree of political stability after 255 to Antigonus rather than themselves and their current leaders. Antigonus would always be, for most of them, a hated scion of hated stock.

Antigonus could not possibly have foreseen the coming of the Romans, but it made his legacy, Greek hatred for Macedonian dominion, singularly unfortunate for Philip V and Perseus. Every time the Roman threat promised to boil over into war, they sought allies among the Greek states; each time, fewer Greeks fought alongside them against the Romans. The Romans exploited this situation. Every Greek state of any significance was divided into pro-Macedonian and pro-Roman factions, and the Romans regularly dispatched delegations to tour the Greek towns and confederacies, and encourage them with threats and promises to abandon Macedon. Even the Achaeans were eventually separated from the Common Alliance.

The relative ease with which the Romans obtained help or at least neutrality from the Greeks was, at least in part, a consequence of Antigonus' repressive measures. We have found no reason to doubt Polybius when he said that Antigonus planted more tyrannies in Greece than any other Macedonian king. He was more responsible than any other Macedonian king for the hatred the Greeks felt for Macedonian dominion, and therefore more responsible than anyone for the Greek turn to the Romans, when they saw that these newcomers intended to liberate them from Macedon.

After the decisive victory of the Roman general Titus Quinctius Flamininus at Cynoscephalae in Thessaly in 197, he simply ordered

Philip V to desist in the future from exercising any degree of control over the Greeks. Flamininus chose the following year's Isthmian Games, held near Corinth, to make the official announcement to the Greeks of their freedom; those states that had been subject to the Macedonians were now, under Roman protection, to be "free, ungarrisoned, untaxed, and subject to their own ancestral laws." The stadium was packed with spectators for the games:

> At first, not everyone heard the announcement, or not well enough, and a confused buzz ran through the stadium, the noise of puzzled people asking one another for clarification and calling for the announcement to be repeated. But when silence fell again, the herald projected his voice more, to make sure he could be heard by everyone, and repeated the proclamation. A cry of joy arose, so unbelievably loud that it was heard on the coast. The spectators stood up; the athletes were forgotten; everyone leaped up eagerly to greet and salute the savior and champion of Greece.

Greek lives had been subject to Macedon for 140 years. The Greeks mobbed Flamininus with such enthusiasm that he had to take refuge in his tent. This spontaneous outburst of joy welled up from the deep resentment they felt about Macedonian dominion. They were not to know that Roman dominion would be just as repressive in its way, and longer-lasting by many centuries.

Notes

Since the great bulk of the new evidence on the third century that has emerged since William Tarn's groundbreaking *Antigonos Gonatas* (1913) is inscriptional in nature, I have been quite thorough in recording the relevant inscriptions, but I have usually mentioned the literary sources only when I directly quote or refer to them, or when they are somewhat obscure.

ABBREVIATIONS

Austin = M. Austin. *The Hellenistic World from Alexander to the Roman Conquest: A Selection of Ancient Sources in Translation*. 2nd ed. Cambridge University Press, 2006.

Burstein = S. Burstein. *The Hellenistic Age from the Battle of Ipsos to the Death of Kleopatra VII*. Translated Documents of Greece and Rome 3. Cambridge University Press, 1985.

CID = J. Bousquet et al. *Corpus des inscriptions de Delphes*. 4 vols. De Boccard, 1977–2002.

F = Fragment

FGrH = F. Jacoby. *Die Fragmente der griechischen Historiker*. Weidmann/Brill, 1923–.

Fornara = C. Fornara. *Archaic Times to the End of the Peloponnesian War*. 2nd ed. Translated Documents of Greece and Rome 1. Cambridge University Press, 1983.

I.Eleusis = K. Clinton. *Eleusis: The Inscriptions on Stone*. 2 vols. Athens Archaeological Society, 2005–8.

IG = *Inscriptiones Graecae*. Many vols. De Gruyter, 1913–.

I.Kaunos = C. Marek. *Die Inschriften von Kaunos*. Beck, 2006.

I.Rhamnous = V. Petrakos. *Ho Demos tou Rhamnountos*. Vol. 2, *Hoi Epigraphes*. Athens Archaeological Society, 1999.

ISE = L. Moretti. *Iscrizioni storiche ellenistiche*. La Nuova Italia, 1967.

I.Thessaly = A. McDevitt. *Inscriptions of Thessaly: An Analytical Handlist and Bibliography*. Olms, 1970.

P.Herc. = Herculaneum papyri

Rigsby = K. Rigsby. *Asylia: Territorial Inviolability in the Hellenistic World*. University of California Press, 1996.

SEG = H. Pleket et al. *Supplementum Epigraphicum Graecum*. Gieben, 1923–.

Syll.[3] = W. Dittenberger et al., eds. *Sylloge Inscriptionum Graecarum*. 3rd ed. 4 vols. Hirzel, 1915–24.

Welles = C. Welles. *Royal Correspondence in the Hellenistic Period: A Study in Greek Epigraphy*. Yale University Press, 1934; repr. Ares, 1974.

INTRODUCTION

Antigonus' attempt to win Aratus: Plutarch, *Aratus* 15. *Peace between Antigonus and Antiochus*: Justin, *Epitome of the Philippic History of Pompeius Trogus* 25.1.1. *Number of third-century Athenian laws and decrees*: M. Osborne and S. Byrne in *IG* II[3] 1.

1. THE DISARRAY OF MACEDON

Flamininus' observation: Polybius, *Histories* 18.37.8–9. *Theophrastus*: *Enquiry into Plants* 5.2.1. *Gold and silver mines*: Diodorus, *The Library* 16.8.6; Herodotus, *Histories* 5.17. *Wedding feast*: Athenaeus, *Savants at Dinner* 128a–130d. *Deaths of Philip and Eurydice*: Diodorus, *The Library* 19.11.2–7. *The Peace of the Dynasts*: Diodorus, *The Library* 19.105.1. *The Fetters of Greece*: Polybius, *Histories* 18.11.5; Livy, *History of Rome* 32.37.3. *Captain of Phila's bodyguard*: *IG* XII 6 1 30. *Phila-Aphrodite*: Athenaeus, *Savants at Dinner* 254a. *"Gonatas" from Gonnoi*: Eusebius, *Chronicle* 1.89. *Antigonus Geniculosus*: J. Martin, *Scholia in Aratum vetera* (Teubner, 1974), *Vita III*, p. 15. *Antigonus short and ugly?*: Seneca, *On Anger* 3.22. *Beware of mocking Antigonus*: Plutarch, *Moralia* 458f (*On the Avoidance of Anger*). *Villa of Papyri bust*: see Fiorenza Grasso, in *Pergamon and the Hellenistic Kingdoms of the Ancient World*, ed. C. Picón and S. Hemingway (Metropolitan Museum of Art, 2016), 123. *Ball games*: Athenaeus, *Savants at Dinner* 15c. *Bon vivant*: e.g., Diogenes Laertius, *Lives of the Eminent Philosophers* 7.13. *Visits to Zeno*: Diogenes Laertius, *Lives of the Eminent Philosophers* 7.6. *Generosity to Cleanthes*: Diogenes Laertius, *Lives of the Eminent Philosophers* 7.169. *Antigonus teases Persaeus*: Diogenes Laertius, *Lives of the Eminent Philosophers* 7.36. *"I have lost the theater of my actions"*: Plutarch, *Moralia* 183d (*Sayings of Kings and Commanders*). *Visits to Menedemus*: Diogenes Laertius, *Lives of the Eminent Philosophers* 2.141. *"Do you owe the dead wages?"*: Plutarch, *Demetrius* 40.2. *Cool-headed Antigonus*: Plutarch, *Pyrrhus* 31.2. *Demetrius careless with petitions*: Plutarch, *Demetrius* 42.2. *Demetrius buried in Demetrias*: Plutarch, *Demetrius*

53.1–3. *King of Greece*: Eusebius, *Chronicle* 1.237. *Justin on Arsinoe's sons*: *Epitome of the Philippic History of Pompeius Trogus* 24.2.2. *No alternative*: Memnon of Heraclea, *FGrH* 434 F 8. *Divine retribution*: Justin, *Epitome of the Philippic History of Pompeius Trogus* 24.3.10.

2. THE PRIDE OF SPARTA

Tyranny of Athenian imperial leadership: Thucydides, *History* 1.124.3, 1.139.3. *Spartan reputation*: Thucydides, *History* 1.18.1; *FGrH* 105 F 1; Plutarch, *Moralia* 859c–d (*On the Malice of Herodotus*). *Friend or foe?*: Plutarch, *Moralia* 233e (*Sayings of Spartans*). *Messenian prowess questioned*: Plutarch, *Moralia* 192b (*Sayings of Kings and Commanders*), 217f (*Sayings of Spartans*). *Plutarch on Spartan resistance to Macedon*: *Moralia* 240a–b (*Customs of the Spartans*). *Aristotle on Spartan women*: *Politics* 1269a–1271b; the quotation is from 1269b32–34. *Leaders, not followers*: Arrian, *Anabasis* 1.1.2. *"All the Greeks except the Spartans"*: Arrian, *Anabasis* 1.16.7; Plutarch, *Alexander* 16.18. *"Battle of mice"*: Plutarch, *Agesilaus* 15.4. *Dormant tradition*: Plutarch, *Agesilaus* 30.6. *Spartans wanting change*: Plutarch, *Agis* 5.4. *Damis on Alexander's divinity*: Plutarch, *Moralia* 219e; Aelian, *Historical Miscellany* 2.19. *Eudamidas I*: Plutarch, *Moralia* 220e–f (*Sayings of Spartans*). *Cleonymus in Boeotia*: Plutarch, *Demetrius* 39.1–2. *Spartans harsher masters than Macedonians*: Plutarch, *Moralia* 219a–b (*Sayings of Spartans*). *Camp of Pyrrhus*: Polybius, *Histories* 5.19.4. *Donation of wheat to Sparta*: Plutarch, *Moralia* 233e–f (*Sayings of Spartans*). *Peloponnese as acropolis*: Strabo, *Geography* 8.1.3. *Importance of Acrocorinth*: Plutarch, *Aratus* 16.4–5. *Importance of Peloponnese as a whole*: Polybius, *Histories* 9.29.10.

3. THE DEMOCRATIC SPIRIT OF ATHENS

Exiles Decree: Diodorus, *The Library* 18.8.4. *Isocrates on footloose men*: *Letter* 9.9. *Xenocrates on Antipater's settlement*: Plutarch, *Phocion* 27.4. *Adeimantus of Lampsacus*: *SEG* XLIII 27. *Stratocles' decree*: Plutarch, *Demetrius* 24.4. *Cavalry monument*: Pausanias, *Description of Greece* 1.15.1. *Epicurus under siege*: Plutarch, *Demetrius* 34.2. *Desertion of Strombichus*: *IG* II^3 1 918–19. *Callias decree*: *IG* II^3 1 911 = Austin, no. 55; Burstein, no. 55. The decree was published in 270/69. See also *IG* II^3 1 985, published in the early 250s, which is the decree thanking Phaedrus. For reasons for retaining 286 as the date of the revolution, see Shear 2010. For reasons for thinking that it was the Ptolemies, not the early Antigonids, who formed the Confederacy of Islanders, see Meadows 2013. *Pausanias wrong about Piraeus*: *Description of Greece* 1.26.3. *Antigonus' instructions to the Munychia garrison*: Plutarch, *Moralia* 754b (*Dialogue on Love*). *"Destroying the hated Macedonians"*: Epicurus, F 112 Arrighetti. *Thanks for Zeno*: *IG* II^3 1 863. *The democracy of all Athenians*: Austin, no. 55 (= Burstein, no. 55), line 83. *Greeks enslaved by garrisons*: Polybius, *Histories* 9.29.5–6. *Two kinds of garrisons*: Polybius, *Histories* 18.4.6. *Unruly mercenaries*: Polybius, *Histories* 13.6.4. *Curse tablet*: D. Jordan in *Mitteilungen des Deutschen Archäologischen Instituts: Athenische Abteilung* 95 (1980): 225–39.

4. THE VIGOR OF CONFEDERACIES

Massacre of Aetolian councilors: Livy, *History of Rome* 42.28.6–7. *Polybius on the Achaean Confederacy*: *Histories* 2.38.6–7. *Polybius as admirer of Aratus' policy*: *Histories* 2.37.9–11. *Celtic fears*: Strabo, *Geography* 7.3.8. *Athenian hymn to Demetrius*: Austin, no. 43; Burstein, no. 7. *Achaean ambassador on the Aetolians*: Livy, *History of Rome* 34.24.3.

5. THE EMPIRE OF THE PTOLEMIES

Cratesipolis ignores mercenaries: Polyaenus, *Stratagems* 8.58. *Ptolemy I's expedition to Greece*: Diodorus, *The Library* 20.37.1–2. *Importance of Greater Egypt*: Polybius, *Histories* 5.34.5–9. *Sotades' tactless crudity*: Plutarch, *Moralia* 11a (*On the Education of Children*). *Theocritus on Greater Egypt*: *Idyll* 17.86–91. *Succession of empires*: Daniel 2.37–41, 7.4–8. *Ptolemaic rule of the entire world*: Callimachus, *Hymn* 4 (to Delos), lines 169–70; Theocritus, *Idyll* 17.92. *"Chicken-coop of the Muses"*: Timon, F 786 (*Supplementum Hellenisticum*).

6. KING OF MACEDON

The war with Antiochus: apart from Justin (below), see also Memnon, *FGrH* 434, esp. F 18; *P.Herc.* 155 F 8.5 (text as in Walbank 1995). *Antiochus' love for Stratonice*: Plutarch, *Demetrius* 38 (even with the fabulous elements stripped away). *Antigonus' third attempt on Macedon*: Justin, *Epitome of the Philippic History of Pompeius Trogus* 25.1–2. *Menedemus' decree*: Diogenes Laertius, *Lives of the Eminent Philosophers* 2.142. *Mercenary pay*: Polyaenus, *Stratagems* 4.6.17. *Obscure pretenders*: Diodorus, *The Library* 22, F 4; Porphyry, *FGrH* 260 F 3; Eusebius, *Chronicle* 1.235. *Apollodorus demagogue?*: Diodorus, *The Library* 22, F 5. *Cyrrhus inscription*: see Hatzopoulos and Gounaropoulou 2013; *Pan statue base*: T. Pazaras and M. Hatzopoulos, "Επίγραμμα ἀπὸ τὴ Βέροια τῶν Ἀντιγονιδῶν," *Tekmeria* 3 (1997). *Pyrrhic victory*: Plutarch, *Pyrrhus* 21.9. *Antigonus' take on his retreat*: Plutarch, *Moralia* 183d (*Sayings of Kings and Commanders*). *Pyrrhus' scorn for Antigonus*: Plutarch, *Pyrrhus* 26.7. *Pyrrhus' inscription*: Pausanias, *Description of Greece* 1.13.3. *Aegae as hearth of the country*: Diodorus, *The Library* 22, F 12. *Pyrrhus' failure to punish the Celts*: Diodorus, *The Library* 22, F 12. *Pyrrhus as gambler*: Plutarch, *Pyrrhus* 26.2. *Antigonus on Pyrrhus' prowess*: Plutarch, *Pyrrhus* 8.2. *Pyrrhus' death*: Plutarch, *Pyrrhus* 34. *Pyrrhus' killer as Demeter*: Pausanias, *Description of Greece* 1.13.8. *Alexandrian* promanteia: *Syll.*[3]

404. *"Like stars around the sun"*: Austin, no. 43; Burstein, no. 7. *Friends of Antigonus and Phila*: *SEG* XXXIX 595 (Hatzopoulos, no. 46) and *SEG* XXXIX 596 (Hatzopoulos, no. 45). *No automatic inheritance of Friendship*: Plutarch, *Moralia* 183d (*Sayings of Kings and Commanders*). *Demetrias inscription*: the text may be found in, e.g., Boehm 2018, 190–91. *Demetrius II letter*: *SEG* XII 311. *Seleucus on the burden of kingship*: Plutarch, *Moralia* 790a (*Old Men in Public Affairs*). *Antigonus letter*: *SEG* XLVIII 783 (another copy: *SEG* LI 796). *Coan* asylia *decrees*: Hatzopoulos, nos. 36 (= Austin, no. 65), 41, 47, and 58 (*SEG* XII 373 and 374); Rigsby, nos. 23–27 (compare Rigsby, no. 68). *Cassandrean judges*: *SEG* XVII 238. *"Money-bags"*: Diodorus, *The Library* 29.29. *Demetrius' revenues*: Aelian, *Historical Miscellany* 9.9. *Flamininus' Isthmian Declaration*: Polybius, *Histories* 18.46.5; Livy, *History of Rome* 33.32.5; Plutarch, *Flamininus* 10.4. *Local maintenance of garrisons*: A. Giovannini, "Le traité entre Iasos et Ptolémée (*IK* 28,1, 2–3) et les relations entre les cités grecques d'Asie mineure et les souverains hellénistiques," *Epigraphica Anatolica* 37 (2004): 69–87. *Demetrius' extraction of money from Athenians*: Plutarch, *Demetrius* 27.1.

7. ANTIGONUS AND THE GREEKS

Ashoka: Major Rock Edict 13, lines 17–18. *League of the Greeks at Plataea*: Austin, no. 63 (*SEG* LXI 352) and *SEG* LII 447. *Slaves, not allies*: Polybius, *Histories* 15.24.4. *Polyperchon's letter to the Athenians*: Plutarch, *Phocion* 34.3. *Antigonus' liberal use of tyrants*: Polybius, *Histories* 2.41.10. *"Greece was thoroughly oppressed"*: Eusebius, *Chronicle* 1.237. *Hero cult of Eudamus*: *SEG* LII 447. *Athenian decree for Aristomachus*: *IG* II^{3} 1 1019. *Aristippus and Antigonus*: Plutarch, *Aratus* 25.6. *Caunus inscription*: *I.Kaunos* 4. *Unpublished Aristides inscription*: see B. Petrakos, "Άνασκαφές: Ῥαμνοῦς," *Ergon* 50 (2003): 15–16. *Chremonides decree*: Austin, no. 61; Burstein, no. 56. *Glaucon inscription*: Austin, no. 63. *Troezen decree*: Fornara, no. 55. *Glaucon's embassy*: *ISE* 53. *Epichares inscription*: *I.Rhamnous* 3. *Thanks for protecting the countryside*: *IG* II^{3} 1 920, lines 8–10. *Arsinoe cult at Rhamnous*: *SEG* LIX 146. *Amphictyonic decree*: *CID* 4.36. *Antigonus on Halcyoneus' death*: Aelian, *Historical Miscellany* 3.5; Plutarch, *Moralia* 119c–d. *Spartan withdrawal*: Justin, *Epitome of the Philippic History of Pompeius Trogus* 26.2.7. *Egyptian effort half-hearted*: Pausanias, *Description of Greece* 1.7.3. *Fish and green figs*: Athenaeus, *Savants at Dinner* 334a. *Antigonus' quip*: Plutarch, *Moralia* 545b (*On Inoffensive Self-Praise*). *Sostratus' quotation of Homer*: *Iliad* 15.201–3 (translated by Anthony Verity). The source of the anecdote is Sextus Empiricus, *Against the Professors* 1.276. *Aegean island inscriptions*: *IG* XI 4 1052 (Syros); *IG* XII 5 570 (Ceos); *IG* XII 5 1008 (Ios); *IG* XII 7 221–23 (Amorgos); Hegesander of Delphi, ap. Athenaeus, *Savants at Dinner* 400d (Astypalaea); *IG* XII 6 150 (Samos; unless the Queen Phila mentioned is Antigonus' mother, rather than his wife); Welles, no. 14 (Miletus). *Delian statue group base*: *IG* XI 4 1096.

8. THE WHEEL OF FORTUNE

Demetrius as joint king: Burstein, no. 54. *"The altars of the kings"*: *IG* XI 4 1036. *Antigonus at Eleusis*: *I.Eleusis* 193. *Apollodorus fragment*: *FGrH* 244 F 44. *Apollodorus of Otryne as general*: *I.Rhamnous* 8 = Burstein, no. 61. *Another dual appointment?*: *I.Rhamnous* 16, lines 2–3. *Demetrius of Phalerum the younger*: *IG* II^{3} 4 28; *IG* II^{2} 1285; *I.Eleusis* 195. *Demetrius' response to the Areopagus Council*: Hegesander of Delphi, F 8, in Athenaeus, *Savants at Dinner* 167d–f. *Athenian statue of Antigonus*: *IG* II^{2} 793. *Athenian renewal of friendship with Antigonus*: *IG* II^{3} 1 982. *Praise for Heraclitus of Athmonon*: Burstein, no. 60 (see also *IG* II^{2} 1225, c. 245). *Demetrius' friends honored too*: *IG* II^{3} 1 995. *Sacrificing for the health of the royal family*: *IG* II^{3} 1 1009; *IG* II^{3} 1 995; *IG* II^{3} 1 1020; *IG* II^{3} 1 1002. *Antigonus a god in Athens and Rhamnous*: *I.Rhamnous* 7. *Callias decree*: Austin, no. 55; Burstein, no. 55. *Phaedrus decree*: *IG* II^{3} 1 985. *Antigonus' stable at Sicyon*: Plutarch, *Aratus* 6.2. *Alexander as king*: *IG* XII 9 212; Suda, E 3801. *Arrhidaeus inscription from Eretria*: *IG* XII 9 212. *Rhamnous in trouble*: *SEG* LI 107; see also B. Petrakos, "Ἀνασκαφές: Ῥαμνοῦς," *Ergon* 40 (1993): 7–8, for an unpublished inscription praising the general Archandros for keeping Rhamnous safe from Alexander's pirates. *Donations for Athens*: *IG* II^{3} 1 1011, lines 10–30. *Thanks for Aristomachus*: *IG* II^{3} 1 1019. *Apollonius letter*: text in Fraser and Roberts 1949. *Boastful Ptolemy*: Josephus, *Jewish Antiquities* 12.93. *Antigonus' quip again*: Plutarch, *Pelopidas* 2.2; but the quip is attributed on this occasion to Antigonus "the elder"—that is, Antigonus Monophthalmus (compare *Moralia* 182c with 360d). *Antigonus' envoy to Delos*: *IG* XI 4 1052. *Judges for the islands*: *IG* XI 4 1052 (Syros); *SEG* XLIV 710 (Cimolos). *Antigonus' lust for Corinth*: Plutarch, *Aratus* 17.1. *Antigonus and Nicaea*: Plutarch, *Aratus* 17.2–5; Polyaenus, *Stratagems* 4.6.1. *Liberation of Corinth by Aratus*: Plutarch, *Aratus* 23.4. *Persaeus' fate*: Athenaeus, *Savants at Dinner* 162c–d; Plutarch, *Aratus* 23.5; Polyaenus, *Stratagems* 6.5; Pausanias, *Description of Greece* 2.8.4, 7.8.3. For other texts, see H. von Arnim, *Stoicorum veterum fragmenta*, vol. 1 (Leipzig, 1905), nos. 435–62. *Ptolemy III honorary Achaean general*: Plutarch, *Aratus* 24.4. *Aratus vs. Argive tyrants*: Plutarch, *Aratus* 25.1–3. *Agis as reformer*: Plutarch, *Agis* 4.2.

9. COURT AND CULTURE

Aristogenes of Cnidus: Suda, A 3911. *Cleomenes' style of kingship*: Plutarch, *Cleomenes* 13.2. *Luxury of Macedonian court*: Polybius, *Histories* 16.22.3–5. *Precarious courtiers*: Polybius, *Histories* 5.26.12–13. *Apelles' downfall*: Polybius, *Histories* 5.26.7–11. *Alexander hunting*: Quintus Curtius Rufus, *History of Alexander* 8.1.14–16, 8.6.7. *Cassander and the boar*: Athenaeus, *Savants at Dinner* 18a. *Early Hellenistic kingship*: Austin, no. 45. *Demetrius of Phalerum on kingship treatises*: F 38 Stork/van Ophuijsen/Dorandi. *"A glorious state of slavery"*: Aelian, *Histori-*

cal Miscellany 2.20. *Despicable diadem*: Stobaeus, *Anthology* 4.8.20 Wachsmuth and Hense (Antigonus); Plutarch, *Moralia* 790a (*Old Men in Public Affairs*) (Seleucus). *Private cult of kings?*: Smith 1988, 11. *Strymon altar*: *SEG* XLVIII 812. *Antigonus and Philip V as gods*: Mari 2008, appendix. *Antigonus as god in Athens and Rhamnous*: *I.Rhamnous* 7. *The Rhamnousian cult interrupted and restarted*: *I.Rhamnous* 17. *Histiaea Antigoneia festival*: *IG* XI 4 1055. *Ios inscription*: *IG* XII Supplement 168. *Worship on Cos*: *IG* XII 4 326 mentions an Antigoneion temple, with altars, but the inscription dates from the first century BCE. *Founder of Iolcus*: *I.Thessaly* 1030. *Antigonus pooh-poohs his divinity?*: Plutarch, *Moralia* 360d (*On Isis and Osiris*); also at *Moralia* 182c (*Sayings of Kings and Commanders*). *Theocritus on the uses of royal wealth*: *Idyll* 17.106–16 (Richard Hunter's translation). *Eratosthenes on doubling the cube*: Eratosthenes, *Letter to Ptolemy*, in Eutocius of Ascalon, *On the Sphere and Cylinder of Archimedes* 90.13–27 Heiberg. *Letters of Antigonus and Zeno*: Diogenes Laertius, *Lives of the Eminent Philosophers* 7.7–9. *Persaeus as lapsed Stoic*: H. von Arnim, *Stoicorum veterum fragmenta*, vol. 1 (Leipzig, 1905), no. 441. *Bion accuses Antigonus of cowardice*: Teles, *On Poverty* 43 Hense. *Bion on money*: F 38a Kindstrand. *Bion on fate*: F 16a Kindstrand. *Antigonus fond of Bion*: Diogenes Laertius, *Lives of the Eminent Philosophers* 4.54; Plutarch, *Moralia* 531e (*On Compliancy*). *Bion teased at court*: Diogenes Laertius, *Lives of the Eminent Philosophers* 4.46–47. *Bion's response to Persaeus*: Athenaeus, *Savants at Dinner* 162d–e. *Menedemus vs. Persaeus*: Diogenes Laertius, *Lives of the Eminent Philosophers* 2.144. *Hieronymus of Rhodes' eloquence*: Diogenes Laertius, *Lives of the Eminent Philosophers* 5.65. *Hieronymus of Cardia biased*: Pausanias, *Description of Greece* 1.9.8. *Antagoras and Antigonus banter*: Athenaeus, *Savants at Dinner* 340f. *Timon on Menedemus*: Diogenes Laertius, *Lives of the Eminent Philosophers* 2.126. *Aratus composed* Phaenomena *at Antigonus' suggestion*: J. Martin, *Scholia in Aratum vetera* (Teubner, 1974), *Vita III*, p. 15. *Acts of the Apostles*: 17:28. *Pella library*: Plutarch, *Aemilius Paullus* 28.11. *Posidippus epigram*: Posidippus of Pella 55 Austin/Bastianini; translation by Kathryn Gutzwiller.

10. A GLIMPSE OF THE FUTURE

Achaean attacks on Attica: e.g., *IG* II^{3} 1 1160. *The fickleness of Fortune*: Diodorus, *The Library* 18.59.5–6. Damnatio memoriae: Livy, *History of Rome* 31.44. *Flamininus' Isthmian Declaration*: Polybius, *Histories* 18.46.5; Livy, *History of Rome* 33.32.5; Plutarch, *Flamininus* 10.4.

Bibliography

This is a fairly full bibliography. Most of the entries are English-language publications, but I have included a few of the most important works written in other languages. In order to save space, I have not separately listed chapters from edited collections of essays where such books contain three or more relevant chapters.

LITERARY SOURCES IN TRANSLATION

Athenaeus. *Deipnosophistae* (*Savants at Dinner*). Translated by S. D. Olson. 8 vols. Harvard University Press, 2006–12.

Diodorus of Sicily. *The Library, Books 16–20: Alexander the Great, Philip II, and the Successors*. Translated, with introduction and notes, by R. Waterfield. Oxford University Press, 2019.

Diogenes Laertius. *Lives of the Eminent Philosophers*. Translated by P. Mensch; edited by J. Miller. Oxford University Press, 2018.

Justin. *Epitome of the Philippic History of Pompeius Trogus*. Translated by J. Yardley, with introduction and notes by R. Develin. Scholars Press, 1994.

Pausanias. *Description of Greece*. Translated by W. Jones. 5 vols. Harvard University Press, 1918.

Plutarch. *Hellenistic Lives*. Translated by R. Waterfield, with introduction and notes by A. Erskine. Oxford University Press, 2016.

Polyaenus. *Stratagems*. Translated and introduced by P. Krentz and E. Wheeler. 2 vols. Ares, 1994.

Polybius. *The Histories*. Translated by R. Waterfield, with introduction and notes by B. McGing. Oxford University Press, 2010.

INSCRIPTIONS

Inscriptions, always important for the study of ancient Greek history, are particularly vital for the third century, since we lack any complete historical narratives. The very many hard-copy tomes are tucked away in libraries, but four open-access websites are essential: Attic Inscriptions Online, the Centre for the Study of Ancient Documents, Inscriptiones Graecae (in Greek and German), and the Packard Humanities Institute. There are also catalogs of relevant inscriptions in Hatzopoulos 1996 (Macedonian institutions) and Mackil 2013 (confederacies). Both these books are included in the list of books, chapters, and articles below, and the Hatzopoulos collection is also on the Packard Humanities Institute website.

SOURCEBOOKS

These books contain translations, chiefly of inscriptions, but also of papyri and, more rarely, of extracts from literary sources.

Austin, M. *The Hellenistic World from Alexander to the Roman Conquest: A Selection of Ancient Sources in Translation.* 2nd ed. Cambridge University Press, 2006.

Bagnall, R., and P. Derow. *The Hellenistic Period: Historical Sources in Translation.* 2nd ed. Blackwell, 2004. Originally published as *Greek Historical Documents: The Hellenistic Period.*

Burstein, S. *The Hellenistic Age from the Battle of Ipsos to the Death of Kleopatra VII.* Translated Documents of Greece and Rome. Cambridge University Press, 1985.

Harding, P. *From the End of the Peloponnesian War to the Battle of Ipsus.* Translated Documents of Greece and Rome. Cambridge University Press, 1985.

REFERENCE WORKS

The Oxford Classical Dictionary, now in its fourth edition (2012), and its fifth edition online (http://classics.oxfordre.com/), is a treasury of information on all aspects of the ancient world; it is rivaled by *The Cambridge Dictionary of Classical Civilization* (2008). Either of these is as indispensable as the best atlas: *The Barrington Atlas of the Greek and Roman World*, edited by R. Talbert (Princeton University Press, 2000).

BOOKS, CHAPTERS, AND ARTICLES

Alexander, J. "Cassandreia during the Macedonian Period: An Epigraphical Commentary." *Ancient Macedonia* 1 (1970): 127–46.

Andronicos, M. *Vergina: The Royal Tombs.* Athenon, 1992.

Anson, E. *Alexander's Heirs: The Age of the Successors, 323–281 BC.* Wiley-Blackwell, 2014.

Apostolou, S. "A Note on Divine Honours for Antigonus Gonatas." *Letras clásicas* 15 (2011): 3–8.

Archibald, Z. *Ancient Economies of the Northern Aegean, Fifth to First Centuries BC*. Oxford University Press, 2013.

Archibald, Z., J. Davies, V. Gabrielsen, and G. Oliver, eds. *Hellenistic Economies*. Routledge, 2001.

Austin, M. "Hellenistic Kings, War, and the Economy." *Classical Quarterly* 36 (1986): 450–66.

Badian, E. *Collected Papers on Alexander the Great*. Routledge, 2012.

Bagnall, R. *The Administration of the Ptolemaic Possessions outside Egypt*. Brill, 1976.

———. "Alexandria: Library of Dreams." *Proceedings of the American Philosophical Society* 146 (2002): 348–62.

Bayliss, A. *After Demosthenes: The Politics of Early Hellenistic Athens*. Continuum, 2011.

Beck, H., ed. *A Companion to Ancient Greek Government*. Wiley-Blackwell, 2013.

Beck, H., and P. Funke, eds. *Federalism in Greek Antiquity*. Cambridge University Press, 2015.

Berrey, M. *Hellenistic Science at Court*. De Gruyter, 2017.

Berthold, R. *Rhodes in the Hellenistic Age*. Cornell University Press, 1984.

Beston, P. "Hellenistic Military Leadership." In *War and Violence in Ancient Greece*, edited by H. van Wees, 315–29. Classical Press of Wales, 2000.

Bikerman, E. "Sur les batailles navales de Cos et d'Andros." *Revue des études anciennes* 40 (1938): 369–83.

Billows, R. *Antigonos the One-Eyed and the Creation of the Hellenistic State*. University of California Press, 1990.

———. *Kings and Colonists: Aspects of Macedonian Imperialism*. Brill, 1995.

———. "The Succession of the Epigonoi." *Syllecta classica* 6 (1995): 1–11.

Bing, P. "Aratus and His Audiences." *Materiali e discussione per l'analisi dei testi classici* 31 (1993): 99–109.

Boehm, R. *City and Empire in the Age of the Successors: Urbanization and Social Response in the Making of the Hellenistic Kingdoms*. University of California Press, 2018.

Bollansée, J. "Persaios of Kition, or the Failure of the Wise Man as General." In *Politics, Administration, and Society in the Hellenistic and Roman World*, edited by L. Mooren, 15–28. Peeters, 2000.

Borgeaud, P. *The Cult of Pan in Ancient Greece*. Translated by K. Atlass and J. Redfield. University of Chicago Press, 1988. First published in 1979 in French.

Borza, E. *In the Shadow of Olympus: The Emergence of Macedon*. Princeton University Press, 1990.

Bourke, G. *Elis: Internal Politics and External Policy in Ancient Greece*. Routledge, 2017.

Bringmann, K. "The King as Benefactor: Some Remarks on Ideal Kingship in the Age of Hellenism." In *Images and Ideologies: Self-Definition in the Hellenistic World*, edited by A. Bulloch, E. Gruen, and A. Long, 7–24. University of California Press, 1994.

Briscoe, J. "The Antigonids and the Greek States, 276–196 BC." In *Imperialism in the Ancient World*, edited by P. Garnsey and C. Whittaker, 145–57. Cambridge University Press, 1978.

Brown, E. "Antigonus Surnamed Gonatas." In *Arktouros: Studies Presented to Bernard W. Knox*, edited by G. Bowersock, W. Burkert, and M. Putnam, 299–307. De Gruyter, 1979.

Bugh, G., ed. *The Cambridge Companion to the Hellenistic World*. Cambridge University Press, 2006.

Buraselis, K. *Das hellenistische Makedonien und die Ägäis: Forschungen zur Politik des Kassandros und der drei ersten Antigoniden im Ägäischen Meer und in Westkleinasien*. Beck, 1982.

———. "Ambivalent Roles of Centre and Periphery: Remarks on the Relations of the Cities of Greece with the Ptolemies until the End of Philometor's Age." In *Centre and Periphery in the Hellenistic World*, edited by P. Bilde, T. Engberg-Pedersen, L. Hannestad, J. Zahle, and K. Randsborg, 251–70. Aarhus University Press, 1993.

Burstein, S. "Arsinoe II Philadelphus: A Revisionist View." In *Philip II, Alexander the Great, and the Macedonian Heritage*, edited by W. L. Adams and E. Borza, 197–212. University Press of America, 1982.

Byrne, S. "The Athenian *damnatio memoriae* of the Antigonids in 200 BC." In *Philathenaios: Studies in Honour of Michael J. Osborne*, edited by A. Tamis, C. Mackie, and S. Byrne, 157–77. Greek Epigraphical Society, 2010.

Caneva, S. *From Alexander to the Theoi Adelphoi: Foundation and Legitimation of a Dynasty*. Peeters, 2016.

Carlier, P. "Homeric and Macedonian Kingship." In *Alternatives to Athens: Varieties of Political Organization and Community in Ancient Greece*, edited by R. Brock and S. Hodkinson, 259–68. Oxford University Press, 2000.

Carney, E. "The Reappearance of Royal Sibling Marriage in Ptolemaic Egypt." *La parola del passato* 42 (1987): 420–39.

———. *Women and Monarchy in Macedonia*. University of Oklahoma Press, 2000.

———. *Arsinoë of Egypt and Macedon: A Royal Life*. Oxford University Press, 2013.

———. "Dynastic Loyalty and Dynastic Collapse in Macedonia." In *East and*

West in the World Empire of Alexander, edited by P. Wheatley and E. Baynham, 147–62. Oxford University Press, 2015.

———. *King and Court in Ancient Macedonia: Rivalry, Treason, and Conspiracy*. Classical Press of Wales, 2015.

Cartledge, P. *Thebes: The Forgotten City of Ancient Greece*. Pan Macmillan, 2020.

Cartledge, P., and A. Spawforth. *Hellenistic and Roman Sparta: A Tale of Two Cities*. 2nd ed. Routledge, 2001.

Chambers, M. "The First Regnal Year of Antigonus Gonatas." *American Journal of Philology* 75 (1954): 385–94.

Chamoux, F. *Hellenistic Civilization*. Translated by M. Roussel. Blackwell, 2003. First published in 1983 in French.

Champion, C. "In Defense of Hellas: The Antigonid Soteria and Paneia at Delos and the Aetolian Soteria at Delphi." *American Journal of Ancient History* 3–4 (2004–5): 72–88.

Chaniotis, A. "Foreign Soldiers, Native Girls? Constructing and Crossing Boundaries in Hellenistic Cities with Foreign Garrisons." In *Army and Power in the Ancient World*, edited by A. Chaniotis and P. Ducrey, 99–113. Steiner, 2002.

———. *War in the Hellenistic World: A Social and Cultural History*. Blackwell, 2005.

———. "The Impact of War on the Economy of Hellenistic *Poleis*: Demand Creation, Short-Term Influences, Long-Term Impacts." In *The Economies of Hellenistic Societies, Third to First Centuries BC*, edited by Z. Archibald, J. Davies, and V. Gabrielsen, 122–41. Oxford University Press, 2011.

———. *Age of Conquests: The Greek World from Alexander to Hadrian*. Profile, 2018.

Cherry, J., and J. Davis. "The Ptolemaic Base at Koressos on Keos." *Annual of the British School at Athens* 86 (1991): 9–28.

Clauss, J., and M. Cuypers, eds. *A Companion to Hellenistic Literature*. Wiley-Blackwell, 2010.

Clayman, D. *Timon of Phlius: Pyrrhonism into Poetry*. De Gruyter, 2009.

———. *Berenice II and the Golden Age of Ptolemaic Egypt*. Oxford University Press, 2014.

Constantakopoulou, C. *Aegean Interactions: Delos and Its Networks in the Third Century*. Oxford University Press, 2017.

Dixon, M. "Hellenistic Arbitration: The Achaian League and Ptolemaic Arsinoe (Methana)." In *Argosaronikos: Practica 1ou Diethnous Sunedriou Istorias kai Arkhaiologias tou Argosaronikou*, vol. 2, edited by E. Konsolaki-Giannopoulou, 81–87. Poros Municipality, 2003.

———. *Late Classical and Early Hellenistic Corinth, 338–196 BC*. Routledge, 2014.

Dmitriev, S. *The Greek Slogan of Freedom and Early Roman Politics in Greece*. Oxford University Press, 2011.

Domingo Gygax, M. *Benefaction and Rewards in the Ancient Greek City*. Cambridge University Press, 2016.

Doran, T. *Spartan Oliganthropia*. Brill, 2018.

Dreyer, B. *Untersuchungen zur Geschichte des spätklassischen Athen (322–ca. 230 v. Chr.)*. Steiner, 1999.

Eckstein, A. *Mediterranean Anarchy, Interstate War, and the Rise of Rome*. University of California Press, 2006.

———. "Hellenistic Monarchy in Theory and Practice." In *A Companion to Greek and Roman Political Thought*, edited by R. Balot, 247–65. Wiley-Blackwell, 2009.

Edson, C. "The Personal Appearance of Antigonos Gonatas." *Classical Philology* 29 (1934): 254–55.

Erdas, D. *Cratero il Macedone: Testimonianze e frammenti*. Tored, 2002.

Errington, R. M. "An Inscription from Beroea and the Alleged Co-rule of Demetrios II." *Ancient Macedonia* 2 (1977): 115–22.

———. "The Nature of the Macedonian State under the Monarchy." *Chiron* 8 (1978): 77–133.

———. *A History of Macedonia*. Translated by C. Errington. University of California Press, 1990. First published in 1986 in German.

———. "König und Stadt im hellenistischen Makedonien: Die Rolle des Epistates." *Chiron* 32 (2002): 51–63.

———. *A History of the Hellenistic World, 323–30 BC*. Wiley-Blackwell, 2008.

Erskine, A., ed. *A Companion to the Hellenistic World*. Blackwell, 2003.

———. "Between Philosophy and the Court: The Life of Persaios of Kition." In *Creating a Hellenistic World*, edited by A. Erskine and L. Llewellyn-Jones, 177–94. Classical Press of Wales, 2011.

———. *The Hellenistic Stoa: Political Thought and Action*. 2nd ed. Bristol Classical Press, 2011.

Erskine, A., L. Llewellyn-Jones, and S. Wallace, eds. *The Hellenistic Court: Monarchic Power and Elite Society from Alexander to Cleopatra*. Classical Press of Wales, 2017.

Flacelière, R. *Les Aitoliens à Delphes: Contribution à l'histoire de la Grèce centrale au IIIe siècle av. J.-C.* De Boccard, 1937.

Fortenbaugh, W., and S. White, eds. *Lyco of Troas and Hieronymus of Rhodes: Text, Translation, and Discussion*. Transaction, 2004.

Fraser, P., and C. Roberts. "A New Letter of Apollonius." *Chronique d'Égypte* 24 (1949): 289–94.

Fuks, A. *Social Conflict in Ancient Greece*. Brill, 1984.

Funke, P. "*Poleis* and *Koina*: Reshaping the World of the Greek States in Hellenistic Times." In *The Polis in the Hellenistic World*, edited by H. Börm and N. Luraghi, 109–29. Steiner, 2018.

Gabbert, J. "The Grand Strategy of Antigonus II Gonatas and the Chremonidean War." *Ancient World* 8 (1983): 129–36.

———. "The Anarchic Dating of the Chremonidean War." *Classical Journal* 82 (1986): 230–35.

———. *Antigonus II Gonatas: A Political Biography*. Routledge, 1997.

Garland, R. *The Piraeus*. 2nd ed. Bristol Classical Press, 2001.

Gill, D. "Arsinoe in the Peloponnese: The Ptolemaic Base on the Methana Peninsula." In *Egyptian Stories: A British Egyptological Tribute to Alan B. Lloyd*, edited by T. Schneider and K. Szpakowska, 55–77. Ugarit, 2007.

Ginouvès, R., ed. *Macedonia from Philip II to the Roman Conquest*. Princeton University Press, 1994.

Giovannini, A. "Le statut des cités de Macédoine sous les Antigonides." *Ancient Macedonia* 2 (1977): 465–72.

Gómez Espelosín, F. "Plutarch and Justin on Aristotimus of Elis." *American Journal of Philology* 112 (1991): 103–9.

Grabowski, T. "The Ptolemies versus the Achaean and Aetolian Leagues in the 250s–220s BC." *Electrum* 19 (2012): 83–98.

Grainger, J. *The League of the Aitolians*. Brill, 1999.

Green, P. "How Political Was the Stoa?" In *From Ikaria to the Stars*, 210–21. University of Texas Press, 2004.

Griffin, A. *Sikyon*. Oxford University Press, 1982.

Griffith, G. *The Mercenaries of the Hellenistic World*. Cambridge University Press, 1935. Reprint, Ares, 1984.

Grilli, A. "Zenone e Antigono II." *Rivista di filologia e di istruzione classica* 91 (1963): 287–301.

Gruen, E. "The Polis in the Hellenistic World." In *Nomodeiktes: Greek Studies in Honor of Martin Ostwald*, edited by R. Rosen and J. Farrell, 339–54. University of Michigan Press, 1993.

Habicht, C. "Athens and the Ptolemies." *Classical Antiquity* 11 (1992): 68–90.

———. *Athènes hellénistique: Histoire de la cité d'Alexandre le Grand à Marc Antoine*. Translated by D. Knoepfler and M. Knoepfler. 2nd ed. Les Belles Lettres, 2006. Originally published in 1995 in German as *Athen: Die Geschichte der Stadt in hellenistische Zeit* (1995); first published in 1997 in English as *Athens from Alexander to Antony*, translated by L. Schneider.

———. "Divine Honors for King Antigonus Gonatas in Athens." In *The Hellenistic Monarchies: Selected Papers*, translated by P. Stevenson, 285–88. University of Michigan Press, 2006.

———. *Divine Honors for Mortal Men in Greek Cities: The Early Cases*. Translated by J. Dillon. Michigan Classical Press, 2017. First published in 1956 in German.

Hammond, N. *Epirus*. Oxford University Press, 1967.

———. *The Macedonian State: The Origins, Institutions, and History*. Oxford University Press, 1989.

Hammond, N., and F. Walbank. *A History of Macedonia*. Vol. 3, *336–167 BC*. Oxford University Press, 1988.

Hannestad, L. "Greeks and Celts: The Creation of a Myth." In *Centre and Periphery in the Hellenistic World*, edited by P. Bilde, T. Engberg-Pedersen, L. Hannestad, J. Zahle, and K. Randsborg, 15–38. Aarhus University Press, 1993.

Harding, P. *Athens Transformed, 404–262 BC: From Popular Sovereignty to the Dominion of Wealth*. Routledge, 2015.

Hatzopoulos, M. *Macedonian Institutions under the Kings*. 2 vols. National Hellenic Research Foundation, 1996.

Hatzopoulos, M., and L. Gounaropoulou. "Un règlement urbanistique de Kyrrhos (Macédoine)." *Comptes rendus de l'Académie des Inscriptions et Belles-Lettres* 157 (2013): 1369–96.

Hau, L. *Moral History from Herodotus to Diodorus Siculus*. Edinburgh University Press, 2016.

Hazzard, R. "The Regnal Years of Ptolemy II Philadelphos." *Phoenix* 41 (1987): 140–58.

———. *Imagination of a Monarchy: Studies in Ptolemaic Propaganda*. University of Toronto Press, 2000.

Heinen, H. *Untersuchungen zur hellenistischen Geschichte des 3. Jahrhunderts v. Chr.: Zur Geschichte der Zeit des Ptolemaios Keraunos und zum Chremonideischen Krieg*. Steiner, 1972.

Herman, G. "The 'Friends' of the Early Hellenistic Rulers: Servants or Officials?" *Talanta* 12–13 (1980–81): 103–49.

———. "The Court Society of the Hellenistic Age." In *Hellenistic Constructs: Essays in Culture, History, and Historiography*, edited by P. Cartledge, P. Garnsey, and E. Gruen, 199–224. University of California Press, 1997.

Hinüber, O. von. "Did Hellenistic Kings Send Letters to Aśoka?" *Journal of the American Oriental Society* 130 (2010): 261–66.

Hodkinson, S. *Property and Wealth in Classical Sparta*. Classical Press of Wales, 2000.

Hölbl, G. *A History of the Ptolemaic Empire*. Translated by T. Saavedra. Routledge, 2000. First published in 1994 in German.

Hornblower, J. *Hieronymus of Cardia*. Oxford University Press, 1981.

Howe, T., ed. *Ptolemy I Soter: A Self-Made Man*. Oxbow, 2018.

Hunter, R. *Theocritus: Encomium of Ptolemy Philadelphus*. University of California Press, 2003.

Juhel, P. "Epigraphic Evidence for Ptolemy Keraunos, King of Macedonia: The Epinikos Decree Revisited." *Historia* 64 (2015): 77–105.

Kennell, N. *Spartans: A New History*. Wiley-Blackwell, 2010.

Kidd, D. *Aratus: Phaenomena*. Cambridge University Press, 1997.

Kindstrand, J. *Bion of Borysthenes: A Collection of the Fragments with Introduction and Commentary*. Uppsala University Press, 1976.

King, C. *Ancient Macedonia*. Routledge, 2018.

Knoepfler, D. "Les *kryptoi* du stratège Épichares à Rhamnonte et le début de la guerre de Chrémonidès." *Bulletin de correspondance hellénique* 117 (1993): 327–41.

———. "Les relations des cités Eubéennes avec Antigone Gonatas et la chronologie delphique au début de l'époque Étolienne." *Bulletin de correspondance hellénique* 119 (1995): 137–56.

Kralli, I. "Athens and the Hellenistic Kings (338–261 BC): The Language of the Decrees." *Classical Quarterly* 50 (2000): 113–32.

———. *The Hellenistic Peloponnese: Interstate Relations; A Narrative and Analytic History, from the Fourth Century to 146 BC*. Classical Press of Wales, 2017.

Kusmin, Y. "The Antigonids, Caunus, and the So-Called 'Era of Monophthalmus': Some Observations Prompted by a New Inscription." In *Deformations and Crises of Ancient Civil Communities*, edited by V. Goušchin and P. Rhodes, 73–85. Steiner, 2015.

Lagos, C. "A Hoard of the Chremonidean War." *Numismatic Journal* 156 (1996): 272–78.

Landucci, F. "The Antigonids and the Ruler Cult: Local and Global Perspectives." *Erga-Logoi* 4 (2016): 39–61.

Lane Fox, R., ed. *Brill's Companion to Ancient Macedon: Studies in the Archaeology and History of Macedon, 650 BC–300 AD*. Brill, 2011.

Larsen, J. *Greek Federal States, Their Institutions, and History*. Oxford University Press, 1968.

———. "The Aetolian-Achaean Alliance of ca. 238–220 BC." *Classical Philology* 70 (1975): 159–72.

Launey, M. "L'exécution de Sotadès et l'expédition de Patroklos dans la mer Égée." *Revue des études anciennes* 47 (1945): 33–45.

———. *Recherches sur les armées hellénistiques*. 2nd ed. De Boccard, 1987.

Le Bohec, S. "Les épistates des rois Antigonides." *Ktema* 11 (1986): 281–88.

Leon, C. "Antigonos Gonatas Rediscovered." *Ancient World* 20 (1989): 21–25.

Lewis, S. *Greek Tyranny*. Bristol Phoenix Press, 2009.

Lönnqvist, K. "Studies on the Hellenistic Coinage of Athens: The Impact of Macedonia on the Athenian Money Market in the Third Century BC." In *Early Hellenistic Athens: Symptoms of a Change*, edited by J. Frösén, 119–45. Finnish Institute at Athens, 1997.

Luraghi, N., ed. *The Splendors and Miseries of Ruling Alone: Encounters with Monarchy from Archaic Greece to the Hellenistic Mediterranean*. Steiner, 2013.

———. "Timaeus' Athens Revisited: Culture and Politics in Early Hellenistic Athens." *Annali della Scuola Normale Superiore di Pisa* 9 (2017): 179–208.

———. "Stairway to Heaven: The Politics of Memory in Early Hellenistic Athens." In *The Hellenistic Reception of Classical Athenian Politics and Political Thought*, edited by M. Canevaro and B. Gray, 21–44. Oxford University Press, 2018.

———. "Kallias of Sphettos between Two Worlds." In *La cité interconnectée dans le monde gréco-romain*, edited by M. Dana and I. Savalli-Lestrade, 273–85. Ausonius, 2019.

Ma, J. "Fighting Poleis of the Hellenistic World." In *War and Violence in Ancient Greece*, edited by H. van Wees, 337–76. Duckworth and the Classical Press of Wales, 2000.

———. "'Oversexed, Overpaid, Over Here': A Response to Angelos Chaniotis." In *Army and Power in the Ancient World*, edited by A. Chaniotis and P. Ducrey, 115–22. Steiner, 2002.

Mackil, E. *Creating a Common Polity: Religion, Economy, and Politics in the Making of the Greek Koinon*. University of California Press, 2013.

———. "Ethnic Arguments." In *Ethnos and Koinon: Studies in Ancient Greek Ethnicity and Federalism*, edited by H. Beck, K. Buraselis, and A. McAuley, 11–28. Steiner, 2019.

MacLeod, R., ed. *The Library of Alexandria: Centre of Learning in the Ancient World*. I. B. Tauris, 2000.

Mari, M. "The Ruler Cult in Amphipolis and in the Strymon Valley." In *Thrace in the Graeco-Roman World*, edited by A. Iakovidou, 371–86. Centre for Greek and Roman Antiquity, 2007.

———. "The Ruler Cult in Macedonia." *Studi ellenistici* 20 (2008): 219–68.

———. "Powers in Dialogue: The Letters and *Diagrammata* of Macedonian Kings to Local Communities." In *Letters and Communities: Studies in the Socio-political Dimensions of Ancient Epistolography*, edited by P. Ceccarelli, L. Doering, T. Fögen, and I. Gildenhard, 121–46. Oxford University Press, 2018.

Mathisen, R. "The Activities of Antigonos Gonatas 280–277 BC, and Memnon of Herakleia, *Concerning Herakleia*." *Ancient World* 1 (1978): 71–74.

———. "Antigonus Gonatas and the Silver Coinages of Macedonia c. 280–270 BC." *Museum Notes (American Numismatic Society)* 26 (1981): 79–124.

McCredie, J. *Fortified Military Camps in Attica*. Princeton University Press, 1966.

McKechnie, P. "W. W. Tarn and the Philosophers." *Ancient History Bulletin* 28 (2014): 20–33.

McKechnie, P., and P. Guillaume, eds. *Ptolemy II Philadelphus and His World*. Brill, 2008.

Meadows, A. "The Ptolemaic League of Islanders." In *The Ptolemies, the Sea, and the Nile*, edited by K. Buraselis, M. Stefanou, and D. Thompson, 19–38. Cambridge University Press, 2013.

Michalopoulos, M. *In the Name of Lykourgos: The Rise and Fall of the Spartan Revolutionary Movement, 243–146 BC*. Translated by M. Kavallieros and M.-A. Niforos. Pen & Sword, 2016. First published in 2009 in Greek.

Mikalson, J. *Religion in Hellenistic Athens*. University of California Press, 1998.

Mooren, L. "The Nature of the Hellenistic Monarchy." In *Egypt and the Hellenistic World*, edited by E. van't Dack, P. van Dessel, and W. van Gucht, 205–40. Peeters, 1983.

———. "Kings and Courtiers: Political Decision-Making in the Hellenistic States." In *Politische Theorie und Praxis im Altertum*, edited by W. Schuller, 123–33. Wissenschaftliche Buchgesellschaft, 1998.

Murray, O. "Philosophy and Monarchy in the Hellenistic World." In *Jewish Perspectives on Hellenistic Rulers*, edited by T. Rajak, S. Pearce, J. Aitken, and J. Dines, 13–28. University of California Press, 2007.

Murray, W. *The Age of Titans: The Rise and Fall of the Great Hellenistic Navies*. Oxford University Press, 2012.

Oetjen, R. *Athen im dritten Jahrhundert v. Chr.: Politik und Gesellschaft in den Garnisonsdemen auf der Grundlage der inschriftlichen Überlieferung*. Wellem, 2014.

Ogden, D. *Polygamy, Prostitutes, and Death: The Hellenistic Dynasties*. Classical Press of Wales, 1999.

Oliver, G. "The Politics of Coinage: Athens and Antigonus Gonatas." In *Money and Its Uses in the Ancient Greek World*, edited by A. Meadows and K. Shipton, 35–52. Oxford University Press, 2001.

———. *War, Food, and Politics in Early Hellenistic Athens*. Oxford University Press, 2007.

O'Neil, J. "Who Attended the Achaean Assemblies?" *Museum Helveticum* 37 (1980): 41–49.

———. "The Political Elites of the Achaian and Aetolian Leagues." *Ancient Society* 15–17 (1984–86): 33–61.

———. "The Creation of New Dynasties after the Death of Alexander the Great." *Prudentia* 32 (2000): 118–37.

———. "The Ethnic Origins of the Friends of the Antigonid Kings of Macedon." *Classical Quarterly* 53 (2003): 510–22.

Osborne, M. "Kallias, Phaidros, and the Revolt of Athens in 287 BC." *Zeitschrift für Papyrologie und Epigraphik* 35 (1979): 181–94.

———. *Athens in the Third Century BC*. Greek Epigraphical Society, 2012.

Palagia, O. "Art and Royalty in Sparta of the Third Century BC." *Hesperia* 75 (2006): 205–17.

Palagia, O., and S. Tracy, eds. *The Macedonians in Athens, 322–229 BC*. Oxbow, 2003.

Panagopoulou, E. "Antigonos Gonatas: Coinage, Money, and the Economy." PhD diss., University College London, 2000.

———. "Between Federal and Ethnic: The *Koinon Makedonōn* and the *Makedones* Revisited." In *Ethnos and Koinon: Studies in Ancient Greek Ethnicity and Federalism*, edited by H. Beck, K. Buraselis, and A. McAuley, 363–83. Steiner, 2019.

Papazoglou, F. "Sur l'organisation de la Macédoine des Antigonides." *Ancient Macedonia* 3 (1983): 195–210.

———. *Les villes de Macédoine à l'époque romaine*. De Boccard, 1988.

———. "Polis et souveraineté." *Ziva antika* 50 (2000): 169–76.

Papazoglu, F. *The Central Balkan Tribes in Pre-Roman Times: Triballi, Autariatae, Dardanians, Scordisci, and Moesians*. Translated by M. Stansfield-Popović. Hakkert, 1978.

Paschidis, P. "The Interpenetration of Civic Elites and Court Elite in the Hellenistic Period." In *Rois, cités, nécropoles: Institutions, rites et monuments en Macédoine*, edited by A.-M. Guimier-Sorbets, M. Hatzopoulos, and Y. Morizot, 251–68. National Hellenic Research Foundation, 2006.

———. *Between City and King: Prosopographical Studies on the Intermediaries between the Cities of the Greek Mainland and the Aegean and Royal Courts in the Hellenistic Period (322–190 BC)*. National Hellenic Research Foundation, 2008.

Pollitt, J. *Art in the Hellenistic Age*. Cambridge University Press, 1986.

Porter, W. "Aratus of Sicyon and King Antigonus Gonatas." *Hermathena* 20 (1930): 293–311.

———. Introduction to *Plutarch's Life of Aratus*. Cork University Press, 1937.

Powell, A., ed. *A Companion to Sparta*. 2 vols. Wiley-Blackwell, 2017.

Pownall, F. "Folly and Violence in Athens under the Successors." In *Folly and Violence in the Court of Alexander the Great and His Successors*, edited by T. Howe and S. Müller, 47–58. Projekt, 2016.

Rankin, D. *Celts and the Classical World*. Routledge, 1987.

Raynor, B. "Theorodokoi, Asylia, and the Macedonian Cities." *Greek, Roman, and Byzantine Studies* (2016): 225–62.

Reger, G. "Athens and Tenos in the Early Hellenistic Age." *Classical Quarterly* 42 (1992): 365–83.

———. "The Date of the Battle of Kos." *American Journal of Ancient History* 10 (1993): 155–77.

———. "The Political History of the Kyklades, 260–200 BC." *Historia* 43 (1994): 32–69.

Rice, E. *The Grand Procession of Ptolemy Philadelphus*. Oxford University Press, 1983.

Robertson, N. "The Decree of Themistocles in Its Contemporary Setting." *Phoenix* 36 (1982): 1–44.

Roisman, J., and I. Worthington, eds. *A Companion to Ancient Macedonia*. Wiley-Blackwell, 2010.

Roy, J. "The Achaean League." In *The Idea of European Community in History*, vol. 2, *Aspects of Connecting Poleis and Ethne in Ancient Greece*, edited by K. Buraselis and K. Zoumboulakis, 81–95. National and Capodistrian University of Athens, 2003.

Rzepka, J. *Greek Federal Terminology*. Oxbow, 2017.

Scharfe, H. "The Maurya Dynasty and the Seleucids." *Zeitschrift für vergleichende Sprachforschung* 85 (1971): 211–25.

Schironi, F. "Enlightened Kings or Pragmatic Rulers? Ptolemaic Patronage of Scholarship and Sciences in Context." In *Intellectual and Empire in Greco-Roman Antiquity*, edited by P. Bosman, 1–29. Routledge, 2018.

Scholten, J. *The Politics of Plunder: Aitolians and Their Koinon in the Early Hellenistic Era, 279–217 BC*. University of California Press, 2000.

———. "The Internal Structure of the Aitolian Union: A Case Study in Ancient Greek *Sympoliteia*." In *The Idea of European Community in History*, vol. 2, *Aspects of Connecting Poleis and Ethne in Ancient Greece*, edited by K. Buraselis and K. Zoumboulakis, 65–80. National and Capodistrian University of Athens, 2003.

Sedley, D. "The Protagonists." In *Doubt and Dogmatism: Studies in Hellenistic Philosophy*, edited by M. Schofield, M. Burnyeat, and J. Barnes, 1–17. Oxford University Press, 1980.

Sellars, J. *Stoicism*. Acumen, 2006.

Shear, J. "Demetrios Poliorketes, Kallias of Sphettos, and the Panathenaia." In *Studies in Greek Epigraphy and History in Honor of Stephen V. Tracy*, edited by G. Reger, F. Ryan, and T. Winters, 135–52. Ausonius, 2010.

———. "The Politics of the Past: Remembering Revolution at Athens." In *Greek Notions of the Past in the Archaic and Classical Eras: History without*

Historians, edited by J. Marincola, L. Llewellyn-Jones, and C. Maciver, 276–300. Edinburgh University Press, 2012.

———. "An Inconvenient Past in Hellenistic Athens: The Case of Phaidros of Sphettos." In *Shaping Memory in Ancient Greece: Poetry, Historiography, and Epigraphy*, edited by C. Constantakopoulou and M. Fragoulaki, 269–301. Histos Supplement 11. Histos, 2020.

Shear, T. *Kallias of Sphettos and the Revolt of Athens in 286 BC*. American School of Classical Studies at Athens, 1978.

Shipley, G. *The Greek World after Alexander, 323–30 BC*. Routledge, 2000.

———. *The Early Hellenistic Peloponnese: Politics, Economies, and Networks, 338–197 BC*. Cambridge University Press, 2018.

Smith, R. *Hellenistic Royal Portraits*. Oxford University Press, 1988.

Sosin, J. "Endowed Eponymous Festivals on Delos." *Kernos* 27 (2014): 127–57.

Spawforth, A., ed. *The Court and Court Society in Ancient Monarchies*. Cambridge University Press, 2007.

Strootman, R. "Kings and Cities in the Hellenistic Age." In *Political Culture in the Greek City after the Classical Age*, edited by R. Alston and O. van Nijf, 141–53. Peeters, 2011.

———. *Courts and Elites in the Hellenistic Empires: The Near East after the Achaemenids, c. 330–30 BCE*. Edinburgh University Press, 2014.

———. "Hellenistic Imperialism and the Ideal of World Unity." In *The City in the Classical and Post-classical World*, edited by C. Rapp and H. Drake, 38–61. Cambridge University Press, 2014.

———. *The Birdcage of the Muses: Patronage of the Arts and Sciences at the Ptolemaic Imperial Court, 305–222 BCE*. Peeters, 2017.

Tarn, W. "The Battles of Andros and Cos." *Journal of Hellenic Studies* 29 (1909): 264–85.

———. "The Dedicated Ship of Antigonus Gonatas." *Journal of Hellenic Studies* 30 (1910): 209–22.

———. "The Social Question in the Third Century BC." In *The Hellenistic Age: Aspects of Hellenistic Civilization*, edited by J. Bury, E. Barber, E. Bevan, and W. Tarn, 108–40. [Cambridge] University Press, 1924.

———. *Antigonos Gonatas, King of Macedonia, 276–239 BC*. Oxford University Press, 1913. Reprint, Argonaut, 1969.

Taylor, M. "When the Peiraieus and the City Are Reunited." *Zeitschrift für Papyrologie und Epigraphik* 123 (1998): 207–12.

Thompson, D. "Philadelphus' Procession: Dynastic Power in a Mediterranean Context." In *Politics, Society, and Administration in the Hellenistic and Roman World*, edited by L. Mooren, 365–88. Peeters, 2000.

Thonemann, P. *The Hellenistic Age*. Oxford University Press, 2016.

Tracy, S. *Athens and Macedon: Attic Letter-Cutters of 300 to 229 BC*. University of California Press, 2003.

Tsaravopoulos, A. "Two More Inscribed Nails from Korone, Porto Rafti." *Grammateion* 5 (2016): 43–48.

Van der Vliet, E. "Pride and Participation: Political Practice, Euergetism, and Oligarchisation in the Hellenistic *Polis*." In *Political Culture in the Greek City after the Classical Age*, edited by R. Alston and O. van Nijf, 155–84. Peeters, 2012.

Vander Waerdt, P. "Politics and Philosophy in Stoicism." *Oxford Studies in Ancient Philosophy* 9 (1991): 185–211.

Van Oppen de Ruiter, B. "The Death of Arsinoe II Philadelphus." *Zeitschrift für Papyrologie und Epigraphik* 174 (2010): 139–50.

Virgilio, B. *Lancia, diadema, e porpora: Il re e la regalità ellenistica*. 2nd ed. Istituti Editoriali e Poligrafici Internazionali, 2003.

Walbank, F. *Aratos of Sicyon*. Cambridge University Press, 1933.

———. "Macedonia and Greece." In *The Hellenistic World*, edited by F. Walbank, A. Astin, M. Frederiksen, and R. Ogilvie, 221–56. Vol. 7, pt. 1 of *The Cambridge Ancient History*. 2nd ed. Cambridge University Press, 1984.

———. *The Hellenistic World*. 2nd ed. London: Fontana, 1992.

———. "Antigonus Gonatas in Thrace (281–277 BC)." In *Studia in honorem Georgi Mihailov*, edited by A. Fol, 503–11. Bulgarian Academy of Sciences, 1995.

———. *Polybius, Rome, and the Hellenistic World: Essays and Reflections*. Cambridge University Press, 2002.

Wallace, S. "The Significance of Plataia for Greek *Eleutheria* in the Early Hellenistic Period." In *Creating a Hellenistic World*, edited by A. Erskine and L. Llewellyn-Jones, 147–76. Classical Press of Wales, 2011.

———. "Adeimantus of Lampsacus and the Development of the Early Hellenistic Philos." In *After Alexander: The Time of the Diadochi (323–281 BC)*, edited by V. Alonso Troncoso and E. Anson, 142–57. Oxbow, 2013.

Waterfield, R. *Dividing the Spoils: The War for Alexander the Great's Empire*. Oxford University Press, 2011.

———. *Taken at the Flood: The Roman Conquest of Greece*. Oxford University Press, 2014.

———. *Creators, Conquerors, and Citizens: A History of Ancient Greece*. Oxford University Press, 2018.

Wehrli, C. "Phila, fille d'Antipater et épouse de Démétrios, roi des Macédoniens." *Historia* 13 (1964): 140–46.

Wheatley, P., and C. Dunn. *Demetrius the Besieger*. Oxford University Press, 2020.

White, K., et al. "'The Base Mechanic Arts'? Some Thoughts on the Contribution of Science (Pure and Applied) to the Culture of the Hellenistic Age." In *Hellenistic History and Culture*, edited by P. Green, 211–37. University of California Press, 1993.

Whitehead, D. "The Garrison Demes." In *The Demes of Attica, 508/7–ca. 250 BC: A Political and Social Study*, 401–7. Princeton University Press, 1986.

Will, E. *Histoire politique du monde hellénistique (323–30 av. J.-C.)*. 2 vols. Université de Nancy, 1979, 1982.

Worthington, I. *Philip II of Macedonia*. Yale University Press, 2008.

———. *Ptolemy I, King and Pharaoh of Egypt*. Oxford University Press, 2016.

Index

Boldface letters refer to the general maps on pp. xvii–xxi.